MW00617789

HERE I STAND

...in a Beautiful State

TAMEKA FOSTER RAYMOND

ISBN: 978-1-7378718-0-4 - Hardcover
ISBN: 978-1-7378718-1-1 - Paperback
eISBN: 978-1-7378718-2-8 - eBook

Library of Congress Control Number: 2021917682

Printed in the United States of America   0 9 0 9 2 1

♾ This paper meets the requirements of ANSI/NISO Z39.48-1992 (Permanence of Paper)

Cover Design by Skania Florestal
Cover Photo by Nasta Belicova

Photos by Robert Ector, Kimberly O'Hara, Jonathan Mannion, and TFR Personal Archives

 Dedication

I want to thank Jehovah God for giving me the strength to write and for the time that I had with my precious son Kile, I will continue to keep his name, legacy and goals alive.

I'm thankful to have been the vessel that carried Kile to watch him grow into the beautiful, creative soul that he was. Though our time was short, I'm better and grateful for it.

I also want to acknowledge those of you that are grieving a loss, especially that of a child. I feel you. I pray that my words and actions align and aid you.

To my sons, whom I love with everything I am. I want to apologize to you, if you were impacted in any way by my life's choices. Remember to always stand in your truth, follow your dreams and be open minded. I will love you and ride for you til the wheels fall off. My heartbeats!

To my loves past and present, "thanks for the ride", memories and blessings.

To my creative friends Isoul Harris, Akeem Jones, Dream Hampton, Jodi Meisner, Kim Alsup, Dennis Ross and Hope Innelli. Thank you for your listening ears, advice and guidance through this process for nearly a decade. Monique Stewart thank you so much for pushing and encouraging me!! I finally did it guys!!

Lastly, this book is dedicated to the little engines that could.... The Black girls that continue to inspire and move the needle with their talent, resilience and undeniable magic... I hope my experiences have or will help you in some way. Albeit cliché, you can totally do it! Don't listen to detractors. Just keep growing onward and upward.

Agape,

~TJR

Foreword

❧

As you enjoy reading this memoir and begin to know the truth about Tameka, you will be inspired by how she shows her inner strength. Early in her life she demonstrated how thorough and detailed she can be by learning not only her part but the parts of each character in the play that she was participating in. I played a big part in her interest in business, travel and fashion. Her caring spirit from her missionary grandmother. Tameka is a stand out for her intelligence, wit and vision. At the time of her fashion pursuit in the entertainment industry, she would have to rely on her true sense of who she was and what she wanted because Tameka was long before her time and women of color were not received openly. The world was not ready to receive her many talents and beauty. We can all be excited about reading this book about how this remarkable woman still stands and stands beautifully.

With Love

Aunt Sadie

❧

I hope my experiences
have or will help you in
some way. Albeit cliché,
you can totally do it!
Don't listen to detractors.
Just keep growing
onward and upward.

❧

Introduction

❧

B est thing about getting older is you learn to giveth no more shits. Worse thing is you're mad you spent so many years giving a shit. I know—here I am, only two sentences into my book and I'm lit already.

Let me backup. Never for once think, as you're reading these pages, that I was sitting in front of my computer beating my chest, imagining myself to be Wonder Woman. Truth is, my keyboard has been wet with tears, and the trash bin next to me is full of Kleenex. Life has a way of getting to you. No matter how much you have, no matter how much you hide from it, life is gonna catch you, grab you by the shoulders, and shake everything upside down. The best thing you can do when that happens is come out and tell your story in your own words. This is my chance to do that.

When I first thought about writing a book, I couldn't think of any other like the one I wanted to put out there. That's when I realized this would be more than a book; it would be a monument. A place where my children could visit years from now and say, "Wow, that was my Mom. The good, the bad, the ugly—this was her life told in her words without spin or remix."

Know that I didn't set out idly to do this. Several things happened over the last few years that have forced me to write. Some of these things made me numb. My mom died in 2015 out of the clear blue sky. The way in which she went, as you'll discover, just stopped my heart. Within seconds, my Momma, "Sweet Lo" or later called 'Granny Lo' by my children, the only girl among seven kids, the chocolate drop, dance machine, always laughing Queen of Comedy, the one-line bandita, *Unsolved Mystery* aficionado, and the woman who gave me life then helped me through some of the more difficult times in that life, was suddenly gone. When you experience something like this, you start to realize that the problem with life is that you assume you have time. You think you've got the whole future to accomplish your dreams, take that trip, procrastinate, go back to school, or whatever it is you've been thinking about doing, yet still haven't. You imagine you always have time, but you don't.

The strange thing is, despite wanting to do so much more, I've packed a lot of living into the time I've had—so much so you'd think I was 98 years old already. This book is a wild journey through some of my most pivotal moments. And when I say "wild", I'm talking "colossal roller coaster wild". Things happened that I would've never discussed a few years ago, but again, age makes you bold. Bold enough now to talk about important relationships I've had over the years, and what I learned in the wake of those relationships. Bold enough to recount a time when I had everything I thought I desired, and yet I sat at home wanting none of it. There's a certain peace in being broke, and an unbelievable stress in having it "all". It's complicated, but trust me, this book breaks it down for you.

Somehow, I have been involved or have spent time with a few of the most intriguing, successful people out there, but here's the catch: some of them didn't become as successful or as wealthy as they are until they met me or shortly thereafter! Maybe, just maybe, I have the proverbial "Midas Touch". I kid, but Energy is everything, and I bring it to whatever I do and whomever I care about. Of course, the aftermath is what counts and I'm proud to have been a part of their history. Anyway, I'm finally cool with talking about all that stuff. I don't mind opening up about my teenage years and my early fascination with urban street boys, or revealing how Lil' D, a former major, err, "street pharmacist" from Oakland who I dated for a while as a teen, later got clemency from President Obama. I can talk about it now… In fact, I want to talk about crazy shit like losing my first love to street violence but never losing hope, being a single mom in Oakland arguing with the welfare office for my dignity, and ultimately making it on my own. I'm happy to set straight what you think you know about me from innuendo and rumors. To tell of the illustrious career that I had in the fashion business styling some of the entertainment industry's biggest names long before meeting either my media mogul or international sex symbol/musical genius exes. And yes, I'll be frank on the subjects of what it was like to be shamed by the media and the public because I was the seemingly unlikely one, in their eyes, to be loved by a heartthrob millions of other women coveted. Oh yeah, I'll even spill the tea on being jilted at the altar, being outed for pursuing lipo, and nearly dying on the operating table. And finally, after years of introspection and serious selfcare, I'm even ready to talk about my five beautiful sons and being gutted by the tragic loss of one of them at too tender an age. Yes, I'll be candid about how I lost myself in love, and I'll be equally forthcoming about how I found myself again in the shattered pieces of life I had to pick up and reassemble after the loss of my boy.

There is a ton I'm prepared to reveal and explore with you. Let me just say before we start, I'm super anxious right now and probably a tad paranoid. I suspect there will be some backlash, finger pointing and tons of denials. Comes with the territory. But at the same time, I feel free…free to tell you my story. There will likey be more to follow, one book is hardly enough. My life has been such a whirlwind, and at times pretty surreal, but I've worked hard to arrive at the graced and grounded space I'm in now. I'm finally free to tell you all the reasons why I've been so numb and how through it all I'm able to still stand. I've mastered the art of not giving a damn, or a rat's ass, oh so very well. My life has not been for the faint of heart, but if you come along for the ride as I relive parts of it, I suspect you'll emerge stronger too.

CHAPTER 1

Pull Up to the Bumper

❧

Everything was hazy as I slowly opened my eyes. At first, the sound was muffled, too. Yolanda was standing over me, mouthing something frantically. I could tell she was screaming, but the ringing in my ears drowned out her words. She was holding one of my shoes; I struggled to understand why. I didn't remember being hit, but I did remember suddenly sailing through the air, tumbling to the ground, and skidding some 200 feet before coming to a full stop. I had flown in the air and made a quick stop at Quik Stop.

My brother Dion's arms were wrapped around his head; his eyes were big like saucers. He wasn't speaking, but his face told me something was off. I started to panic. It was sort of like when a baby falls and the adults' reaction makes the baby cry. The timeline of my life is dotted with different near-death experiences. As much as I hate cats, I've always felt as if we had something in common— some minute but considerable quality that has stuck with me ever since I was a 9-year-old kid lying dazed and confused on that pavement.

The champagne-colored Cadillac Seville continued halfway down the road before the driver threw the gear into reverse and backed down 14th Street to where Yolanda stood, still frozen in fear.

"Oh God!!! Is she ok?" the man asked as he exited his car, leaving the driver's-side door hanging open while he ran over to see. Later, I would recall that he wore faded blue jeans and had on a light brown button-up. His short black Afro was picked out and neat. He looked like an ol' school "Lenny". Yolanda shook her head *No* in response to his question and as she did, her feathered hair— newly cut in a Dorothy Hamill bob—swayed from side to side. She had called my name over and over, more times than I can remember.. Tears tumbled down her cheeks. I began to cry too as the numbness gave way to surging pain in my limbs. "My legs hurt!" I blurted out. I had a terrible road rash on my forearm, my hip was throbbing, and the knee of my new Sassoons was frayed from its brush with the asphalt.

We never got his name. He'd nearly run me over and was kind enough to drive us back home, but "Lenny Plenny" sure didn't stick around to speak with my daddy. To say that my father was upset would be an understatement. Every other word out of his mouth was "mutha-fuck", "got-damnit", and "shit." No wonder the driver sped off in such a hurry. My daddy was too upset to get an explanation from either of my siblings. He simply said "OHH-MY-GOD!! Get out of my sight!" Fortunately, I sustained minimal injuries and fully recovered. I've been knocked down plenty of times in my life... but I've always gotten back up.

❧

I've been
knocked down
plenty of times
in my life...
but I've always
gotten back up.

❧

Black Excellence — My Family

From left:
Auntie Sadie + John Dawson.
Granny Lou and my Grandfather John Earl Foster.
Louise Cotton
My Great Grandmother Katie's husband George and herself.
1947

CHAPTER 2

Love and Happiness

❧

Who is Tameka J. Foster?

As far back as I can remember, my Momma's and Daddy's families were as oxymoronic as one could imagine. Both great, but polar opposites. Down to the foods they ate, the music they loved, and the way they celebrated. I saw neither side as *better* than the other — just totally and utterly different.

My maternal family was Southern, down to earth, and always kept it 1,000!! My paternal family was fit, polished, poised, and a tad bit persnickety. Nevertheless, both had great philosophies on life and a strong moral compass, which was significant in establishing my foundation. I can't imagine not having stood on both sides of the fence during my childhood; I find that I'm most often largely misunderstood because few understand whence I came.

I'm a staunch believer that who we become as adults is a direct result of how and by whom we were raised as children. No one can tell me different. Most of our personality traits, mannerisms, work ethics, and habits are influenced by our upbringing. The things we witness, experience and are taught, shape us for the better part of our lives. When you encounter extremely studious people, it is generally due to their parents' beliefs and style of child-rearing. When you encounter people who are racists, live with biases, or are prejudiced, theirs is typically learned behavior. Children are not born with these characteristics. Attitudes like these are taught. Childhood is so important. Things become ingrained into our very fiber during these formative years, which brings us back to me— the "Jehovah's Baptist" or "Baptovah Witness". I was raised learning two different faiths from two very different grandmothers, so I just combined them. Still perplexed.

"A child is born with no state of mind, blind to the ways of mankind..."
-Grandmaster Flash

My parents were married — well somewhat married. Their union was common law I suppose…or at least, I think it was. Hell, I don't actually know more than the bare facts. All I can be sure of is that they were a couple and we all lived together until I was 14. Although my mom adopted my dad's last name, I never saw any evidence of their nuptials or even a wedding photo. My assumption is that they never made it down the aisle. They were together, however, for 21 years—from the mid-1960s through the mid-1980s. During that time, their life was seemingly traditional. My mother maintained the house and cooked, my father worked, and for the first 13 years of my life my mother was primarily a stay-at-home mom. They went through a lot together, they were in a major car accident months after I was born. My mother was driving a blue AMC Javelin and was in a coma for a week, my father was thrown out of the passenger window and luckily it was down. Thank God, they survived or my life would have been a lot different. I was the only child that they had together. My older sister Yolanda— my mother's child— lived with us, but I had over a dozen other siblings (my father's offspring) all over Northern California and some in the southern region. My mom also had a boy— my older brother Dion— who lived with his paternal grandmother since he was young.

My mother, Lorene Foster, née Hadden, was from Shreveport, Louisiana. She stood about 5'4" tall, was beautifully mocha-toned, and had killer legs. She was a dancing machine, an excellent cook, and was always laughing, albeit she was a no-nonsense woman. She was the eldest of seven children, the only girl amongst my six uncles. Having all brothers meant that my mother did not play games, and that she had developed a thick skin over time. My mother was built Ford tough and she raised us to be the same way. God tends to make things come full circle; this early life experience enabled my Mother to teach me how to better manage life with my five sons. She was a loving mother, but as I write this, I realize there were a few things that were unique about my childhood. Though my mother never dropped the ball when we were around, I can't say that she was a complete model citizen. There was definitely something notably, umm...un-*soccer-mom*-esque about her. My mother wasn't what you'd imagine a mother to be, though I wouldn't say she was a bad mother either. When I was a little girl, there was something about her I couldn't quite identify—something that age and experience would reveal to me later. People say that one's vices are often virtues carried to excess. I wonder if some of my mother's vices were developed in the company of the same exact type of guys I started to date and in the very lifestyle that I grew to love.

I got my early-bird genes from my dad. My momma slept-in

most mornings because it wasn't "her shift." Early mornings were just not her thing, especially on weekends. I remember my dad making breakfast and the air being filled with the smell of hot buttery pancakes, cinnamon, and sausage, and with the sounds of Dr. Buzzard's Savannah Band singing, *"I'll play the fool for you... oh girl"*. We kept our Marantz record player spinning with stacks of vinyl beside it; great music was always in rotation. My parents were oddly, well versed musically. They loved white artists as much as black artists. The Doobie Bros, Bee Gees, Kenny Loggins, Hall & Oates, were all music staples in our house. My dad would take me to T's Wauzi Records or Leopold's Records and let me pick out 45s of my favorite artists. The Sylvers, Prince, Michael Jackson, and The Debarges (I know it's Debarge but we always called them "the Debarge's") were my favorites back then.

My mom had a few girlfriends that she would hang with, like Mary Jean and my godmother Curtis Faye. I can still recall the mixed scents of my mother's Kool Filter Kings menthol cigarettes, musk incense, her favorite Rive Gauche fragrance by YSL, and Posner's Groovy Grape on the lips. She rarely drank, so I knew she was about to exit stage left when I saw a brandy snifter with her Hennessy VSOP in it. Going out with my godmother Faye and Mary Jean always caused a heated exchange with my Daddy. I think the three of them together signified trouble in his eyes. Uh-oh, 3-the-Hard Way!

My mother's friend, Mary Jean, had a daughter by one of the men in my father's singing group. Our home-life structure was a little different than that of my cousins Dawn and Dwayne's. Their mom, Aunt Cassandra, was a conservative woman and she ran a certain kind of household. They were on an organized schedule. Aunt Cassandra worked full-time preparing meals while raising a family, taking care of my Uncle Melvin, and making it to Sunday service and bible study. I used to watch her and wonder where she went to get plugged in. Yet on the same token, my mother's house was meticulously clean, and we had a home cooked meal, every night.

When I was a young girl, my dad, John Foster, was a serial rolling stone— a ladies' man, if you will. (Hence, all the offspring.) Daddy is about 6'1, 195 pounds, and has always been quite lean. He is an attractive, latte- colored biracial man with keen features, a beauty mark on his nose, and wavy black hair, but he doesn't much embrace the 'white side" of his heritage. When his father—my grandfather, John Sr.—was born, he was given his mother's maiden name of Foster because his biological father, Hosea Ely, was a white sheriff in Hearn, Texas and would not claim a biracial child. Given my father's unusually diverse background, he had a profound knowledge of the solar system, American history, and was rather well-versed on world events and politics. As a young girl, I remember him teaching me that the nearest star to Earth, other than the Sun, was called Alpha Centauri and that it was four and a half light-years away and traveled at 186,000 miles per second, and that the Sun was only eight light-minutes away. Yep, he was more or less well-rounded. He was also part of a singing group in the '60s and into the early- '80s called "The Ballads." Two years after I was born in 1973, my father made an acting debut in a Blaxploitation movie called *The Mack*. *The Mack* was filmed in Oakland and starred Max Julien, Richard Pryor, Frank Ward and others. My father always reminded me of Richard Pryor because of his thick moustache, candor, and swift sense of humor. He was a *"bad-mutha-shut-yo-mouth"* that travelled around performing with his group and... .err... bouncing between different "lady friends". The Ballads opened for acts such as Marvin Gaye, The Temptations, Patti Labelle, Ike & Tina Turner, Stevie Wonder, Smokey Robinson and the Miracles as well as Harold Melvin and the Bluenotes in venues such as the Apollo Theater, the Oakland Coliseum, and the Hollywood

Palladium to name a few. The Wu Tang clan actually sampled one of my dad's songs called "Dizzy World" for a song with Snoop named "Conditioner". (*Cut the check Wu Tang.*) They performed all over the U.S. My daddy just loves music and people so it became a bit of a hobby toward the end.

Around 1975, he stopped performing quite as much and was home more working as a longshoreman in the ILWU local 2 union in San Francisco, and scuba diving as a hobby during his time off. He was gone a lot, but when he was home, he was quite present. I remember the day my sister and I entered the house after school to find all new furniture. He had just signed a new record contract. I swear I thought we were so rich; the funny thing is my dad's group was independent so the money they made was relatively nominal. But as a ten-year-old child I thought we were sky ballin'. This was at a time when I saw a wad of $1 bills and swore it was thousands!

Daddy loved his Javelins, a total muscle car in the '70's, and he loved to work on it. I guess that's why I'm drawn to men that are skillful. He kept buying the same car, I rode with him everywhere in that car, listening to and singing old R&B classics, and I remember it had a small hole in the floorboard where I could literally see the pavement move. By the time I was in seventh grade, I remember asking him to drop me off a few yards before the front of the school. I told him that his car had "hips" and one fender had a gray primer patch where he had done some work on a dent or ding. When he reminded me that it still got us from A to B. I responded, *I knowww, but daddy where was the final paint and buff part?*" FML. He was super proud of his car and did all the repairs himself. I was definitely his road dog. We used to ride out early in the morning while my mom slept, and we'd visit his friends, both male and female— the latter of which I often called "aunts." Though I never saw anything inappropriate, in hindsight, the fact that I was there at all was a whole violation. These said "aunts' ' almost always had a gift or ice cream for my troubles. On occasion we would also swing by a couple of my siblings' houses too. Somehow, I instinctively never told my mother. I was intuitive as a girl; Somehow, I just knew better. Sharp as a tack.

Both of my parents were wonderful in their own ways. My mom was passionate, protective, and caring while my dad was wise, fun, and doting. They both had an affinity for comedy and music; if loving music is hereditary, then I definitely got it from those two. Music is in my bones…an intrinsic part of my being. It was a huge part of my childhood. The radio was always on blast and *Soul Train* was on our television during Saturday clean-up around the house. We never missed it. My mother loved Maze, Rick James, The Emotions, and Marvin Gaye. I remember my daddy coming home many nights after drinking, turning the music on, *"Though you may not drive a great big Cadillac",* and her fussing. "Turn it down, the kids are sleeping." Fact is, they were both night owls. He loved the Chi-lites, Bee Gees, and of course his fave, Marvin Gaye. On second thought, Mom was likely mad at him for his other indiscretions. Music was never a problem for us. We all loved music and movies. For years, I thought for sure my daddy was an alcoholic; this was until I became an adult, took him out, and turns out he was just a total lightweight with a two-drink max. The man just cannot drink.

I was the hella quick-witted, sarcastic, smart-aleck, sassy type. Always had a mouth. Urban myth has it that one day, at 4 years old, I woke up early, got myself dressed, grabbed a few books and proceeded to waltz my narrow ass out the house, where I walked totally alone to the corner store. My parents, in a complete panic, looked everywhere until they found me sitting there nonchalantly behind the counter. My mom enrolled me in kindergarten ASAP… a year early. She changed my birth certificate from 1971 to 1970. I started Bella Vista Elementary, and by 2nd grade had the same teacher that my father had in grade school. Her name was Mrs. Frances. At age six, I was cast in the annual Christmas pageant as a fairy, and while I loved the performance aspects of it, I would fuss about everything else. I could be heard complaining, *"I don't like my hair!"* or *"Why do I have to wear these itchy tights?!"* before going on stage. Always the shit talker.

At nine years of age, I was already a latch-key kid, always forever wearing the green yarn around my neck and given the instructions "DO NOT ANSWER THE DOOR FOR ANYONE!... Only make peanut butter and jelly sandwiches or ham and cheese…DO NOT TURN ON THE STOVE!!" blah blah blah. Well they forgot to tell me not to sneak in their room and play with matches, because that's *exactly* what I did. My curiosity led me right down the hallway to their bedroom on a sunny weekday afternoon. I had been watching my favorite after school shows— it was either the *Flintstones, Leave It To Beaver, The Brady Bunch* or *Happy Days,* and when it ended, I started looking in their armoire, opening drawers, flipping through Dad's *Playboy* magazines. *Ewww gross*! Then, while I was snooping under their bed, I found my dad's cigar box for his little weed stash. He also read the newspaper every morning so there was an accumulated pile of folded papers halfway under the bed. Well, guess who decided to try her hand at campfire building? ME. I lit the end of the paper and it started smoking hella rapidly, so I began to fan it. Umm…*not smart.* The fire began to move quickly, I grabbed my dad's bedside water gallon, only to find that it was almost empty. #MajorFail I then ran to grab a cup of water to douse it, but it was travelling fast underneath the bed. Smoke was billowing. I saw the sheets in flames, I was like OMG exit stage right! The whole time I was running down the stairs I was thinking, *Oh shit! Oh shit!* I ran next door to our neighbors' house—the Pruitts— and they called the fire department. Needless to say, I was mortified, and never told the truth about how the fire started until I was grown and on my own. My parents thought it was due to their failure to turn off their electric blanket. Retrospectively, I wonder why my momma or daddy didn't think to just take me with them after school because those were also the days when we ran loads of errands with our parents, waited in the hot-ass car with the windows cracked, the doors locked, and the radio volume low . As kids we were used to it and complained the whole way home. But that didn't happen on that day. Instead, I made my grand debut as President of *Shit Show Productions*.

My mom and dad were grateful I was unharmed; nonetheless, we were displaced as a family. They found another place quickly, but they needed time to furnish it. That's when they sent me to Clearlake to live with my grandmother. Clearlake is a small resort town of about 15,000 people in Northern California, named after the oldest natural lake in America, which is located there. 72 percent of the town's population is white and only about 4 percent is black, so umm...yeah it was like moving to *the Ozarks*. It was considerably different from Oakland. Racism was prevalent and I still cannot imagine why my grandmother elected to retire there. I'm still scratching my head about that choice. I lived with my father's mother Louise, whom we called "Granny Lou", and her second husband "Granddaddy Sam". I spent my third and fourth grade years attending Lower Lake Elementary School and boy were those kids racist. I don't remember having one friend, black, white, or otherwise. I rode the school bus daily, with my backpack and my pink Hello Kitty tin lunch pail and thermos. I always sat in the front because the white kids were loud, mean, and rowdy. They would pick on kids randomly, harassing and making fun of them. One day as the bus made its way to my stop on the corner of

35th, I gathered my things and began to get off. That's when I noticed that the ringleader and a few of his ruffians were disembarking their *ignant* asses off the bus at my stop too. I'm thinking *Great!! Sucks teeth*. As expected, they started laughing, skipping rocks toward me, and repeating, "Haha Nigger," "She's a nigger," "Hurry up Nigger." Yep, with a hard "R". I remember I kept looking back at them. My heart rate was ramping up while I tried to turbo speed walk to my grandmother's driveway. As soon as I got to our property line at the edge of the fence, I took off and started running like a young *Flo Jo*, while yelling my grandmother's name at the top of my lungs the whole way. "Granny Lou!! Granny Lou!!" I flung the door open and explained to her quickly what had happened. She was perturbed; I had never seen her so mad. She threw the towel down, stormed out the screen door, and waited until the boys got within ear shot. Then she threatened them, saying that she knew where they lived and dared them to ever say another word to me. I'm over there peeking out the screen door thinking, *Shit man, they're **really** going to get my ass tomorrow. Dammit to hell.* Needless to say, I was highly concerned; I had the bubble guts and spent the evening nervously biting my nails down to the quick, yet I was beaming with pride. At the same damn time, it was then that I realized I was different; I never saw color before that day. Growing up in Oakland I had friends of every ethnicity, but I didn't look at us as different in an unfavorable way. I guess you could say I was color blind; I knew that people were unique, but I never viewed our differences as something to shy away from. It was definitely eye opening. Incidentally, I was nine and didn't know yet about the "can of whup ass" method. That came several years later.

My parents thought the school system would be better there, or so they said. I was a total bookworm, I really loved books, I literally used to read the dictionary. I would pick out cool, usually polysyllabic words, write them down, and learn the definitions. I did this on my own. In retrospect, I wonder if they were just on the outs or wanted to send me away so that I wasn't around to pick up on their issues or other things that might have been going on. Daddy was a player, as I mentioned before—a definite ladies' man— and my mom had her own iniquities. There was probably some *ish* going down that they didn't want me to bear witness to. So off I went to Clearlake and Yolanda went to her Father's.

I call this season of my life, "sewing, fishing, and Jehovah!" Always in the background of Granny Lou and Granddaddy Sam's fully-equipped, double mobile home — quite the norm for Lake County — was Jehovah, scripture, more Jehovah, and the deafeningly quiet family dinners. They had a big oval wooden dining table and I was in charge of setting it for dinner nightly. After dinner we would sit around the television — volume on low — to watch the '*80s Dating Game* and *The Lawrence Welk Show.* "Ah one, ah two, and ah three" was Lawrence Welk's nightly band countdown ritual. That was the closest we got to the secular world. My grandmother was a Shaklee Vitamins and Forever Living Aloe Vera products representative; she was truly about that herbalife and swore by the effects of Aloe vera as a part of her daily regimen.

A couple times a month, we would stop by the bait shop to pick up a container of worms, and with our fishing poles in hand, we would go out to the lake and quietly sit at the edge of the shore for hours. I remember the banks of Clearlake being full of fish skeletons and dead carp; it was like a fish cemetery. We always took an empty 5-gallon bucket in case we were successful. We were often lucky— catching bluegill, bass, crappie, and mostly catfish, which we would then take home, go downstairs to my Granddaddy Sam's shack to scale, clean, before cooking and eating it. I remember Granddaddy Sam saying:

"Be careful with the gallbladder, you'll ruin the meat and we'll get sick." Ironically, I won't eat fish to this day. Gallbladder? Little liver? *Zoinks*! I guess battle fatigue from all the weekly fish autopsies performed back then. It was also on that level of my grandparents' property that they maintained a small chicken farm, complete with a chicken coop, and the little dark wooden shed where the chickens lay their eggs. We also had rabbits. It was like pioneer living.

On Sundays, we hopped into the Ford station wagon (yes, complete with wood panels on the side!) and headed over to the Kingdom Hall. Everyone looked like they could have been cast in *Mr. Rogers Neighborhood*. A cardigan cornucopia, pressed khaki trousers, pocket protectors, and sensible shoes. I would often be called upon to do "impromptu talks", which required going on stage to speak about a chosen Biblical topic with little or no preparation. Yep, I also did "field ministry", aka going door to door. I had my spiel down: "Hi, I'm Tameka Foster, with the Jehovah Witnesses. If you were to die today, do you know where you would go?" Hey, don't *knock* it till you try it! No pun. Looking back, I learned so much during this period of my life. I also took gymnastics and piano lessons. We canned fruits and made homemade mayonnaise and the most delicious ice cream. I was also taught how to juice fresh fruits and vegetables. Fast forward to today: I absolutely love juicing! I learned valuable nuggets that I have carried throughout my life, from my Granny Lou. She was kind of like, part Stepford wife, part June Cleaver, part Diahann Carroll. All Jehovah.

I compare living with Granny Lou to attending finishing school. She taught me how to sew, properly set a table, to exude modesty, how to be and act like a lady, and to watch my figure. She prepared me for my splendiferous teenage and adult years. Lord, if she saw me now—thicker than a snicker, part *heathenish,* and anti-fish— she would laugh.

I would stay with Granny Lou and Granddaddy Sam during the weekdays and then head back to Oakland with my parents on weekends, during school breaks, and on holidays. On regular weekends in Clearlake, I helped my grandmother at the flea market. She had a booth and sold random vintage furniture and clothing, home accents, and tchotchke items. We would get up at 7:00 on Saturday morning, eat a quick breakfast, then head over there to set up by wiping down mirrors, hanging garments, dusting-off chairs, and laying out trinkets. This was an early start for my love of entrepreneurship. In Clearlake, I was a prim and proper Jehovah's Witness and in Oakland…well I was Baptist…half Baptist and slightly uncouth. As a JW, we tranquilly sang from a hymn book, and in a Baptist setting, there was lots of spontaneous, unbridled praise for the Father, Son and the Holy Ghost. You get what I'm saying about the oxymoronic-ness of it all now? The energy was most definitely different.

My grandmother Estella, we called her "Grandma Hadden", my mother's mother, was a down-home, Southern, bible-thumping Baptist woman. Photos of Mahalia Jackson, the Kennedy's, and Martin Luther King were permanently perched on her fireplace. For the longest I thought they were family. She had a powerful demeanor. We would walk into her house, all excited to see her, and she would just put her cheek out for us to kiss; sometimes not even making eye contact. She was stern. She raised her children with high morals and good southern values. She made it clear that hard work was a must. As a result, my uncles all had solid union jobs and kept those jobs for 30 to 40 years until their retirement.

Photos of Mahalia
Jackson, the Kennedy's,
and Martin Luther
King were permanently
perched on her fireplace.
For the longest I thought
they were family.

CHAPTER 3

That Girl

❧

My parents separated when I was about 12 years old; my mom had finally had enough of my daddy stepping out. The final straw was when he got his brother-in-law's sister, Diane, pregnant, and my youngest sibling, a baby girl named Venus Mignon Foster, was born in July 1983. We moved in with Grandma Hadden as a result. At Grandma's, I was comfortable; I had my own pre-furnished room with a queen-sized brass bed, a beautifully detailed, scrolled dresser with a large mirror and burnished brass circular pulls, and two matching nightstands. As a teen I was thinking, "Dang, this is old fashioned!!" Now I would kill to get my hands on these very same pieces. Her house was a huge two-story Victorian with spacious bedrooms and walk-in closets. I felt like a princess living there, although it was smack dab in the middle of East Oakland. I immediately started my Michael Jackson wall collage which enshrined two floor to ceiling walls. While Michael was singing about living off the wall, I had him all over the wall. I'm talking eight full-size posters of MJ and no less than 40 glossy magazine covers with small cut-out photos of him performing. I saved every concert ticket and album cover and kept a shiny glove and a collection of pin-back buttons as well. I was totally obsessed. I was a complete "fan-addict" -–that's a next-level fanatic. Needless to say, I personalized my room and it was amazing. My mom, grandma, and uncles approved. I've always been creative, and they pretty much supported that quality in me. *Man, that poster of Mike in the yellow sweater vest and crystal brooch was every-damn-thing.*

I went to church with my grandmother, sang in the choir, liked a boy that played the drums, had a tambourine and all. I loved it! Church was mandatory in Grandma Hadden's house. She would say, "If you can get up and find the energy to go and hang out, you can get dressed for church to give thanks." I was fine with that. I was already accustomed to being at the Kingdom Hall a couple days a week. Besides, I was intrigued by the distinctiveness of the Baptist church. I grew fond of the vibrant ensembles—men in their well-pressed suits and the women in their patterned frocks, kitten heeled pumps, and glorious crowns; the smell of musty pews; the dampness in the air from the baptistry under the choir loft; the constant hollers of "Hallelujah!", "Preach Preacha!" and "Take your time!" the hilarity of church mothers shouting during the praise and worship medley and then nodding off during the sermon —nothing like it.

It was also at Grandma Hadden's sky blue, two-level home on the corner of 90th and Olive that we would have the most epic family gatherings. I'm talking get-togethers complete with tipsy uncles, cousins doing the "bump", wooden doorway beads, plastic-covered saffron-colored velvetine furniture, shag carpets, family *Soul Train* lines to "Use Ta be My Girl" by the O'Jays, pool shooting, and kids outside playing tether ball, backgammon, tunk, and domino games that would sometimes end in huge blow-outs. My uncles were the epitome of the Black power poster, complete with the fist, hair pic, corduroy suits, and polyester disco shirts. I still remember my gorgeous single uncles, Bruce and James, pullin' up to the parties in their T-topped Trans Am or Camaro, with some bad chicks on their arms. My Uncle Melvin would roll up in his brown *Scooby Doo*-like van with my cousins Dawn and Dwayne. My mother and Grandma in the kitchen debating about trimming the fat off the meat. *Alexa play, Marvin Gaye." "Make me wanna holler, the way they do my life"* Yes, that was exactly the vibe.

My mother ended up working two part time jobs after the split—three days a week at the Campbell's Soup factory in Sacramento and the grave-yard shift as an in-home care worker. Whatever you do, don't work the doggone third shift if you have a hot-ass daughter. I crept out at night a couple times, and whenever I was at home, I always snuck on the phone late at night. I was super grown... or so I thought. I spent a lot of time with my older sister Yolanda, cousin Dee Dee, and their buddies. We would ride all over the city in Dee Dee's midnight blue Fiat Spider convertible. Top down and cruising by Lake Merritt or just hanging out in Berkeley to grab a slice from Blondies and window shop. We also would run into guys along the way; of course, four cute girls in a convertible always worked. I loved being with my sister and her crew, I learned so much from them. They were all fashionistas and I emulated a bit of each of their styles. One evening, after a long day of fun in the sun, Dee Dee decided to stop by Sonja's house and she and my sister ran inside for a minute. They left the car running with me in the backseat. Alone. At this point I made a strangely impulsive decision. I decided to take Dee Dee's car for a quick spin— a joy ride, if you will. The idea was to zip around the block with the one good time with the quickness. Right? Wrong!!! It was a terrible idea, because as soon I took off and made that right turn at the corner, I commenced to side-swiping three parked cars and nearly hit a pedestrian. The part that I hadn't considered was that I didn't quite know how to drive yet, nor did I have a driver's license. The little roadster was just so cute and petite; I assumed it would be as easy to maneuver as it looked. I whipped back around the corner, parked the car in the same spot, and hopped in the backseat as if nothing had ever happened. The damage to Dee Dee's car wasn't immediately known, but witnesses began to come forth calling and saying that they saw the tiny cabriolet involved in a hit and run. *I merely swiped them with the same delicacy that one would use when applying blush. I mean... what was all the fuss about?* I think it was around this time that they started calling me Lucy. *I Love Lucy* was one of my favorite TV shows, and like Lucy, I always ended up in scenarios that mimicked the character on the show. It was as if I was in my own real-life situational comedy; I always had some slapstick shenanigans underfoot. Never failed.

In the sixth grade, once I moved back to civilization from Mayberry USA, aka Clearlake. *Thank you, Jehovah Jireh, Jesus, Yahweh, and the 12 disciples, The Father, the Son, and the Holy Ghost, and the Kingdom Hall elders!* I auditioned for the annual school play. That year they were doing Shakespeare's *Hamlet*. Hamlet was a play about Prince Hamlet of Denmark, about his revenge against his uncle Claudius who murdered Hamlet's father to take over his throne and steal his wife, which was Hamlet's mother Gertrude. I auditioned for the part of Ophelia, Polonius' daughter. Let me tell you, I rocked that audition so masterfully, That I not only learned Ophelia's part, I knew Gertrude's, Horatio's, Rosencrantz and Guildenstern's parts. I aced the audition and was offered the leading role of Hamlet!!! My favorite teacher Ms. Gloria Durflinger encouraged me to accept the role. I was so reluctant, because Hamlet was a dude, but hey we were all 5th and

6th graders and once I memorized my lines, had my costume fitted, and added the fake moustache, it was *lights, camera, action*!!

During a handful of summers in the '80s, I would go to Sacramento for a few weeks to visit my daddy's daughter, Valencia. She had three children— two boys and one girl. Her daughter, my niece, Eboni, was four years younger than me and was already a singing child prodigy. She won talent shows and was gifted vocally well beyond her years. My young precocious business mind was already at work; I drew up an amateur marketing plan and an entire handwritten management contract, complete with two signature lines. I neatly printed every word. I remember writing certain parts with different colored ink pens. When I think about the research I did— looking on the back of my six favorite album covers to identify various record labels, locating the executives' names in the credits, and tracking down their contact information— I'm still pretty impressed with how my brain was wired. If it's true that the human brain stops growing in size when we're about 15 years old., then my brain at age 12 had to have been going through a growth spurt! It was also during this time that my daddy got back together with one of his baby mothers and married her. I never asked my mother how this made her feel, but I can only imagine it must have stung, hard. *Men.*

Around this time, I noticed boys. I discovered that I had a certain magnetism. They liked me. I mean I always knew that I liked them. That was evident when I fell for the drummer named Raymond at church. But once I discovered that the attraction was mutual, this became a whole new way of life. One Saturday, my sister Yolanda did my hair and picked out a cute outfit for me, which consisted of white jeans and a pastel shirt. We caught the bus to North Oakland to her best friend Anna's house. Well, Anna had a little brother named Lamont who I decided to show off for because I thought he was cute.

Anna lived in a building that had a small playground in the front that was constructed of rusted metal, chipped paint, and a dirt floor. I proceeded to grab onto the *Meka-go-down*— I mean, *merry-go-round* and started running aggressively like a track star, I inevitably tripped and was dragged by the Meka-go-down, only stopping after about eight rotations when I finally thought to let go. My hair was mangled, elbow scuffed up, outfit and face dusty. I had to jump up fast as hell and pretend that nothing hurt as the boys looked on. My whole body was wrecked; I needed a Got damn Calgon bath, bad! It was the most embarrassing moment in my crush loving career. I still can't look him in the eye, because I was so darned **molded.* They never let me live that one down; I still get clowned about it on occasion.

As I reminisce, I realize that I was always the very cool, entertaining girl that guys felt relaxed around. They trusted me and often confided in me because I was emotionally consistent and pretty forgetful when it came to petty negativity. I was less reactive than most girls my age, and if I did have reason to get mad, I wasn't one to hold onto grudges. I was pretty open-minded when it came to boys and I was always okay with having a platonic relationship. I became a complete boy magnet. *By the same token, mosquitoes love and are attracted to me too.* The young lady in me understood the male mindset; once I mastered that, I decided boys were my thing! We just got along, meshed well, and other girls sensed it. I've always had a great sense of humor and even that annoyed chicks. Unfortunately, this ease with guys posed a bit of a problem keeping certain friends as life progressed. Girls would find reasons to start beefs with me and by high school it became both predictable and laughable.

I have always had a big ol jubilant personality. Some have told me that they find me to be authentic, energetic, motivational, well versed, and imaginative and I like that they see the real me.

I've always had a great sense of humor and while it has annoyed some chicks, it has amused most people I meet. I've learned that some folks have an infectious vibe. It has nothing to do with physical appearance, status, or style. And people who have vibrant personalities, don't always need to be the center of attention to captivate an audience. In part, it's about mastering the art of conversation, reading body language, and understanding others. When you got it, you got it. One guy likened dealing with me to receiving a box of chocolates. He said, "You never know what you're gonna get—you can be sweet, sometimes salty, and always surprising." Hey, I'll take that! Fact is, I think of myself more like water, the way my fellow Oakland native, Bruce Lee, spoke about the element. He encouraged everyone to be formless and shapeless like water. He reminded us that when you pour water in a cup, it *becomes* the cup. As he would say, "Water can drip or it can crash." Just like water, I've always flowed and adapted.

Whenever difficult situations arose, I didn't let fear overtake me, and I never had an energy of helplessness. I also didn't let my past control who I was. I never limited myself. By middle school, or junior high as we called it, I started liking really smart, popular, preppy, nerdy guys. Nowadays, we would call these guys "metrosexual". I don't know why; that's just where my eyes went and the types I gravitated toward. The summer of eighth grade, while attending Bret Harte Junior High, this was further made abundantly clear after a close friend, Rena Hudson, was killed and disposed of in a dumpster allegedly by one of her street associates. At least that was what was reported to us as kids. I remember crying and feeling haunted at night just thinking about what happened to her. I was afraid of the dark at 13, because of this. Square guys became even more attractive after this.

This was until I was introduced to Alan Lee at church after bible study in the 9th grade. Alan was a slim attractive kid from Buffalo,

New York. He was refreshing and distinguishable from other guys in Oakland. First, he had a strong East Coast accent and a clean-cut style, always with a fresh line up for his fade. Alan was also the best dressed guy I knew in 1984. He would wear suede Pumas with fat laces, Polo everything, and the flyest sweat suits. What's more, he adored me. I met his beautiful mother Veronica, a Pan Am flight attendant, who affectionately called him "Toot". They were sweet. I adored them because she was a single mom and she doted on her son. When I met her, she took to me immediately. She even brought me my first Louis Vuitton bag back from a trip she took to Asia. This was before I knew about knockoffs; nevertheless, it was the kindest gesture and my first designer bag. I was just flattered that she grew to like me so much in such a short amount of time. Her son was smooth, but not slick. We would sit on the phone for three hours and just talk about life, hip hop, fashion, life after high school, you name it. One night he informed me that his mother would be gone for a couple days on an international trip. Alan and I decided that it was time for me to come over and potentially end my virginity. While we were talking about it, I was so scared. The next day I left my house at 7:00 am and per usual got on the AC Transit 40B bus headed toward my school, passed my school en route to Alan's house.

Once I got to his door, I knocked and rang the doorbell a couple of times, I realized that he wasn't home. I couldn't believe it; he stood me up and took his ass to school knowing that we had a plan. I contemplated this day the entire night before. I was ready though. I guess when you know you know, so I hightailed it over to Oakland High and snuck on campus. My cousin, Ingrid, worked in the office and found out what class he was in, and where it was located. Within minutes, there I was peeking in the window waving him down and hoping his Algebra teacher wouldn't catch us. Alan looked up, smiled at me, and just covered his face laughing. I hung out in the bathroom until class was over, and we left and walked back to his house. Everything about this was so risky— first, me cutting school; second, me sneaking onto his campus; and third, me preparing to give this young man some "snacks" after several months of dating. We childishly giggled and walked back to his house. Once there, we made food. I was relaxed; the day went as planned and my first experience was awkward and scary but pleasant, nonetheless. The decisions we make in our youth always fascinate me. We have so many misconceptions about what our first time is supposed to be like. We're always envisioning candlelight, bubble baths, and romance. He made me feel comfortable and respected, so I went over and we had sex. It wasn't awkward, or weird, and it wasn't this especially magical moment either. Fifteen years old may have been too young, but no one could have told me that he wasn't going to be my lifelong boyfriend at the time. Even when we broke up, I never had any regrets or hard feelings. In fact, we didn't end our relationship due to a disagreement or anything like that; he simply relocated back to his hometown of Buffalo and we eventually lost contact. *Damn, just like that my first real boyfriend was gone.*

After Alan left and I got to high school, I dated a couple of other nice guys. I definitely had a type, until it occurred to me that in addition to preppy nerdy guys, I had a thing for bad boys as well. There was something about their exciting, hyper-masculine bravado that took over my rational thoughts. I think I admired their sense of freedom. Despite the fact that this quality made them unsuitable for long-term relationships, the challenge made them so attractive to me that it was seemingly worth the potential heartbreak and subsequent drama. The sweetest taboo is that we always like something that we can't or shouldn't have, our longing for it grows exponentially. And where I was from, these guys usually had money, weren't riding the bus, looked nice, and talked a damn good game.

Since my mom and I were no longer living with my father, the boys I befriended or dated became my new male influences. They were the masculine figures I apotheosized. My uncles were a presence at my grandmother's house, but they were more like authoritarians. I felt comfortable around guys because there was no jealousy, competitive spirit, or insecurity issues to contend with the way there were with some of my female peers.

Clearly, my childhood influences were all over the place. Many people impacted my life during this pivotal time, but the sum total of my experiences with my high-definition, colorful families on both sides definitely molded me into the Tameka that I am today. shaping everything from my eclectic tastes to my vivacious personality. My early years were so simple ... and then things got complicated.

CHAPTER 4

Rapture

❧

Darrin Lorenzo Banks, aka DB (some friends also called him "Lucky" was about 5 '10", with smooth brown skin, teeth were strong and white like ivory— straight and perfect. I mean, those pretty teeth were like that of a Colgate ad, and he managed to smile often and it would light up any room. His face was very masculine and had beautifully ethnic features— almond-shaped eyes, full lips, a broad nose, and high cheek bones. He was a total cutie pie with a hearty laugh and easy spirit. He was street smart, though wise enough to understand the importance of education. A rare breed. And he was mine. I didn't always believe it, but time has revealed this. He was just too good to be true.

Darrin was just different. He wasn't the cliché "street guy" type. He never wore much jewelry outside of a nice watch, and never had flashy clothing or wore big logos or baggy jeans. He had a classic style, studious and fly as hell. He wore Gucci, Brioni, Zegna, and

Brunello Cucinelli casualwear. That man loved Italian fashion. No logos. If you knew, then you knew. His personality was charismatic. He had a genuinely good disposition; it is so hard to describe. You know how some guys are so kind, a wee bit square, and have a light positive spirit that just emanates from them? Darrin was that guy. He was the complete opposite of those types with a dark, negative aura who are actually so insecure they overcompensate with "things" or excessive big-dick energy. You could walk right past him on the street and never assume anything about his wealth, hobbies, occupation or goals, yet when he entered a room his presence was felt, it's this polarity that made him so hard to describe. He was full of integrity. Just like I like 'em. Envision a human mash-up between Dre's quiet energy, Obama's smooth likability, and Ace's good looks and low-key hustle in the movie *Paid in Full*. Side note: I swore that movie was based on him back then. So many similarities it was eerie. Real always recognizes real. We were inseparable ... well at first.

One sunny day in 1986, I was riding with my cousin Dee Dee in the Fiat convertible in North Oakland, we turned a corner and he pulled beside us. There he was, all fine, chocolate, and smiling with those damn gorgeous teeth. He was driving a shiny black S500 Mercedes. I could smell the air freshener and feel the cool breeze of his air conditioning looming from his driver's side window. There was no loud music, no big chains, a crisp Polo and a clean cut. I knew it then. I just liked him. Period. End of discussion. I said, "Who in the hell is HE??" Bear in mind, I'm 15 going on 36. My little grown ass. It was love at first sight. Straight UP. He spoke to my cousin and smiled at me. That was enough; I just fu*#ing knew. We exchanged numbers... Well, he gave me his and it was on!

We would have such a great time going to movies, outdoor concerts, sporting events, visiting restaurants, and jet-setting off to

Vegas. Family birthday dinners were a must. (I swore he sounded like a sommelier speaking about corkage fees, legs, bodies, and aromas), We'd drive to Sausalito on weekends, staying all day having both lunch and dinner. I loved to shop in San Francisco—Wilkes Bashford was his favorite. And during the holidays, I would do all of the shopping for his family and mine. I took the CHSPE test (much like the GED) in the beginning of 12th grade, finished high school at 16, and attended Heald Business College. (Remember, I started kindergarten at 4 and skipped a grade in elementary). Sometimes I wonder, who does that? Why start your senior year in high school, take senior pictures, only to test out and quit going? I was just too grown for my own good. I was smart as a whip and felt that high school was too slow at that point. My mother was beyond frustrated at this point and my father was just living his own life with his new wife. Divorced kids have it rough. But I digress.

At one point, Darrin and I enrolled at Diablo Valley College (DVC) together, I studied Criminal Justice, although he was far more focused than I. A transfer to UC Berkeley and a Business degree was his ultimate goal and I wanted a degree in Law. I always dreamed of becoming an attorney and having two children, a boy and a girl. Obviously, God had other plans.

I loved Darrin and wanted us to be accepted by our families, but neither my parents nor his mother were huge fans of our relationship. (Story of my life.) I truly don't think his mom disliked me as a person, but she didn't approve of me dating her son either. She was a devout Pentecostal woman and had very clear values and ideas about what she believed was right. I think because I wore jewelry, makeup, and pants — all big no-no's in the Pentecostal faith — she didn't feel that I was the right girl for her son. In hindsight, she would have likely preferred that he dated someone in "the church." She didn't yell, was never rude, nor did she raise her voice. She just let me know in very subtle ways that her son shouldn't be dating me. The five-year age gap between us probably didn't help either — I was a young buck ok a doe if you will, only 15 years old when we started dating; Darrin was already twenty. It sounds nuts to me now, but I lied to him about my age. I was a young girl who was far beyond her years. I had a maturity level and understanding of things that surpassed most of my peers. I had put away childish things long ago. While most were thinking of cheerleading, prom, cotillion, senior trips, and other rites of passage, I was thinking beyond all of that, trying to figure out how to get a good job and how to "stack" money. I padded my resume, exaggerated my skills and landed my first job at 16 as an assistant manager at United Colors of Benetton on Post Street in San Francisco, while attending Heald (yes assistant manager, keys and all!). Fortunately, I had retail experience from working for my Granny Lou and Aunt Sadie. I also worked at Pier 1 Imports in Concord briefly. That's where my mind was. Many girls my age dated older people. Where I'm from, it wasn't as taboo then. I can't say precisely why that was true. We just grew up and dated guys in an environment where dating older was part of our upbringing. I also think that older guys offered us basic necessities and some desired goods too. They were meeting both our material and nonmaterial needs. These incongruous relationships presented strategic choices, whether we were in the pursuit of survival or status. Remember, that as young girls, fitting in and being cool was still job one. There were many psychosocial attributes, involved in this type of dating, but for me it was always consensual. Despite the age difference, Darrin's siblings were pretty kind to me... well maybe there were a few *(like a million)* side glances and eye rolls, here and there. Looking back, as both a grown woman and mother myself, I can see both perspectives, I get it now. I'm grateful to Mrs. Banks for always managing to muster a smile and for being the strong mother that she was.

Fact is, Darrin lived a complex life. Raised in West Oakland by a single mother, he inherited a hustler's mentality and most definitely knew how to *get to* the money. I don't mean by any means necessary, as in violence, robbing, or stealing, but he was pretty financially efficient. He seemed like a former boarding school student— well-spoken, cultured, and so refined— but he also kept his ear and his business to the street. Once we started dating, I was always by his side; definitely a ride or die; in exchange he took care of me and made sure that I was polished, never worried about money or "staying fresh." At 16-17, this is all a girl wanted, right? Wrong… I wanted a 100% faithful man in an environment where that didn't even exist?? *Does it anywhere?* I digress... that's another chapter or book altogether. Funny thing is, people always judge or look down upon people that may not follow every law, have criminal pasts or may have committed systemic crimes, but I can tell you this, some of the most generous, honest, solid and good natured people that I know have come from the streets. Far more integrity than some of these square, seemingly "perfect" clowns. Just sayin'. There are good and bad apples in every bunch from the Fortune 500 boardrooms to the block. Be slow to judge.

Let me backup a minute by giving a bit of context. Oakland in the late 80s, the "crack" epidemic had begun, and our normal working-class people began using drugs. It likely began socially and then became habitual. Oakland was somewhat of a war zone growing up. There were lots of murders and other nefarious activity on the streets. Over time, we became desensitized to the TV news reports and Oakland Tribune headlines that read "Man Gunned Down…" Black-on-black crime sadly became the norm. I would hear of legendary turf wars: East Oakland versus West Oakland. North Oakland often fell somewhere in between. The city of Oakland was both thriving and dying at the same time. Hustlers and playas were glorified. On any given day you'd see young guys riding up and down the street in their drop-top classic cars that had been restored to the nines. Speakers blaring, girls had their heads on a swivel to see the hot boy coming down the block. Hair was whipped with a fresh asymmetrical cut, ten perfect nails covered in garnet red or cotton candy, designer crossbody, and Wet n' Wild 521 lip gloss. Girls were moving narcotics around for the guys, lucky for me I was never asked or required. They became hometown heroes because they had all the money and clout. Sadly, the boys in high school didn't stand a chance. No phone? No money? No whip? Boy bye. Oh, how sadly we were mistaken. These guys would have friendly "*sideshow*" car battles to show off their refurbished 66 Mustangs, Falcons, Chevelles, box Chevys, Caprice Classics, or their old school Cougars. They almost always had to have "*Trues & Vogues*" *or* the car was considered incomplete. Another staple was their "hella bumpin' sound systems. Back then you had to have a "Zapco" board and at least four 15" woofers. You literally could feel the vibration of cars bumpin' "Computer Love" coming from blocks away. The guys were fly as hell— super neatly dressed and intact. They wore things like derby jackets with their neighborhood (aka turf names) embroidered on the back. They also sported Levi's 501 jeans with the hard creases, Fila velour sweat suits, Nike Cortez sneakers, sweat suits, and a Pirates baseball cap. Never leaving their donkey rope and chunky jewelry at home. Not Darrin though. He just moved different than the average.

I remember when he took me on my first trip to Los Angeles from Oakland. We stayed at a hotel on Wilshire, near Westwood. It was a double date of sorts with his friend Anthony "Stringfield" and my close friend Teresa. I lied to my mother and said I was sleeping at my friend's house. He was the first gent that had ever taken me on a vacation or shopping (hell, he should have been!! I was hella young and taking a huge risk in going. I loved risking it all… Oy Vey!!). Anywhoo, back to the shopping, I mean big time, spoiled shopping —"Junior Trap Queen" shit. Let's just say, I was very well taken care of by Ellesse, FILA, North Beach Leathers, Gucci sweat suits and sneakers, nugget jewelry, EK glasses, and a herringbone chain. Sounds so trivial now, but in 1988 you couldn't tell me nothing. At all. He always made sure that I had a nice amount of spending money in my wallet. In those days, I didn't think much about growing my money, investing in things like stocks or real estate. I just didn't know any better…but I did know enough to save and save I did well. Even at 17, I was always a Capricorn woman… thereby a G.O.A.T especially during that moment in time.

Our relationship was very dichotomous in nature. On one hand it was fun, toxic, risky, and perilous, on the other it was full of solid life lessons, game, love, and adventure. Initially, as a teen I snuck around to be with him, eventually moving in and becoming straight-up hooked on him. If any girl got out of line, I would call or check her ass on sight. Neva scared. Pure foolery. Shaking my head.

Dear, Young Meke — keep your single, envious-natured, thirst trapping, girlfriends away from your cute, generous, hood-rich, charming, outgoing boyfriends. This will prevent tons of beat downs, confrontations, keyed cars, prank calls, spontaneous 'pull ups', tire replacements, restraining orders, and other unsavory behaviors — *signed, Grown Meke.* I was totally with the shits about Darrin, and I did not care about the consequences either. Periodt.edu I was like a Federal Agent on him—like white on rice. Now some 30 years later, I'm quite sure that I was suffering from obsessive love, because I lost hella sleep, friends, weight, edges, appetite, brain cells, and my right mind over him. I guess I was caught up in the "Rapture of Love", our favorite song. I took it literally. Just sayin'. The relationship was so turbulent at times, I once tried taking a box of Actifed allergy medicine in a pseudo-attention-getting-suicide-attempt. I ended up being rushed to the hospital where I survived with the clearest sinuses ever. #MajorFail! Childish per usual. Our break-ups were treacherous and frequent. I didn't quite know how to handle that man, I was young and uber intense about his ass.

When we were on, we spent tons of quality time together. In fact we were en route to Game 3 of the 1989 World Series (Oakland A's vs. SF Giants) when the big Earthquake happened in San Francisco on October 17th, 1989, at 5:03 pm. Strangely enough, we had decided at the last minute to take public transportation to avoid game traffic and BAM, there we were stuck on the B.A.R.T train underground, well underwater for nearly an hour. Thank God we didn't drive because a portion of the Bay Bridge collapsed, and lives were lost. We were stranded in San Francisco with his eight-year-old nephew, Kevin. It was dark because the power was out, people were running, crying and it was just purely chaotic. The following month, late November 1989, I found out that I was a month pregnant. I didn't tell many. Not my parents, uncles, sister, or many of my girlfriends. Although Darrin knew, he wasn't particularly excited. It wasn't because he didn't care about me or love me; it was because our situation just wasn't ideal. We had gone through a lot over the course of our relationship. During one of our breaks, I found out that he had cheated on me with a friend named Pam— like my bonafide, same church, fellow Capricorn (the kicker!), true-blue homegirl... I terrorized her for 3 years straight— went to her job, house, and if I ran into her at an event, I didn't hold back. On sight it was like, *"Oooh, There go that bitch!!"* He caught hell too. I didn't only hold her accountable, because my commitment wasn't with her. But as my girlfriend, she certainly should have known better. More importantly, she should have known *me* better. I didn't stop tormenting her until I discovered that I was pregnant. I also found out that he was creepin' with at least two other girls that I knew of. A mess! The infidelity made me batshit crazy, quite literally. Theoretically, he wasn't always cheating, his rendezvous were during a breakup, but the way my loyalty meter (loyaltometer) is set up I didn't believe that he should be messing around during that time. I would drive around looking for him with a flashlight in the daytime. Then at night, pull-up to wherever, park outside, beep him "911" on his Skytel pager incessantly. These were the days when you would beep a person and expect a quick return call, but if they didn't you would then drive to a near-by pay phone hoping that they would call back the anonymous number. What was even worse is that my boyfriend became familiar with the pay phone and wouldn't call that number back either. This become a full day's work and tank of gas! Because you then drive to a different pay phone in another area to page him yet again. Oh, and you dared someone to touch the handset while you were awaiting that call back. I was definitely trippin'. Oh, to be young...

Bear in mind, this was between me working and going to school. As emotionally intelligent as I thought I was entering into the relationship, it really tested my 18-year-old sense of security. I still needed so much more maturing. The sad part was that in hindsight I should have known where I truly stood. We had been together for four years. I had full access to everything while most didn't even know where he lived. He totally took care of me, bought my first car (a convertible Saab, which was a big-ass deal in 1988 and at 17), and he NEVER took anyone around his immediate family, especially his "Ma-Ma" (pronounced Mah Mah). I never condone cheating, but you have to understand what you are fully signing up for when messing with a dude in the streets or someone in certain higher-demand lines of work. It was just 'par for the course". Sad but true... This concept never made sense to me and I fought it tooth and nail. Always. That said, the trust had been broken in our relationship, and I didn't know how to handle it. We took a few relationship breaks. By mid-December, just shy of my upcoming 19th birthday, we had both established that it wasn't the right time for either of us to bring a child into the world, mainly because we were both in school and I was too young. I booked the soonest available appointment; the procedure was scheduled for just after the New Year. Then things took an unforeseeable turn for the worse. Never in my wildest dreams could I have fathomed the twist of fate that would unfold in the coming weeks....

On the night of January 14^{th,} I had gone to Darrin's place in San Mateo, about 25-30 minutes outside of Oakland. I think he initially got that apartment to hide from my super sleuth ass, a spot where he could safely creep. Until I found out about it and persuaded the landlord to open his unit and let me in one afternoon. *"I'm not going to be ignored Dan"*, Fatal Attraction voice. I was banoodles crazy about him.

Truth is, he got the place there to be closer to the college and also because he always believed in living on the outskirts. The following morning, January 15th, I recall feeling super nauseous while taking my shower. I had the first- trimester blues. Literally leaning against the wall, he brought my juice into the bathroom. When I finally got dressed, he asked me to switch cars with him. I took his car, a mustard yellow Corvette (I know, I know, but I promise he was otherwise NOT flashy) and he drove mine, a 1989 Black drop Saab. He told me that he "had to do something" and that he would see me a little later. That was at about 10:30 am. I went straight home from his place, changed my clothes and got comfy. I still had the huge, slightly deflated bouquet of mylar birthday balloons and a withered floral arrangement in my new, quaint, Art Deco apartment on 29th

Street. I was bopping around the place, snacking, flipping through magazines, and washing my hair. It felt like a particularly slow day. I was shuffling back and forth between the bathroom sink and my bedroom, to watch *The Oprah Winfrey Show. Cue music: "Oprah's Onnnn".* Anyway, her show on that day was devoted to the life and legacy of Martin Luther King, Jr. It was his birthday and her guests were contemporaries of Dr. King. They were recounting details of his life and work I'd never heard before. The show really had my attention; I was intrigued. I'd scrub a little bit during commercials, wrap it in a towel when the show came back on, step over into the bedroom and watch a few more minutes. Water would eventually start dripping down my neck forcing me back into the bathroom again. At about 3:20 pm I received a phone call that would change my life forever…. It was my cousin Dana in a panic, "Girl, where are you!!?" …. "Ok… well where is your car?" She was on the phone asking some random Lo-Jack-rep sounding questions.

"Huh?" I responded. "Parked outside, why?!"

I'm thinking, *Why is her crazy ass calling asking all these questions?* Then she gave me random instructions.

"Turn on the news."

This time I paid attention. Helicopters were hovering over the freeway not far from my house. All lanes blocked.

"That looks like your car," Dana said.

Something didn't feel right. Didn't know what it was, but something. I looked closer.

The news chopper was hovering almost at freeway level.

I saw what she was talking about.

"You're right," I said.

"That damn sure does look like my car," I mumbled slowly while squinting at the screen. Then I remembered; my car *wasn't* outside. I didn't drive it that day. We had switched!!

I normally drove the Saab, and the car on the screen was indeed a black convertible Saab. Same body style. Same tan interior. Same black canvas top.

"Police got everything blocked off, ...there was some kind of accident. Just glad you're ok," she said. My end of the line went silent.

"Hello?!!" Dana asked.

I raced out of the door—wet hair and all—got in the car, jumped on the freeway at the Harrison Street (21A) entrance. I got to the police roadblock at the very next exit, which was Grand Avenue (21B)— got out of my car and started running toward the flashing lights. Officers were yelling "Get back in the car!!" I said, "Officer that's my......" I finally complied and got back in my car then sped off to his sister Linda's house to learn that the family was already headed to Highland Hospital where he had been transported.

Once I arrived at the hospital, I was met with the unimaginable. A complete stranger heard me frantically asking the doctors and nurses if an ambulance had brought a man in from an incident at the Grand Avenue exit. The stranger—a wheelchair-bound man sitting in the lobby—looked me straight in the eyes and said with a slurred, slightly southern accent, "Oh that boy they brought in here? He gone baby. He dead baby."

I absolutely lost it. "Shut up! You don't even know me!!" I yelled back.

I started shaking uncontrollably. Tears poured down my cheeks. I was scared and confused. It felt as though the trauma center was spinning all around me. *What happened?!!!* I hated that the stranger said what he said, but something inside of me knew he was telling the truth. *Is Darrin really dead?* I was with him only 5 hours ago!!! Now, I was standing in the middle of the emergency room lobby looking for him. I hadn't found any of Darrin's family members yet. One of the nurses finally led me to a small chapel-like room where the doctor confirmed my— *our*— worst fear. He began with the words, "We did all we could but…." Darrin's older sister, Linda Kay, fell to the ground immediately; she had fainted. I swung the door open and ran out of the room, down the hallway, sobbing and shouting, "NOOOO!!" In that moment, and many moments after, I just wanted to die. Later that night his sister and I had to go to the coroner's office to identify his lifeless body. Somehow, I hoped that they were wrong, and that it would all turn out to be a case of mistaken identity. He was the love of my life, my friend, and my guiding compass. At 19, he was all that I knew. He was indeed my everything.

On January 15, 1990, at 3:13 in the afternoon, my beloved Darrin had passed away due to multiple gunshot wounds. He had been ambushed and gunned down execution style at the freeway-exit traffic light in broad daylight by an "unknown" assailant. It is sad when you have enemies hiding in plain sight. Oakland is only so big, so the process of elimination was simple in my mind. He had to have known them. Sad. Jealousy is real, Hate is also real. Not everyone could handle his amazing light. He just wasn't like them. I don't think he even owned a weapon. Never saw one in four years. He was so positive that he probably didn't think he needed one.

I shared my dreams with him and would sit and listen in awe as he shared his with me. We went through so many phases together. He was now gone, and my world was shattered into a million tiny pieces. So many people mourned "He was one of the good ones," they said. There were some cold-blooded guys out there, scandalous in nature, but he was truly a good dude and the city grieved his loss. Retaliation began. I would hear about it, but I steered clear. Living above the fray, and stayed in my own world, trying to pick up the pieces. Praying daily for comfort, discernment, and protection for my unborn child and me. I kept thinking, why did he want to switch cars? Did he feel something was off? Did he owe someone? Where was he coming from or going? I couldn't quiet my brain. I was uneasy. I didn't sleep for a week.

Darrin's soul was taken to Heaven before he could ever meet his son. Yes, I said Heaven! At 19, I was left without my rock while carrying his child. The life that I knew and loved was ripped to shreds. Unbeknownst to me, this was the moment that would prepare me for many more tragedies to come. It gave me another layer— a new coating of armor, if you will. I thought I was going to give up. I even contemplated suicide multiple times, but past experiences taught me better. I kept going. This first experience of heartbreak and tragedy would show me who I was-– a strong and resilient fighter. I was bigger than I thought. I was going to be that *somebody* Darrin always knew I would be. Four days later, on January 19, the day of my scheduled abortion, I stood alongside his family and privately laid him to rest at Rolling Hills Memorial Park. Somehow, he was more beautiful in death than he was alive—the mark of a man who had fulfilled the soul contract that God had planned for him. Darrin had positively impacted so many lives, mine especially. He showed his loved ones what was possible. We didn't have to stay a product of the environment we were from. There was more for us, our potential was infinite, and no obstacle was too great to overcome. He was in my heart and an incredible part of him was in my womb. Knowing this made the entire experience that much more moving for me.

I remember Mariah Carey's song "Vision of Love" was just being released. I repeated the lyrics regularly to my unborn child. I had written a page goodbye letter that I put into his casket along with photos of us. The news headlines surrounding Darrin's death read: ***"Banks Led a Double Life."*** It was true. In the months leading up to his death, Darrin had enrolled at the College of San Mateo as a Business major. He attended school three days per week, and on his days off, he invested in real estate. He saw hustling as a means to an end—a way to take care of his family-- but he had far bigger ambitions. Having said that, history has proven that you can't have one foot in and one foot out when you want to change your life. It just doesn't work that way. You must fully commit to the change. Point blank.

After his death, I hit rock bottom. His family was grieving amongst themselves and shut me out completely. I also had very little support from my own family. They just didn't understand or feel my devastation. Honestly, young black men were being killed every day in Oakland—no one seemed to care. I was just another 'baby momma" in most eyes. He was my everything, and I couldn't understand a life without him. But I had to pick up the fragments that remained. Needless to say, I decided not to terminate my pregnancy. I am and was a loyal woman, killing his child given the circumstances was not an option. My friends took me to visit Los Angeles in my seventh month, since I was thinking about relocating. When my water broke, I was alone. I drove myself to the hospital and stayed as calm as I could while timing my contractions. My first born, Darrin Lorenzo Banks II made his grand entrance on the evening of June 19th, 1990, five months to the day we buried his father. I was 19 years old. My son gave me a renewed sense of purpose and motivation — one that was even greater than my will to succeed when I was dating his father. Being a young, single mom was difficult, but my courage and willpower were greater. At one point, I tried to receive public assistance, but that process was equally degrading and motivating. Me being some kind of county mom, pushing a stroller down the street on East 14th in Oakland, sucking on a lollipop just wasn't an option. I just knew it. I wasn't that girl. Me and the public assistance system just didn't get along. I tried…they were talking to me crazy when I applied, and I was talking crazy to them back. The social workers were so rude and insensitive. "Was the father like a drug dealer? Can you furnish a death certificate?" They berated me, "And you are *how old*? and he was how old? Did he ever work? Did he have a job?" Their noses were turned up and I kept thinking, *Wow!* The way they spoke to me was so demeaning. Their attitudes were the worst ever—I mean over-the-top nasty. The manager— a woman who hates her job, her thighs, hates you, and hates that you just got her up from watching Jerry Springer, while she was eating a Hot Pocket in the back office— came out and said some condescending crap that I'll never forget.

These workers were speaking to applicants as if the applicants *wanted* to be in the position they were in. They had no idea how much of a toll it takes on a person to ask for public assistance.

I moved on and got a job as a new-account representative at the bank a few months after my son was born. I was in complete hustle mode. "By any means necessary" was my mood. "Scared of going broke" was the theme. I felt panicked, desperate and alone, yet determined. By the time my son was four months old (nine months after Darrin passed), I started going out with my girlfriends, attending concerts, and beginning to meet guys here and there. Overall, I stayed home and took care of my baby boy. On my very first date, nearly a year after Darrin's passing, I was hanging out with a guy and my breasts started to leak milk — talk about embarrassing! But I pressed on, leaky boobs and all. The guy was so nice about it, he and I are still friends till this day, quite the inside joke. The Demi Moore-Patrick

Swayze movie, *Ghost* came out in the fall of 1990 and I would watch it all the time and cry. I missed Darrin so much. I felt abandoned; people tend to disappear when challenges arise. I was under a lot of pressure and trying to figure out my next viable steps. I had more than myself to think about then. Definite learning curve.

I moved out of my cute tiny place into a brand new building for more space, security plus private parking, and I ended up living right next door to Terry Ellis of the group EnVogue. I've always thought that living in a nice place inspires you to do well. I was blessed to be approved and be able to live in such a nice building, bear in mind I was still only 19. Eventually, I decided to move again about 8 months later, but this time it was out of Oakland to start fresh. I packed my shit. My mother and my grandmother were like; *"You ain't taking that baby out of town! You don't even know what you're doing!"* They thought they were my bosses because when I came home from the hospital I went directly to my "Grandmas" house. Her house was always a central point. First stop… it was large, and she had a huge presence, it was Big Momma's House. She was that house where you would go if you were sick, going through a break-up or you just had a baby or whatever it was just the stop you *had* to make. I needed to go, I had severe PTSD from the trauma of losing Darrin. All the on-going murder and drug raid reports only further exacerbated this. I would duck if someone drove too close, circle blocks if I felt followed, never gave out my home address, peek out of my blinds, never sit with my back to doors in restaurants, I was traumatized. Sadly, it had become so common that it was routine, but it was not normal. It was during this time that I was driving down the street in Walnut Creek, and a woman crossed three lanes, to make a sharp right turn into a bank parking lot. I nearly ran into her because of her recklessness. I blew the horn at her and she stopped, rolled her window down, and blurted,

"Shut the f#@k up you nigger bitch!" Nigger with a hard *"R"*. Uh oh!!! Not that word again. I could not believe my ears; this was the absolute wrong time in my life to be saying this to me. I politely turned my car around, drove into the bank parking lot, locked eyes with her as she started to rush into the branch and stood nervously in the teller line. I left my car running and followed right behind her, where I demanded to know, *"Did you really just call me a ni#@er b%*ch!?"* Before she could make some lame excuse, I slapped that woman so hard, quickly exited, and scurried back to my car. Was I wrong? In my 19 year old mind, it felt justified. I bet she'll think twice before saying it again to a random black woman unprovoked. She had truly lost her mind and I was at wits end with everything going on in my life. We clearly both had lost our minds. My teenage years were not normal, and I recognized that it was time to go. I needed a change. I felt subjugated in that life. This season was preparing me for more precarious situations. I was always this concrete rose, never been one to let obstacles stop me.

'Long live the rose that grew from concrete when no one else ever cared.'

–Tupac

By Spring of 1991, I packed up my then eight-month-old son, my personal savings, and all of our belongings into my new blue Honda Accord EX and a 17' U-Haul and made the five-hour trek from Oakland to Los Angeles for a fresh new start. Times had changed.

CHAPTER 5

Back 2 Life

❧

I've had a love affair with fashion for as long as I can remember. My Aunt Sadie opened a pre-owned clothing store called "Eureka" when I was three or four years old. I remember working at her store feeling the different textures of the fabric, noticing designers, bold patterns, and colors. Her store was a consignment shop, which entailed evaluating each item and determining which ones she would accept and which she'd give back to the consignors. I recall people coming in with huge trash bags full of clothes and Aunt Sadie showing my cousins and me what was considered quality and what was cheap as hell. "This is junk!!" she would scream. I began visualizing outfits in my mind by putting different pieces of clothing together creating looks and thinking about how I would rock them when I got older. I also learned the business side—watching her take inventory and calculating commission payments. When I arrived in Los Angeles, I knew I was in the right place to live out my dreams in fashion.

I moved to L.A with no real plan, but I felt so much more alive. I felt as though I had a chance. I finally had total autonomy over my life. I had about $16,000 of my savings left …yes, I had my *own* money. Some people assumed that Darrin had left behind a bunch of cash for me or that I was stashing his money. That was not the case at all. Hell, I wish he did; I gave birth to his child and felt that I deserved it. But he didn't keep money at my house, nor did he involve me in his business very much. I was actually good at saving what he gave me, and I always kept my own mini stash. Besides, I was also working and…well, siphoning money from my 9-to-5. I'm not proud of this, but don't judge me—I was now 20 with a fatherless newborn, no help, and scared shitless. I had to do what I had to do. I paid restitution for my wrongdoings in more ways than one. A scarcity mentality makes people believe there will never be enough. This thinking applies to many things—recognition, love, and emotions, not just money.

The "scarcity mindset" also caused me to make poor decisions. When you're worried about your bank balance, for example, you might put off opening the bills, pay them at the last second, or even pay them late. But the issue won't go away on its own. In fact, it will only get worse, thereby increasing the feelings of scarcity. I always had solid core values and would never hurt anyone, steal from friends or family, or sell my soul or my body, but I was down for anything else. A vicious cycle and I had it bad! I was down for any come up, this for me was survival of the fittest. I focused on the short term of everything, my mind couldn't fathom having abundance again. I was young, anxious, and short-sighted. What I didn't know then was that, what you think you become. I soon learned.

I lived off my savings after Darrin's death. I gave myself a nice fully catered baby shower (paid cash) in a suite at the Hyatt Hotel in Oakland (*where were my friends though?*) I also paid for my prenatal care and hospital delivery in full upfront, and I bought a modest new car. Cash was king and I had that shit.

When I got to L.A, I was hell-bent on finding a good sitter, working and going back to school, and securing an apartment. I had to think long and hard before jumping into an expensive place alone. Despite my savings, I had so much anxiety about finances, it still felt like I was thirty cents shy of a quarter with a child and no job. I was rich to some but broke compared to the lifestyle I had lived before. Can you imagine this much life responsibility at 19? A baby, bills, grief, a new city, so many decisions and so little help. I pushed through…. I did it alone, tired, scared, broke, and broken.

Fortunately, I knew a couple of people who were living in L.A. at the time. I stayed with my friend Francine for about two months. She had a nice one-bedroom duplex apartment in the Mid-City area and kindly allowed me to crash with her until I could figure out a more permanent living arrangement. My son Darrin and I slept between Francine's bedroom and her living room. This worked for us in the beginning, but then we started bickering. Eventually, it seemed like we were arguing over every little thing—whether it was debating about the sky-high cost of every call on the phone bill, the thermostat setting, who drank the last of the juice, whose turn it was to clean, or whose hair was on the floor. We grew more argumentative and at odds with each other by the hour. I was already tired from raising my baby on my own, and the quarreling only made me feel more drained. BTW: I kept the U-Haul as storage this *whole* time. Yep, another poor decision. To be fair, my logic was that it would total the same amount as a storage unit plus movers, and I would have 24-hour access to it. Shit, I was 19. I also knew that Fran's place was temporary. I moved out after a huge blow up where her boyfriend Carlos got involved and put us out. I was so embarrassed and angry therefore needless to say our friendship was on pause for a few years. Bye Fran… for a bit. FYI: Francine is one of my nearest and dearest friends now. She's like a sister. We have both matured so much since then. Unfortunately, her then boyfriend Carlos also passed away and we both ended up being single parents.

My first year of motherhood was tough. Baby boy was growing fast, and his needs were constantly changing. He was crawling, being introduced to new foods, and outgrowing clothes and toys. Thankfully, my sons' father's family came around and started to spend time with him. I would drive him back to Oakland so they could have him for a couple of weeks at a time. This was helpful as I was still discovering L.A, stumbling a bit, starting to date, and learning my way around the city. I didn't have any caregivers that I really trusted to help me with him and had no consistently available family or friends in the vicinity. My living situation was unstable, and my savings were running low. Even when I would go out on lunch or dinner dates with guys, I would always think of my young son and order him something or pack up my meal for him. And if my date's conversation lacked intellect, was shallow, or just focused on getting some ass, his tab reflected it. What do I look like? A fool? Nope. My bullshit tolerance was low, and my bullshit detector has always been high. In L.A., my friend Kelly and Auntie Sonya babysat on occasion. For the most part, I was doing it on my own.

I ended up getting a nice spacious place in Mid-Wilshire (now Koreatown) and finding a cool-ass roommate, named Desiree, through our mutual friend Kelly. She was 18 and I was 20. We went out a lot, met guys and hung out while my son was gone. I still had the huge responsibility of being a full-time single parent, so it was fun and refreshing when I got those breaks. Desiree was pretty and had an hour-glass shape. Men flocked to her, but she only dated the most popular fly guys. I wasn't too shabby myself, so life was good on the dating front. We had a ball and every day was an adventure. For example, during the 1992 Los Angeles riots, Des and I were so glued to the television and outraged by the verdict that we decided to join in the protests. We hopped in her Volkswagen Rabbit Cabriolet and drove into the melee on La Brea Avenue. We got in on some of the looting action; I just remember us lugging a huge television from Circuit City and then going to Blockbuster to get VHS tapes and candy, throwing it all into her convertible. It was like *"Be Kind and Please Rewind"*. It felt good to serve justice for Rodney King!! *"Can't we all just get along?" Power to the people!* In our eyes we were right! But hey, we were also young and dumb.

I joined a couple of talent booking agencies for work as a model and video girl. HATED IT! Sitting at auditions in a room full of pretty, yet mostly vapid vixens, and being cast in videos with desirous directors and creepy artists was not for me. I was not about that *"casting couch"* life. Be clear; I did my share of dating but only on my own terms. This was a whole new world coming from Oakland. Back to the newspaper classifieds I proudly went; I always did well during interviews. I found a job in West Los Angeles at Tishman Realty & Construction corporate office, that was short lived, because I was always late and falling asleep at my desk, which just happened to be the huge one in the MAIN lobby right in front of the elevators (aka the visitors center!) Yikes!! I would be so exhausted from juggling motherhood, early daycare drop-offs, and being out in the thriving Hollywood nightlife, there was no way I could keep my eyes open. It was there, however, that I met my best friend and my boys' godmother LaNita Thomas. Lanita is that friend who will come to your aid no matter what, and be a strong shoulder to lean on. The "clean your kitchen when you're depressed" type of friend. Real friends are hard to come by; I value her so much. She is the one positive thing that came out of that job.

I was beginning to find my footing in L.A. My girlfriend Donyale and I were out and about on the regular. She was a part of a girl group called 5AM (I was in the elite scene or in "the places to be" with them. We were wild as hell. We would get into parties with one + one on the list and then pass the wristband back to our girlfriends. The events were so lit back then, it was *that* serious. Truth is, we didn't need any formal invites to nuthin'; all we had to do was get dressed and be there. I was young, cute, had an I.D, and on the circuit. (Sidebar: My girl Kelly created the popular concept of "Bottle Service" at clubs, so wherever we went we were always welcome.)

After the clubs (Bar One, Carlos'n Charlie's, Century Club, String Fellows, Paradise 24, The Roxbury, etc.) we would hit up Pennyfeathers or my favorite, Larry Parker's Diner—a popular late-night hot spot that was ALWAYS lively…. Loud bangin' music, a DJ, TV screens, and the owner Larry was super chill and never made me wait for a table. Just a real cool vibe. Reminded me of a hip Arnold's Drive-in on *Happy Days*. On any given night, Larry's would be packed with hella guys— the who's who of Hollywood—and the tables had interconnected phones!! Bingo!! It was a single girl's dream— "A-Listers" and fine single men of all types… producers, actors, singers, bad boys, rappers, athletes, "rap-lethes". (*Baby, everyone wanted to try their hand at rap back then!*) What a time to be alive! It was there that I formed several lasting relationships — some guys I dated, some I hated, some went on to become business acquaintances, and others became brothers. I ended up falling super in love with one well-known rapper/producer in particular, and we dated on and off for quite some time. I was by his side during a very tumultuous period in his career. Let's just say we were together, I moved to Atlanta…. and I forgot the rest. The athletes were fun to look at, hang out with, and *not* seriously date, because they were for everybody (although, I broke down and dated a couple of draft picks). We referred to those guys as "community property" back then. It sure didn't stop us from liking them, but it put our goals in far better perspective.

Once my big sister Yolanda and cousin Dee Dee moved to L.A, things got real. Gangs all here, I was now of legal age and had all the access. Before age 21, I was running around using my cousin or sisters IDs to get into clubs. By now I had befriended many of the promoters, power players and "cool" people in town. Always being a people person and ready to dance, I was now formally on the invite list for many of the relevant socials, award shows, dinners, fashion events and swanky soirees. Having an agent didn't hurt either.

The private events were epic, like the Soul Train Awards after-parties and the 1993 "Uptown Unplugged" on the Universal Studios backlot. That was an awesome night; Mary J Blige, Jodeci, Christopher Williams, Father MC, and Heavy D closed the show with, *"Is It Good To You?"* The event was so much fun that the performances were a blur. The year that Magic Johnson shut down Six Flags Magic Mountain for a private event and threw himself the bash of the year, it was called *"Midsummer Night's Magic,"* which was associated with his charity. It was there that I met young NBA prospect, Shaquille O'Neal, as well as my soon-to-be boyfriend "O", a dancer who also worked in TV production on *"The Fresh Prince"*. We dated for a couple of years, even living together with my son for one of those years. I was happy to have a positive male role model around my child. We had fun going to clubs and doing the classic dating thing. We went out until his neighborhood sweetheart, April, moved to California from his hometown of Philadelphia and shit hit the fan. Long story short, we dated for two years, she and I spoke, it went left, and he was caught in a few lies. We broke up, but April and I have remained friends till this day. The End. This was the first of many instances where I learned never to be mad at the other woman for your man's indiscretions. The loyalty is supposed to come from *him*; he made the commitment, not the other woman. Another woman cannot be a home-wrecker, because it's not her home to wreck; it's *his*. Unless she's a friend or chick who knows about you, then that's a whole nutha ball of wax. But even in those instances, he's still at fault. If only the walls could talk.

Now, I did go to Las Vegas once in the late 80's with Darrin, but this was a totally different trip as a single 21-year-old. The fights in Vegas became a girl's getaway for me and my friends. My sister Yolanda and her crew would go as well. There were always a few separate groups of us. I was never one to be seen with a pack of females. Anything more than four felt like a herd to me—one or two others was my preference. I didn't like to roll into places "deep." We would plan the trip and choose our outfits based on (1) pool (2) Casino; and (3) night life. I would pack my Joan & David shoes, Joan Vass and St. John knit dresses, Benetton shirts with short denim skirts, bright Esprit tops, Guess jeans, and a North Beach Leather dress. I was always modestly attired, as if I was Blanche of the "The Golden Girls", even at age 21. We were always a classy bunch, never half naked or in the wrong circles and respected by all. We were hella cool like one of the fellas. I was always live and funny AF, though.

We never slept a wink while in Vegas, my friends had to do shifts, because someone would always tap the hell-out. Eyes burning, feet tired, and bodies cold from the freezing A/C. We would walk the full distance of the Great Wall of China by the end of the weekend, laughing all the way. *Jingle Bells, bihh.* We'd come home with casino carpet on the bottoms of our shoes from doing our walk-throughs. We would forget about ALL our responsibilities back home…well almost.

The casinos were accessible 24 hours a day; clubs were open till 5 am and the restaurants were open all night. Even shopping was available around the clock. Wall-to-wall ni%gas!! It was overwhelming!

High rollers came from every state and every country to witness their favorite fighter win or lose in the competition. It would be nothing for a baller to stunt by inviting my entire friend group to dinner, shopping, and then to the fight. Some would simply want us at the table while they gambled. No strings attached. Of course, some folks hooked up—back then, there were very few with a shy thigh—but the majority were just having fun winning and sharing the wealth "*Big Willie*" style. It was their playground. Someone once said: "closed mouths don't get fed, crime books don't get read, and sad thighs don't get spread". We were just in the sandbox with them. I would always keep my "*gifted*" chips, and cash them in. I could not stand watching folks gamble and lose thousands. I hated the wastefulness of it. It still irks my soul to this day. My mind just isn't wired that way, I'm always thinking of what could be done with that money. We had the time of our lives; there was just nothing like it. Chile, we were so turned up, but we truly enjoyed ourselves and the friendship-bonding time. I like to call it our first "team building" exercises. It was just magical! I was young, wild, and free. There was just no comparable era.

I tell you the 90s as a whole were the best; I had more fun living in Los Angeles 1991-1997 probably than all of my other years combined. Under 30 the greatest memories were made hands down.

The early '90s weren't only about partying; I networked big time and was able to secure a meeting with Arsenio Hall, who was the hot late-night TV host at the time. I researched and wrote my first ever serious treatment to pitch a talk show concept. I wanted to be the next Oprah Winfrey. I felt that I had the personality, maturity level, and that je ne sais quoi that it took to effectively captivate an audience. I went to the UCLA library (don't ask me how I got in) and researched the history of talk shows, and how to reach certain demographics, but I primarily studied all things *Oprah*. I really wanted to know how she garnered the success that she did. I was always an Oprah aficionado.

I had an agent to help me in this pursuit and he later arranged for me to audition for films as well. In L.A all the cute girls and a "modeling" or talent agent. I guess being cute and singing a little was my talent. *Deep Shrug.* In fact, I auditioned for the lead role—the part of Angela—in the 1994 movie, *Low, Down, Dirty Shame.* It was eventually given to the beautiful Salli Richardson, but I was so honored to be submitted and considered, especially given the fact that I had no prior professional acting experience. Preparing for the audition made me focus and study like I never had before. It was then that I knew I had it in me to do whatever I set my mind to. It was time to buckle down. It was clear that Los Angeles had a wealth of resources and opportunities for me. I knew I had to regroup and think about what I really wanted. It was then that I decided the niche my heart was set on was fashion.

CHAPTER 6

It's All About the Benjamins

❧

In 1994, I enrolled at the Fashion Institute of Design and Merchandising (FIDM) as a Merchandise Marketing major, where I learned everything a buyer needs to know to succeed in the fashion world —from color theory to the psychology of buying and marketing. This education led to me becoming a stylist. There went my teenaged plans to pursue a career in law!

While in school we were required to intern in the fashion world for one of my classes, I was a dresser for a Giorgio Armani fashion show that took place in Beverly Hills. It was my first experience working as a dresser at a fashion show, somewhat like an air traffic controller, always giving direction to keep things running smoothly. Changing a full look takes time, making it a literal race to get ready for the runway. In the disorderly backstage environment, the dresser can be a calming influence for models before and during showtime. I was bitten, I loved it and I was offered my first styling gig before I even graduated from school. This opportunity launched the career of my dreams, years of being paid for something I would do for free.

My friend, Todd Russaw, was a new A&R at Biv 10 Records and offered me the opportunity to style some of their new talent. Todd was a super cool, industry guy that my friends and I knew. He always loved my personal style and he knew that I loved fashion, but styling was an entirely new concept for me. To be honest, I never even knew that a career as a stylist existed. I was in school as a fashion marketing major. I remember the creative team at the label called me and asked what my day rate was; I told them to hold on, cause quite honestly, I didn't friggin know. I said $300 a day, not having a clue that stylists could charge upwards of $1,500 a day. They must have laughed their asses off. This was in 1994! I also didn't realize that I was supposed to ask my client (the label) for a credit card, so I put my rent money and debit card on the line for the clothes…chile! Wrong again.

Biv 10 was a joint venture imprint with Motown Records that was led by Michael Bivins — founding member of New Edition and Bell Biv DeVoe. My first gig was to style the up-and-coming girl group 702 for their first music video "This Lil Game We Play"— a duet with R&B group, Subway. My first meeting with the ladies of 702 was at a cool little boutique, Stussy Union, on La Brea Avenue. I knew the owner Eddie, who had recently opened the store and I figured what better place to support. There were four members in the group at the time, and they had driven up in a van together from Las Vegas. I remember when they all got out of the van, they were so young, never waxed, hair in ponytails, and new to it all. I selected three or four urban, *well...* young R&B looks as options for them from stores across L.A. The video was shot in New York; I was so excited to work in another city, I couldn't believe that I was actually getting paid to do this!! On the morning of the shoot, the girls came into my wardrobe trailer one by one sad about their makeup. Shhhh, ladies not a problem. I politely redid their cute faces and continued to style the job. I remember watching the final cut for the first time and thinking, *"Damn, I did that!"* This gig would lead to me styling several other Motown acts like MC Brains and jazz artist Eric Reid. It would also open doors for me to work with Warner Brothers, DreamWorks, MCA Records, and others. Great style, personality, and a solid work ethic leads to referrals in the fashion game. You also must be prepared professionally to go above and beyond the call of duty. It's a business that is so relationship driven, and rife with nepotism. Fortunately, I was finding my rhythm, working often, and doing my thing.

My little boy Darrin, who we called "Noonie" was four years old by now. Noonie got his nickname as a baby from my girlfriend Leslie in Los Angeles, she said he looked like a "Noonie Bug". It stuck with him, my family all started to call him that while he was in diapers. We dropped the "Bug" by the time he was in kindergarten.

It was very important that I ensure a quality education for him— to invest in proper schooling and behavior would guarantee this— so I enrolled him in a private school called the University of Islam, in Inglewood. I wanted my son to have a chance, male influences, and be more than a statistic. They were a bit strict for my taste, so then I moved him to another independent private school, Marcus Garvey. Both schools were a serious commute for me daily, however it was one of my non-negotiables. Along with his daily vegetables and weekly home haircuts courtesy of me. Now in my early 20's, I was a young mom learning the ropes, but I knew that my son deserved the best from me. I have always felt that children were innocent beings and they didn't ask us parents to be here. The least we can do is give our best. There was certainly a lot I could have done better I'm sure, but I tried hard.

Fortunately, I could now comfortably provide for us both. In addition to giving him a solid education, we always had a nice place to live and the latest and most current style. I made sure of that. It was just the two of us. I was slowly making a name for myself. I lived and breathed fashion and continued to study popular culture closely. I was comfortable with my career and cash flow... and then a chance encounter propelled my career to new and unimaginable heights.

It was a dry summer day in Los Angeles, and as usual, I was on the move. Today, I was at the historic Wyndham Bel Age Hotel. Beverly Hills 90210 devotees know exactly where I'm talking about. The swanky hotel was home to many historical moments on the show, including Kelly and Dylan's infamous pool scene; the "Donna Martin Graduates" prom incident; and, of course, it was also where Dylan lived before he moved into his house. On this day, the hotel would be the backdrop to a historical moment for me too.

I trudged into the lobby, schlepping about a dozen heavy garment bags. I was headed to the penthouse to style a photoshoot for rapper Suga Free. As I stepped into the elevator, the door jammed. I lifted my head up, and in walked Lauryn Hill and her entourage. *Oh. My. God.* You know how they say that the favor of God can change your life? Well, unbeknownst to me, this was my moment of favor.

I had a full-on fangirl moment. "Lauryn! I'm such a huge fan! I love your music," I calmly said.

Then, I looked down at her feet and noticed that we were wearing the same shoes—brown strappy Steve Madden heeled sandals. I pointed that out to her too, of course...LOL! Lauryn was cool, she looked over at me, smiled and said few words. I'm sure she just wanted me to stop freakin' talking. Nah! No ma'am. Too excited. Before I got out of the elevator, I handed her assistant, Miriam "Mim" Farrakhan, my card and then turned to Lauryn and said: "Call me if you ever need anything."

The next day Miriam contacted me; Lauryn's stylist had dropped the ball…*say no more*. I picked that bitch up, bounced it, flipped it, and ran with it for over a decade.

I traveled the world with Lauryn and her team. My first official job was a magazine shoot at Smashbox Studio, then I was hired to style the "Ready or Not" video from her early days with the Fugees, and I remained with her straight through to *The Miseducation of Lauryn Hill* album. I was responsible for most of her iconic looks during that era. Working with Lauryn was an incredible experience; she is hands down one of the greatest teachers I've ever had. She is a mastermind. She's super meticulous and very hands-on with her craft. She has genius-level talent and is just an all-around dope individual. I consider my time working with Lauryn and family one of the greatest experiences in my career. After several years, I passed the ball to fashion newcomer Marni Senofonte, who was always of tremendous help to me while working at the Norma Kamali boutique. I'm proud to have played a vital part in Marni's career as a fashion stylist; her present-day career and achievements are so astonishing. It's what I call an alley-oop.

People often ask me how I got my start in the entertainment industry. That question always makes me wince because I don't view myself as someone that's *in* entertainment per se. I'm not an entertainer, nor do I even consider myself a celebrity. I've worked behind the scenes as a fashion stylist for many years and, as a result, have kind of been *"grandfathered"* into the entertainment industry, so to speak. If I had to identify a defining moment in my career — and truthfully, my life — styling Lauryn Hill was my big break.

It's important to remember that a large percentage of what you see in the media is controlled and is never 100 percent true or even favorable. This has been particularly true in my case. My marriage, and the subsequent media fodder that followed, overshadowed my pre-existing and successful styling career. It's understandable why the majority of people know me for being married and not for being Tameka the cool style coach. But styling is how my ex-husband and I met.

I've been fortunate enough to have a career that I not only love, but that's provided me the opportunity to travel extensively. One of my favorite memories is speeding on the autobahn with Lauryn Hill in Germany. Having no federally mandated speed limit means the drivers totally throw caution to the wind. We were in a caravan of six Mercedes Benz S500s topping speeds of 150 mph. It was both exhilarating and scary as hell. My eyes were tightly shut 75 percent of the time. I was praying, laughing, and sometimes screaming!

Styling has taken me across the globe more times than I can count. I've gone vintage shopping in London, Greece, Paris and Japan. I've been flown out to do shoots for Harper's Bazaar in Europe and for Top of the Pop's in England. I've worked in London, Paris, Milan, Beijing, Sydney, Seoul, Madrid, Barcelona, Tokyo, Amsterdam, and Belgium. I'm not new to this. I was a stylist before styling was considered cool or trendy, and I've helped a lot of younger stylists go on to secure niches in this industry.

Admittedly, I haven't always been the easiest or most pleasant to work for, but that's a part of the learning process and the cost of having a seat at the table. Anyone with a peacoat and 10k followers on Instagram is a stylist now. Just because a person works in the mall and "loves to shop" that doesn't make them have the ability to consult someone on their image. The title has lost a lot of its meaning because the market is so oversaturated. There's nothing wrong with wanting to style or design, but *real* fashion styling is more than putting outfits together. A real stylist has influence and understands aesthetic value. A real stylist is able to create a time-stopping look in service of his or her client.

Toni Braxton confided in me that she was pregnant before the 2001 Grammys. Being a mother myself, I understood where she was going with her request. A woman's body changes after having a baby, so naturally we wanted to go for something a little provocative that would show off her pre-pregnancy physique. Opinions about the dress varied, but the media ate it up. The infamous silver dress Toni wore at the 43rd Grammy awards is still considered one of the sexiest red carpet looks, period. Toni still has an amazing body and looks fabulous in everything she wears.

Before my on-screen à la public life, I lived an incredible behind-the-scenes life as one of the go-to fashion stylists for some of the biggest names and curated looks for some of their most iconic moments. I was living my dreams and making a solid 6-figures a year creating iconic looks for industry A-listers like Toni Braxton, Jay Z, Dr. Dre, Patti Labelle, Chris Brown, Lauryn Hill, Chaka Khan, Aretha Franklin, Gerald Levert, Ciara, TI, Ginuwine, Nas, Mary J. Blige, Keith Sweat, Maxwell, Timbaland, and so many more.

Those who wanted to follow in my footsteps studied and worked with me as my assistants. I like to call them partners. I was a proud mentor to several people. Many of my partners have gone on to become today's top stylists in the industry. I was a tough teacher; under my tutelage you would learn how to shop, prep a fitting, pack up returns, set etiquette and more. As one assistant said, "Working with Foster—*wooo*— were some of the most pivotal yet hardest and best times in my learning process." I wasn't always well liked, but my assistants were well taught. Of course, it is innate to want your assistants to like you, but you can't effectively teach or lead if that is your focus. Teaching requires you to take people out of their comfort zones and people HATE that. My methods weren't always fun, but they were effective. I think all of their present-day successes and bank accounts would agree. Although some won't acknowledge how they learned a lot of what they know or who they learned it from, those who know... know.

I met Tameka right after The Score was released and we instantly started talking about style, taste and clothing. She was keen on convincing me that she understood my style and appreciated it. I approved her first pull and the rest is history. She indeed 'got it' and became the person I trusted to style me (and the guys would soon follow) for many years following that first encounter. If my style is iconic, I had an early translator who understood the language of fashion and what I was trying to convey. It was informal and formal, old and new, rugged and refined. It mixed vintage, designer, genres and sensibilities in ways that everyone would eventually try to emulate. Tameka is definitely one of the people I have to thank for 'getting it' (early), and helping to bring that vision to life.

~Lauryn Hill 2021

Not a fan of cats, yet history has shown we have similarities.

1976

Body language experts would say I was not feeling Santa. My issue was likely the Mrs. Claus dress.

December 1974

My favorite velour sweater. From JCPenney or Mervyn's *"At Mervyn's today we'll help you find a way"* but it had a Missoni vibe.

1980

Pink terry cloth and greasy pressed hair. This was not my best picture day.

1978

"Look back at it!!" Here is the exact reason God never gave me a daughter. Mind you this is like 1980.

In my Oh la la Sassoons!

Purple Reign. This is around the time when I started putting together my own looks.

1981

Flipped and flippant.. I was always ready for ruffles! First year of junior high.

1982

Fresh off my Jheri Curl, I had to blow it out for Picture Day. My cardigan was Michael Jackson inspired.

1983

This is where, the hippie, bougie, and hood girl collide. Hence… the gold chains, the Armani collection moment and the shaved hair. Such confusion.

1985

…and the boys arrived, and so did The Gucci sneakers.

1986

"Sweet Love"
San Francisco
Darrin and I.

1989

Game 1 of the World Series.

1989

I baked my daddy a cake. But get into my drop waist wrap dress and wooden bangle.

February 1983

Young Meke - 19 with a
child... it's "go time".
December 1990

I'm not sure what look I was going for,
but my schoolboys were almost bigger
than my face. Me and Vonda.
1983-4

Me and my best friend LaNita decided
to go short!!
Circa 1994

I learned valuable lessons of
strength and prayer from this
woman: my maternal grandmother,
Estella Hadden.

Granny Lou and Aunt Sadie taking a stroll.

The Infamous Larry Parker.

My daddy on the left and
his group The Ballads.

1968

MMQ PRODUCTIONS *presents...*

NEW CLUB 80
2021 FRUITVALE AVENUE · OAKLAND, CALIFORNIA
FEATURING,

★ *The* ★

BALLADS

"Angel Baby", "Dizzy World"
and "God Bless Our Love"

DAP HARRIS
AND

THE AGELESS BAND

☆ SUNDAY · FRIDAY · SATURDAY · SUNDAY ☆

DEC. 1, 6, 7, 8, 1985
— — 2 SHOWS: 10:30 P.M. and 12:30 A.M. — —

My dad's group was always
performing around town.

1985

My dad always had the coolest Aviator shades.

Meet the Parents.

1970's

My grandmother Louise on the far right and my great-grandmother Katie, boy she had a mean side-eye game ...Whence I came!!

1945

Of course, these two had a baby on New Year's Day. Yep, they made me. End of discussion.

1970

Momma, Mary Jean and a Kool Filter King.

The other Jacques Cousteau. My dad on one of his scuba-diving expeditions.

My baby boy, Darrin "Noonie" I kept him super clean.

My grandfather and father both named John Foster. Together they were a mess.

Best friend, Nyeisha, Sister, Rashida and I. LA nights.

Back stage with Dr. Dre at the 1993 Soul Train Awards. He was a styling client in the 90's.

Everyone in LA had to try their hand at
modeling and the short cut. I did both,
we have Halle Berry, T-Boz and Toni
Braxton to thank for this!!

1994

CHAPTER 7

Share My World

❧

As a young girl, oddly enough I never wanted to be married, I just didn't see it, I envisioned myself having two children, a law degree or a career in neurosurgery and a Mercedes Benz. Well, I got half of it right. Fact is I've always been the type of woman that was *in fact meant* to be married. And I'm fortunate. I've had some true beauty in my life, true love, deep passion, some real romance.

The first time I was married, it was to my high school crush Ryan. Lord, did I adore him during that first semester of 10th grade. I mean *goo-goo ga-ga*. Thick, dark, silky brows and lashes, cinnamon brown eyes, gorgeous brown skin, and shiny wavy hair. He was athletic, an absolute alpha male, and also a great son to his mother. I was gone—hook, line, and sinker! I went to Berkeley High, but he was at Kennedy High in nearby Richmond, California. We dated for about four months. He was popular, a star athlete, and all of the chicks knew him, so naturally that meant he was quite booked and busy with the ladies. I used to skip school, take the BART train from Oakland to El Cerrito, get off and walk my skinny ass, two miles UPHILL to see him, only to find out that he had a car the whole time! Ain't that a bitch. I should have known then, he was trouble. Yeah, I liked him, liked him!! I had his letterman's jacket, so you could tell me absolutely nothing... well, until I misplaced it. After high school he left and went off to Howard University for college. It seems that I lost the jacket and the boy simultaneously. Talk about being crushed.

We reconnected some nine years post-high school during a chance run-in at the Fontainebleau Hotel Miami. It was 1997, and I was there doing styling work at an urban music conference called "How Can I Be Down?" My client, Patti LaBelle, was being honored, and I was hired to style her for the weekend and the awards ceremony. He looked exactly as I remembered him, and the attraction was clear. Only there was one catch: I was rushing through the lobby with 'Ms. Patti', her team, and security, and there was simply no time to exchange numbers, emails, cards, or anything at all. Ryan was there with his associates to promote their label/production company called "Noontime Music". They were new to the business and the conference provided the ideal environment for networking. It was great seeing him after all those years. On top of not having an opportunity to exchange contact information, the other issue was, I had begun dating a nice guy in Philadelphia. He was most definitely marriage material and we spoke about it often but, I didn't see a long-term future for us because he was younger and at the time was not fully independent. We went on vacations together and I adored his family. And though I was ready for total commitment, I was concerned about relocating from L.A. to a new city. I had to think about my son and career, and Philadelphia was not conducive to either.

Life is unforeseeable. Here's why…

About two months later while living my best life on a dinner date with a friend at the Soul Café in New York, (I know what you're thinking, I ain't shit, but I was young, and considered myself single until married from my POV) my date introduced me to a female associate that we ran into while at the restaurant. Her name was Shante Paige, they were chatting a while about record label work and Shante mentioned that she was also consulting for a new company called "Noontime Music." Sounded really familiar, I looked up quickly, because I remembered that being Ryan's company name that was mentioned in Miami.

My date finally introduced us by saying, "Oh, I'm sorry; I'm being rude. Shante, meet my friend Tameka Foster. She is a great stylist in the industry. She works with….and she's here visiting from Los Angeles." He likely thought that the introduction might lead to her becoming a new client for me because she was an A&R at a label.

Shante then looked at me and said, "Oh My God!!! Do you know Ryan Glover?!! He told me about you. He mentioned that he saw you at "How Can I be Down?" but didn't get your number." She was so excited. "He's looking for you I promise!" she continued. By the way, she didn't even bother to consider that I was there on a date with a handsome guy as she kept talking. I didn't know what to say… I mean… I was dumbfounded. I was beyond flabbergasted. I was thinking, *This cannot be life.*

Serendipity at its finest I tell ya. She had to be telling the truth because she had just met me that day and was spot on about where and when Ryan and I recently reconnected. I did indeed see him at that music conference in Miami. It was like something out of an urban version of *The Notebook.* Truth is stranger than fiction; at times what actually happens is more bizarre than anything that can be imagined.

My date said "Wow, you should give it to her for him," referring to my number. He was sort of being cheeky and nonchalant, so I did and Ryan called me in the following days.

Talk about whirlwind… He asked me to join him in Oakland for Mother's Day a few weeks later. We were both from the Bay Area and he was going to visit his mother and I would visit mine. It was a great plan and a nice way to meet in the middle to catch up. Well, that was in May 1997. We started seeing each other soon thereafter. The only problem was that I was still talking to the guy in Philadelphia and beginning to lie about trivial shit. It felt awful, because I loved him. Philly really was a great guy. The relationships began to overlap, but Philly wasn't ready to move forward or make any solid future plans. Eventually the long-distance relationship had to end, and the one with Ryan took off full speed ahead. I mean, non-stop… Like foot on the gas fast... pedal to the metal. It was clear that we wanted the same thing.

We met up in New York while we were both there on business, then he came to L.A for a visit. I started making frequent trips to Atlanta, and we knew fairly quickly that we were meant to be together. He would come and pick me up playing Mary's new "Share My World" album and we'd ride for hours listening to it on repeat. The song *"Everything"* became a bit of a theme song for us. That entire album has been a life soundtrack.

"You are my everything, you are my everything, youuu, my everything, everything, everything... it's all because of you I'm never sad and blue."

We were like-minded in our goals, had similar personalities, were kindred spirits, and were both on a trajectory to career success. I liked his hustle, he was smart, a people person, definitely a "finesser", but overall, I appreciated the way he moved. I believed in his dreams and I loved his friends, some of whom I have known since high school. We disagreed over a few petty things initially, like his sticky jade-green "Martin" leather sofa (man I hated that thing) or late-night calls from past flings, then we would make up for days at a time. I remember my first weekend visit to Atlanta; I went to Bed, Bath, and Beyond and bought new towels and bedding. I was such a huge germaphobe and was fiercely allergic to the thought of past "overnight guests". I have always had weird idiosyncrasies and that was one of them. He was the proverbial bachelor until he wasn't. By late Fall of 1997, he arranged for me and my son Darrin to move to Atlanta. He was very assertive and clear about it. I moved gradually and was finally entirely in Atlanta by the new year. I was initially afraid that living in Atlanta would hurt my career and that I would lose clients. I had always been overbooked and in demand in Los Angeles, but Ryan assured me that I could work from anywhere because most of my clients flew me out and covered travel expenses for jobs anyway. Didn't I say that he could sell ice to an eskimo? He also pointed out that we could buy land and build a dream home there. So, I took a chance on love and on him, and decided to make Atlanta my home. It was a great city after all. *Cue Mary "You are everything and everything is you..."* I was gone again, sprung.

Moving to the south was a huge cultural adjustment for me. I really had to get used to their accents... I was seriously convinced that no one had finished third grade until I started sounding just like everyone there. *Dayuum shawty*! The 285 freeway was ridiculous and a big-ass circle; I think I was lost on it for at least the first 72 hours after I landed!! Learning to navigate a new place is always daunting. The other issue was that my boyfriend had been single and eligible for many years there, so I had to regulate a few things on the boundary-setting front. I dealt with a few residual relationship issues, but they were all tied up into a neat little bow quickly.

I was a little savage-minded in the 90's as a whole; thank God I've been delivertttt. Charge it to my young age, not my heart. Honestly, you didn't have to like me, but *respect* was mandatory. Sorry... not sorry.

We broke ground on our first home in early 1998. It was a custom home, as promised. I loved the building process; I made the selections for the flooring, tile, appliances, fixtures, lighting, paint colors & textures, down to the stain and wallpaper, while he essentially came up with the design details. In retrospect, I was putting the cart before the horse, because we were not yet married, but there I was designing and spending thousands on a home that I didn't truly own. Hey, I was 27, ill-advised, and head over heels in love. The bottom-line is we were DOING IT!!! We were building a totally customized house from the ground up! I was on site almost daily, between styling jobs and prenatal doctors' visits, because I was pregnant with our first son together, Ryan Mekai. I was still working, traveling to jobs, and holding down the construction project all at once. Our home wound up being featured in "Heart & Soul" magazine. I was so proud. Not bad for my first interior design gig.

Around that time, I styled my first Atlanta artist, Lathun, for his "Freak It" video. Yeah, I was getting worried—that's not exactly what I had in mind. Then came Ciara, Killa Mike, Ludacris, Lloyd, Jagged Edge, Joe, T.I., and Donell Jones among others. I was just getting into the Atlanta swing of things when I was put on bed rest and told not to board an airplane until after I gave birth. I still had my other clients as well, so I had to hire assistants to handle a few of my regular clients. We had finally moved into the new house, so the bed rest order worked out well; I stayed home nesting, decorating, and preparing the nursery. RG, as I called him, was on cloud nine. He treated me well. He was attentive, and as the family chef, he cooked most of the meals. He also helped out tremendously with my son Darrin. It wasn't perfect, but what is perfection? In March, I had a tremendous baby shower at Atlanta's "Justin's" Restaurant; we reserved the entire place for the event. It was such a big deal for us. Friends and family flew in from California, Texas, and New York.

Ryan 'Mekai' Glover was born April 21st, 1999 at Crawford Long Hospital. The delivery was fast, easy, and my newborn was as cute as a button. I mean Gerber Baby cute. Dimples and all. His father was over-the-moon; he followed the baby and nurses to every station and room, never letting his son out of his sight… I didn't see those two for nearly an hour after the birth. Hell, I thought he took him home! Ryan was great with the baby and he even let me sleep in most mornings. The apple doesn't fall far from the tree—my mom hated early mornings too.

When Ryan "Mekai" was nearly five months old, I was still nursing, so he just about always slept in the master bedroom with us. One day when I went into the bedroom to feed him, there were a series of strategically placed "Post-It" notes that eventually led me on the sweetest scavenger hunt all over the house until finally I was led back to the master bedroom to look *"underneath the baby"*. And there it was: a red box with a ring inside and a final note that simply read, *"Will You Marry Me?"* I'll never forget that moment or how it made me feel. We stayed engaged for nearly two years and then planned a destination wedding in Negril, Jamaica for my 30th birthday. 1-1-01. It was so sweet. It felt somewhat like a big family reunion too, because we bonded and all hung out for days beforehand. It was a triple celebration: my 30th birthday, New Years, and our wedding. It was fun, romantic, and pretty. Such a memorable week! We invited 40 of our closest friends and family, it was such a fun group. We then jetted off for our honeymoon to my favorite place, St. Barth where we stayed at the Carl Gustaf Hotel. While there, I purchased a few rare furniture pieces for our home. I immediately fell in love with the weathered mahogany and grey teak wood that covered nearly every deck. The reclaimed wood pieces were a perfect fit. I was also six months pregnant with our second child, Kile Ishmael. I spaced the boys two years apart.

After the honeymoon, I quickly went back to work for two months, until delivery. It was a busy career season for me. I was still styling Lauryn Hill; I had just gotten Toni Braxton as a new client and she was super busy; there were videos, the Grammys, and countless photo shoots and I was literally sketching concepts for Ginuwine while in the hospital awaiting birth. I even recall asking the nurse to send faxes to my designer in LA. I styled Timbaland and Royce virtually. I never stopped.

Kile Ishmael Glover was born March 29th, 2001. While his was my most painful delivery, he was the sweetest little baby. He had tiny lips and the brightest eyes on the planet. I was a newlywed, but not acting as such; I think I took my husband's patience for granted. He got the least of me. I was so overwhelmed though; I had 3 kids, one of whom was a newborn, and I was running my styling business, managing a creative agency, and designing a clothing line all while juggling tons of bills, paperwork, a home life, and a husband. I became a bitch on wheels. My mother came to live with us for a while to help out, which probably only made it worse, and I also hired a part time nanny. Yet there was still much to do. I had gotten Usher as a client and the promo schedule for his new album, *8701*, was rigorous. I was also working with Ryan's company, Noontime, styling their acts and doing image consulting. They had recently signed young NY newcomer Ashanti, had Absolute, Jene, Cha Cha and others. I was doing about two to three jobs per week. I had invested money into his studio, and in talent that was being acquired for the production company because I believed in them. Many felt that I was "down like 4 flats" both supportive and resourceful. Sidebar: I was not long ago backstage at a So So Def concert event in Atlanta and I ran into one of my favorite producers and songwriters. I felt proud when he gave me my flowers by praising me to everyone in the room and stating plainly that his first music industry check came from me. It made me feel a little embarrassed (hot faced) but I felt quite honored, because people rarely give you credit for the way that you helped them. Most only make it a point to mention you when relationships sour. In 2004, my husband had also started another company; this time it was a fashion brand with friends, Kenny Burns and Derek Dudley, aptly called *"Ryan Kenny"*. I helped inspire him, invested into this venture as well, and was proud to have my clients represent the brand whenever possible. I believed. He was a go-getter and a brilliant businessman; it came as no surprise when his endeavors took off, exponentially. As a result, he began to travel a lot more— frequent trips to LA and Italy became the norm. By this time, I was working with Jay, Aretha, and Mary. I was so excited, but all this new business meant something had to suffer. I loved both my career and family, yet I could feel them butting up against each other. *Career Success vs Marriage Failure.* I was at my bandwidth for sure.

The relationship often got the short end of the stick as our respective careers flourished. We were just doing too damn much. I realize this now, of course. It is truly hard to balance work, family, and new ventures, especially when travel and finances are involved. Fact is, I needed to work; our overhead was just too high. Eventually, we grew apart, and things went cold. Communication got harder, infidelity began, trust was broken, and the damage became irreparable. I also think that respect gets weary for a woman when she pays for things and has doubts about her man's loyalty. My love language became foreign. Respect may be more important than love in the end. The problem is that things don't always stay fun, romantic, and pretty. My marriage didn't, and I'm not even totally 100 percent clear as to why. Young, prideful, and bullheaded, I wasn't open to counseling. I was not empathetic nor was I very reasonable. This was before therapy became as common as going to a nail appointment. It all unraveled. The 'pride before the fall' I suppose. I started working with a realtor to find a 4-bedroom home with a yard— somewhere within an "excellent school district". I wanted the boys and me to be in a new place by Fall 2005. He was totally against it. Our mothers really tried to help. It all got a little nasty. I moved out and did not take as much as a dish, fork, bed, or sheet, paid every bill and I even left him with my 7 series BMW because I remembered the ugliness of a close friend's divorce. Her man cheated. She left her husband and cleaned out their home while he was traveling on business. Boy was she pissed. I always felt that this reaction was too harsh for their kids to witness. I definitely didn't want this to be any harder or potentially embarrassing for my boys. I really wanted a smooth transition for them. Besides, I wasn't particularly mad at him, it just wasn't working.

Although I curated and bought most of the art and décor in our home, it just wasn't worth it for me to take it. I left it all behind. It is what I viewed as decorum. After the move, I always told the boys, "It's nice, because now you have two homes with everything in them. Mommy and Daddy just want (umm... need) separate places." Hell, I tried! Yet I got no credit for any of this, yet he led friends to believe that I left him for dead. Could not have been further from the truth. This narrative eventually made its way to my boys, which for me was the real problem. I had never truly cared about people's opinions of me, but my sons, however, are a different ball of wax.

Material things can be replaced, my kids' childhood experiences could not. Breakups are tough as it is.

Co-parenting was an arduous task. There were many times when I felt I was being alienated, but in the end, we made it work. We both loved our boys and will till the end of the Earth, and that was most certainly the hardest part. The rumors began. I heard he was cheating. Folks said I left him for another man. Cheating is never the answer — it is the ultimate cop-out, and we were both guilty of it. What I will say is that our issues were real and existed before and aside from any 3rd party *entanglement* on either side. Oh, and people actually claimed and believed that I left my boys behind. I suppose that he had something to do with that portrayal as well. Never in life! You got to be fucking kidding me!! Me? A deadbeat mom? I would never leave my children for anything and especially not a man. That could never happen as long as I had breath in my body. My kids were and will always be my pride and joy, so I didn't bother correcting them; I had to let my life speak for itself. But that was ONE thing that pissed me off to the highest level of pissitivity! In fact, I spent a great deal of time with our boys, we would travel, have amazing personal time, I even taught them the importance of philanthropy and giving back. Case and point, one Christmas Eve, Ryan and Kile kept asking for gifts while we were doing some last minute shopping in Toys R Us. I got mad and decided to turn our entire cart into giveaways for the less fortunate children in shelters. We left Toys R Us with the car full of things to take to the nearest shelter downtown Atlanta. I felt that this would be a great experience for the boys, I explained to them the importance of philanthropy, the principal was every time you get something new you should give something away. Our friends were divided; folk always think they must choose a side and ice the other one, or believe a painted scenario during a break-up, and they're usually always wrong. Most of ours definitely chose his and he played right into it. Hey, maybe he never said that I left them, but he never did anything to try and change the perception that I did. Let's just say that he omitted the truth. The false narrative of events that traveled amongst our circle was negative, patently false and it hurt. It became a bit of a show, it was one I wasn't interested in starring in. Bottomline is…..

Truth is woman starts out treating you how she wants to be treated, then she ends up treating you how you treat her. As a general rule. *Cue Mary's "Not Gon Cry"* …. Told you this album resonates.

By Spring 2007 our divorce was final. From the onset, of the more challenging things was to go over and pick up or drop off our boys at the home that I put so much energy into from its inception. Second to that, it was seeing my friends (our mutual) hanging out over there. Kicking it hard in my shit!! I don't know which was worse. Lord knows he loved to host a good, hearty kickback BBQ complete with cocktails on tap. Question? Why do friends not feel that it's a wee bit taboo to hang out at someone's former home with their ex? This concept baffles me to this day. Most of my associates that do things like this have never been married and may not truly understand.. It's truly about respect for a person's feelings and in this case marital property. I guess they figured, hey he's single now it's fair game. Nevertheless…. Awkward to me.

The respect was gone, though I always felt that mutual love was still present long after the break-up. I knew that we were set in our ways – both of us were stubborn, prideful, and old fashioned when it came to the fairytale idea of marriage. Hindsight is always 20/20. Yet life moved on. We both remarried, moved into new homes, and acquired more money and "things". Happiness and experiences, of course, are truly all that matter in the end. Money can't buy that and possessions don't equal joy; they are only a Band-Aid. The things that cost nothing hold the most value. I do not hold onto grudges; I usually either move-on, forget why I was mad, or my love for the person supersedes the anger. Life is just way too short and wonderful. Did I mention that he wound up selling his shares in his company and acquiring millions? He's doing quite well now and I'm happy to see it. You can love someone for life without it being romantic or physical. When you marry someone it's truly a life contract, you shouldn't throw them away just because the relationship didn't work out. I wish that more thought about it this way. My thinking between ages 30 and 35 was far different from the emotional intelligence that I possessed in my forties... Some felt that I'd jumped out of the frying pan into the hottest fire possible. I say, don't shy away from living life in the face of risk or challenges. Learn from your daily experiences; observe your personal path so that you know how to behave as you move forward. Experience is the best teacher; you can either ignore it or learn and grow from it. The decision to make the best of life's lessons is up to you.

Lastly, remain calm at all costs.

I do not hold onto grudges; I usually either move-on, forget why I was mad, or my love for the person supersedes the anger. Life is just way too short and wonderful.

CHAPTER 8

Full Moon

❖

Even before my divorce with Ryan was finalized, I moved out of our marital home and bought a moderate new five-bedroom, three-story house in a gated community in Alpharetta, Georgia. It wasn't as spacious as the custom-built home that I once shared, which is why I say "moderate", but it was newly built, gorgeous, and for the first time, I was investing in a property that was solely mine. My name was on the deed. It felt good. Great actually. The only drawback was the location. Alpharetta was an Anglo-Saxon, umm... hella white community north of where we previously lived. It felt like we were far away from…well, *everything* including people that looked like us. It was 35 miles from the airport and a 50-minute drive to the boys' school in morning traffic. I was also starting to feel the residual effects of leaving so much behind after the separation. I would go to cook something and quickly realized that I didn't have basic essential items, like a cheese grater, colander, or a blender. I didn't have any furniture at first either. All of the beautifully collected tables, chairs, and mirrors that I had shipped from Saint Barth, Los Angeles, and Italy were left behind. Even the art I purchased from local designers was left behind. Damn, I loved my reclaimed wood bed!!

I spent time learning the area, buying furniture, and getting the place together. The first room I focused on was the boys' room. Then, I created a playroom for them. I was happy that they continued to feel at home while with their dad, but it was equally important to me that they felt comfortable and happy in the new home that I was creating for us as well. The house was a three-story townhouse style, with a three-car garage, a huge second floor balcony, and a small yard. It was perfect for us. Curb appeal was out of this world too. It was a new construction; we were the first to live there, and the small lake community had only 25 homes. On my first night there, one of the only Black families in the community came over and said hello. They graciously welcomed me to the neighborhood with a gift basket and a bottle of wine. Jennifer Scott and I are still friends to this day. That gesture made me feel hopeful and gave me a bit of comfort with my decision. It felt a bit lonely initially, even with the kids there.

For the most part, Kile and Ryan, whom we called "Mekai", adjusted well. Darrin, on the other hand, who was now 16 and a sophomore in high school, was left without a father figure. Ryan had essentially been his dad since he was seven, but after the divorce, the relationship ceased to exist; it came to a screeching halt. This made no sense to me. It was unfair to him and I did the best that I could to fill the void. When men get mad, it's nearly impossible to bring them back around. It's just tragic for kids. Being mad at Mom just doesn't make it right.

While adjusting to my new normal, my career was still rockin' and rollin'. I was busier than ever. I was well known in the industry now for being well-prepared and for my attention to detail…OCD even. It was a gift and a curse. The styling was always impeccable, but I was often late for jobs—not because I was unprofessional or purposely tardy, but because I was overly meticulous and needed everything to be just so. I always had too much on my plate as well. Honestly, I would select a whole rack of clothes, choose each of the looks, and then completely second guess the direction. Always thinking, *If I could just get that one brooch or visit that one showroom to pick up that unique item, I could complete the look.*

Welp, one day the universe taught me a most valuable lesson. I was booked in Los Angeles to style Jay Z' *"PSA Public Service Announcement"* video. This wasn't my first-time styling Jay. It was actually my third video and I had done a few photo shoots, as well as the Black Album concert film, but per usual, I was a nervous wreck. It's Jay Z for goodness sakes! Every time I styled him; I went the extra mile. I wanted to make sure that he had as many options as possible. I pulled several pieces for him…everything from jewelry and cufflinks to the sneakers, right down to the socks, were carefully selected. His look was pretty much complete until I became fixated on his most well-known accessory…the New York Yankees hat.

"Allow me to reintroduce myself my name is Hov' H to the O-V, I used to move snowflakes by the o-z, I guess even back then you can call me CEO of the R-O-C Hov, fresh out of the pan into the fire, I be the music biz number one supplier… "

I wanted him to have as many color options as possible…so there I was, running around LA at the last minute trying to find Yankee hats in new color variations. Fanatical. That was mistake number one. Why? Because I had 15 hats already! I had pre ordered them from 'New Era' directly. Not to mention that Los Angeles would not have the greatest selection of Yankee ``fitteds' anyway. Furthermore, a classic blue Yankee is always best. Duhhh. Mistake number two? I sent my assistants to set with all of his other looks but kept his main look with me (the outfit he would wear in the first scene of the video!) …I didn't want anything to happen to it…I wanted to protect it at all costs. Again, taking things to a whole 'nother level. I was being *micro-managey*, because well, it was HOV after all! I acted like I was chauffeuring Jacob's Coat of Many Colors. *Note to Self: Always remember that you f*#k up when you try too hard.* Deep sigh.

Back to the hat…I eventually found one. It was exactly what I was looking for. I hopped in my car and booked it to set. There was one real problem. I was in L.A. Call time was 5 pm— Traffic hour! And lots of it. Everyone knows the City of Angels is traffic hell. I was living in Atlanta now and totally forgot about the 110! There I was stuck on the freeway; I mean in complete gridlock. Like, "shut your car off and kick your feet up" jam packed. I was going to be late for the shoot, and there was no fast way around it!! To make matters worse, Jay happened to arrive exactly on time that day. I was trapped in my car sweating bricks, completely beside myself with anxiety, when Jay's assistant Carlene called and ripped me a new one—like reamed me. When I arrived to set, no amount of apologizing could fix the situation; you could feel the tension in the room. Even my girl Chaka was quiet. That shit was thicker than a Popeyes biscuit with no jelly. You would think I had the actual cure to cancer, not just an outfit with me. I was mortified but pulled myself together and delivered. The looks were on point, hell I was on point; but the lesson I learned that day — priceless: Do not overthink things. Follow your first mind, and don't ever doubt yourself. Yes, it was Jay, one of the greatest rappers of our time, but he too is human, just like you and me. I had put so much pressure on myself that I literally psyched myself completely out. He is hands down one of the coolest and most easy going people on the planet, I was overanalyzing for no reason. Straight panicked. Yikes.

The styling game isn't an easy one. It's all about relationships, but your work ethic and professionalism will go a long way. The best stylists aren't always the top stylists. Read that again. Some gems for my "freshman" fresh getters in the industry—Punctuality is key. Arrive ahead of your call time, to be on time is to be late, and be prepared to serve your client. I learned that the hard way. Tip two—Mind your business. Your client isn't your homie; keep your head in your clothing rack. You may overhear a lot of private conversations and be privy to sensitive information. It may be tempting to chime in and give your two cents… don't, unless asked, and even then, be diplomatic and thoughtful with your responses. Remember you are there to work, not to make friends. And lastly, be original; don't focus entirely on trends. The key is to select classic, timeless looks that fit well.

Luckily, the mishap with Jay wasn't damaging to my career. I kept working and business was good overall.

In true "Lucy" fashion, though, I had another memorable near disaster. On this occasion, it was my *"grand-media-shit-storm pre-party"* and all the internet trolls were invited. This ordeal rolled out the red carpet for years of defamation and the start of my name besmirchment.

Here's how it went down. I was in New York in February 2005. It was fashion week and the streets were lively. I was in town just for a few days to hit up all the major showrooms. It was a workday and I had been pulling for a client. I was wearing just a T-shirt and jeans but thankfully I did have on my Yves Saint Laurent mink coat.

I remember it being freezing cold outside and I felt underdressed for any kind of fashion soiree but my girlfriend, Leanne, wanted to swing by the Gansevoort Hotel for a Pat Fields Rocawear party. I was in talks with an up and coming stylist named Tiffany Hasborne about signing her to Swanky Image Group, so I suggested that she meet me at the event as well. As I was walking into the hotel, I saw Wendy Williams and her entourage leaving.

Simultaneously, I saw one of my showroom contacts at the door. He introduced me to Wendy. He briefed her on who I was, told her a little about my career, and said it would be great for me to go on her show so I could share a little about my styling business with her listeners and maybe garner more business. I was always down for an opportunity to promote Swanky and myself.

My girlfriend also agreed that it would be a cool opportunity. But no one informed me that Wendy was a friggin' "shock jock" and that most of her commentary revolved around spilling the tea on her guests and celebrities. Unbeknownst to me, she had previously quarreled with Whitney Houston, Will Smith, Puff, Jay-Z, and others.... and here I was excited and all gung-ho to do her radio show. Granted, I'm pretty savvy, but at the time I didn't know East Coast radio personalities all that well. My happy ass had no clue what her persona or claim to fame was. I also didn't realize that her interviewing style was more of an interrogation peppered with negative innuendo.

Anyway, the next morning I had to be there pretty early. I was staying at the W Hotel on Park Avenue, which was relatively close to her station. Once there, I had to wait in a green room for about 10 minutes; then it was my turn to go on. I don't remember hearing how she introduced me, although it may have been playing overhead. Admittedly, I was super nervous. I always have a little stage fright when it comes to speaking publicly or being on camera. This was my first time doing a radio interview. I was led inside the studio, offered water, and then Wendy asked a few routine questions about my career— who I worked with, how long, and maybe even how I got started. I don't recall it all. Within 2.2 seconds, she was like "now onto the juicy stuff". My eyes got big and my heart started to race. She began asking personal questions about Toni Braxton, most of which I knew nothing about. I was her stylist, but I didn't hang out with her or witness any personal exchanges. Then I remember her switching the topic to Usher, asking offensive questions about his mother and their working relationship, things about his sexuality, backstage etiquette, etc. FYI: This was prior to us dating. Somehow, I thought she was just playing in the beginning, but it was soon apparent that my reluctance to spill dirt royally pissed her off. Had I been more familiar with her shock-jock style of interviewing, I would have never shown up. Should I have done my research? Sure. But sadly, I didn't. She abruptly ended the interview, which was fine with me because I was not prepared or willing to touch on the topics she was bringing up. The personal lives of my clients have and will forever be off-limits. She went on to tell her listeners that I was drunk when she met me the night before and that I had promised to tell-all on her show. Not true at all — in fact, I didn't have one drink that night. This was a lie to corroborate her story that I had gotten cold feet.

I was well known behind the scenes in the industry at this time, but virtually unknown to the public. This two-minute interview gave the blogosphere the first unsavory introduction of me, so when photos of Usher and I vacationing together in St. Barth popped up a short while later, many bloggers were like, "Ah! Right…Tameka, the girl that Wendy kicked off her show." It made me look nutso and painted a picture of me as an opportunist with a shady past. FIRST of all, each of the clients she asked me about were currently on my roster. They were people who were paying me great money. When she asked me if I was willing to dish "dirt", I thought she meant like styling drama, at least fashion related things like clients being late to set, wardrobe malfunctions, my favorite client, perhaps even their attitudes. I never in my wildest dreams thought she was referring to personal information. Secondly, I am from Oakland California; I don't care what I may witness, I would never go on a radio show and dish personal details about *anyone*. Outside of myself that is, and even then, it wouldn't be anything incriminating. On the radio? It is simply not in my DNA.

Needless to say, a radio jock has a far larger reach and amount of time with the public than I could have had. Because she berated me and talked such crap about me, I got to the point where I really wished we could meet up and speak (or throw hands) in person, off air. I literally spent about three years hoping to run into her anywhere. I was infuriated, she never let the subject go. Then when I got divorced and it became known that I was dating Usher, she started talking again. She even talked about my mother and children, which made me mad. My mother was livid. I never understood how a black woman could tear down another for money, clout, ratings, or laughs. It started to feel a bit obsessive; every other day some friend or another would call me and say, "Did you hear what "Wendy" said about you today?" I thought to myself, *Wow, I must've made a real impact.* I couldn't be the source of her tirade just because I wouldn't snitch about my clients' personal lives. That just doesn't make any sense. How could I ever continue to work for them if I went around discussing their personal matters? I would be shooting myself in the foot and for what reason?? I'm just not built that way. I'm usually very sharp and I felt game goofy to not have done my research on her before just signing up to do her show. Had I known who she was, I would have been prepared to combat her bullshit, because I'm as quick witted as she is and I feel she got the upper hand in that round. All good. We will meet again.

Usher was now also a regular client of mine and our professional relationship was starting to blossom into something more. It began innocently; we were each other's confidants. Contrary to my golden rule of "keeping your nose in the rack". Don't judge me… Do as I say not as I do damnit. *insert eye roll. He was there for me as my relationship with Ryan had started to fall apart. He didn't know Ryan, but they met once or twice when I started working with him. For me he was a listening ear, a voice of reason, and I was the same for him. He would share his relationship issues with me, talk about various girls he was seeing, and more often than not, I would take his partner's side. (What can I say, I am a true girl's girl.) We spent a lot of time together on and off the road and truly became best friends. Feelings started to develop…but he was adamant that he would not date a married woman and encouraged me to make my marriage work, even suggesting that Ryan and I go to counseling. I wasn't at all interested in seeing a marriage counselor — I thought it was too taboo. Once it became clear that there was no fixing my marriage and I was definitive about getting a divorce, we decided to take things a step further. I was not legally divorced, but it was clear to both that Ryan and I were done. We were first sleeping in separate rooms and I eventually moved out, because he wouldn't. We were done… done. Separated and living apart, dissolving a marriage takes time but once it was over, it was ova. *Ovarian*…. Finito.

Usher's and my first official trip together was to Aspen. We flipped a coin to decide where to go. The options were to go to a hot or cold climate. I wanted a 'beachy and frothy' destination …He won the toss and wanted to go somewhere cold and snowy, so Aspen it was. We stayed at a charming boutique hotel nestled in the mountains called

The Little Nell. We cozied up in the most cute idyllic suite, complete with a huge fireplace, and a big tall wooden poster bed. We ate their world-famous truffle fries for days, drank hot toddies, shopped in Aspen's local boutiques and gift shops, went for long walks, and talked for hours. It was romantic and would be the first of many blissful getaways.

We were quite enamored with each other. He loved to stay up late at night, and we spent early mornings talking for hours about everything from new music ideas to fashion, life, the future, and kids. You name it and we covered it. We are both movie buffs, so we did a 'movie marathon' one day. I would also have a front row seat for the wee-hour private rehearsals and mini Marvin Gaye concerts he would put on. Truly, we entertained each other and the chatter in the world around us didn't matter much. We got along well and had similar interests. I am a music lover— always dancing. We shared playlists and swapped stories. Life was incredibly enjoyable for a while.

One year, his mother threw a birthday dinner for him in a private section of the Capital Grill and I was invited. There were about 5 tables, seating 10 guests each. I came in with three large gift boxes. I bought him a Breitling watch, a suit, and some shoes. Things were heating up between us and I felt inclined. I also had two dozen balloons and a cake delivered to his house earlier that day. We sat at separate tables, but kept smiling and flirting with each other. He sat with his family—his Mom, grandparents "Nanny" and "Pop", brother, etc. The dinner was nice. Toward the end of evening he opened his gifts, then one of his friends, Devyne, stopped in to say hello. My heart sank, because I felt that Devyne being there could only mean one thing: a party was to follow. Once, the dinner ended and we were all heading out, Usher came over to me and said, *"Hey, the guys want to take me out for my birthday. I'll call you later when I'm headed back toward the crib...*" My heart sank, I was so disappointed because I had hoped we would spend the rest of his birthday together. He hung out with his friends the entire day, then there was the dinner party, and now a club??? I went home and tried to sleep. Finally, at about 2am, I woke up realizing that I hadn't heard from him. I called his cell; no answer. Then I called the home phone and his house manager David answered, "Hey sis, Boss man is sleep!" I'm like "Huh?". Ok well, *"Go in his room and wake him up! Tell him I'm on the telephone!"* He puts me on hold for about 3 minutes and the phone is making that intercom-system beeping sound. He comes back and says, "Aye T, I tried. He's out like a light." Meanwhile, I'm getting dressed fast as hell. I'm fuming, because I knew this was some bullshit and he always called me before going to sleep. Nothing was adding up. Club, then home in bed, and asleep by 2?? Who do I look like Boo Boo the Fool??? Yeah ok. I drove over to his house, got to the main gate, and told the guard where I was going, "Raymond Estate". The guard didn't even ask my name; he just opened the gate. I found that odd because he lived in a very secure gated community and the Country Club of the South didn't play about letting folks in without calling. I got to his street and as I was driving down the block, I noticed that there were several cars parked on both sides of the road. This was unusual in his community. I turned on his corner to see his driveway packed with cars—everyone was blocked in. All the lights were on in the main house and the guesthouse was fully lit. Oh he's having a party, party??! I clearly wasn't invited, so I parked my car on the street and walked up to the side door near the kitchen. Ironically that door was locked. I caught a glimpse of the balloons that I sent floating in the air near the cake on the counter, although the kitchen was empty. I heard music vibrating from somewhere; it was bumping. I proceeded to walk through the parked cars to the side gate, and to the staircase, which led to the pool level. I skipped down the stairs passing several people hanging out and smoking by the pool. Girls in short dresses and stretch denim jackets were giggling and walking back up the stairs. Meanwhile, I'm dressed like I came to handle business—sweatpants, t-shirt, and sneakers. I walked through the basement bedroom door to find a gaggle of tattooed and pierced strippers laughing and getting oiled up. They had either just finished a performance or were just about to start one. The room was humid and smelled like sweat, baby oil, and Victoria's Secret "Amber Romance". I saw friggin' RED...**REDRUM!** I said, "Excuse me" while pushing past woozy women. The entire basement was dark except for the light from the huge aquarium. The music was blaring *"Where dem dollas at?"*. I'm looking everywhere for Usher and finally I find him sitting on the staircase leading up to the main level. He was leaning back on his elbows with some chick in front of him!!! His belt was unbuckled. I lost it. I pushed her out of the way and pulled him into a corner. I was going off and then it happened... I snapped! I slapped his ass so hard it was like you could hear the needle slide across the record. It was like the scene in *"The Color Purple"* when Squeak slapped Ms. Sophia. *"Welp, time ta go"*. Everybody heard or saw it somehow and started to clear the basement. Maybe they didn't see or hear, but the place damn sure cleared out within minutes. He snatched me and took me upstairs to his room. I was crying and upset. Once he left me to go back downstairs, I got in my car and left. I was so done. He was done. We didn't speak for at least a month after that. Eventually, I wrote letters, sent flowers, and called back-to-back. He iced me and I was sick. Isn't it funny how men can do wrong and then use reverse psychology and we end up apologizing? Why was I apologizing? He lied and got caught. Now the cat was pretty much out the bag about us dating. We started talking after several weeks and I apologized because I had zero right to put my hands on him.

90

I totally blacked out. It was wrong and unacceptable. I realized then that I had fallen in love, I was in a bit of a predicament. I had some tough decisions to make and a lot to think about. Was this what I really wanted? Did it make sense? Confused, but happy and excited inside. Very perplexing. I knew it would be hard, I just didn't realize how hard.

As our friends started to find out that we were really together, there were mixed opinions all around. Some of my friends thought he might be too young for me; others thought that we were "cut from a different cloth." He had few personality traits that they didn't love but had to forgive. Others said "Yes!! Go for it, he's good to you, enjoy every minute". His friends didn't welcome the idea of him being "locked down". I mean, he was the walking all-access pass to clubs and women—oh, and he had the money to finance it all, too. So, umm... yep, I'm sure I was a cause for concern. Once we started dating heavily, the club outings started to slow down, the random broads in the guesthouse days simmered, and the strip club attendance was at an all time low. The seven-year age gap wasn't a big deal; he had dated older before and besides age is just a number when you're a total old soul like he was. We set boundaries and put the drama behind us. Sometimes we all hung out doing things like group bowling, movies, or "caking." "Caking" was what we did when it was any one of the crew's birthdays. Usher would go and buy between 5 and 7 sheet cakes and then we would surprise the person by smashing them from every direction. We returned the favor by getting him too. We also did things like taking drives in his GT Porsche Carrera—*Vroooom*—speeding down highway 400 late at night, always listening to new music. We would sometimes grab our favorite char-grilled wings, french toast, and chai tea at R. Thomas and head home. Usher was a very special, unique being. His true personality would have surprised most people. He is very much a family man and he actually knows how to make chocolate candy like a true confectioner. I swear the turtles and pecan rolls he makes are the best. He loved going all out for holidays, sometimes going completely overboard during Christmas and Thanksgiving. I'm talking full décor, logs on the fire, roasting marshmallows, turkey basting, and tons of Christmas music and traditions. The guy was not only truly spontaneous, but he's super creative at planning surprises and giving gifts. He was so generous-hearted. that he literally gave just to see the reaction on a person's face. When you are the object of his affection, there is no better treatment—but when you're not, he shows you that you're not. He can run very hot and very, very cold. There simply is no in between.

In 2006, Usher got the opportunity to perform on Broadway. He was invited to join the cast of the musical "Chicago", playing the leading role of Billy Flynn. His mother was initially less than thrilled. It wasn't her idea, and besides, he was just coming off the success of his *Confessions* album. But I think Broadway had been a long-time aspiration for Usher, so he accepted the role. This meant six weeks of pre-rehearsal in New York. He asked me to join him there and I agreed. He got a stylishly furnished 2-bedroom apartment in a Manhattan high-rise adjacent to the theater. Obviously, I had to commute back to Atlanta sometimes to spend time with my boys during my visitation weeks. Other times, I had my personal assistant, Toni, or my best friend, LaNita, who is also the boys' godmother, bring them up to New York so that I could stay. Usher was a man that didn't like being alone much. He was very dedicated to the role of the shiesty yet debonair attorney and he learned the work of Bob Fosse. He also studied actors that had previously starred in the role. I rehearsed his lines with him, often playing Roxie or Velma and we watched tons of films. I connected especially with Roxie Hart's *"The name on everybody's lips is going to be Roxie Hart"* character in more ways than one. Although, I loved Brenda Braxton personally who played the role of "Velma Kelly". We remain in touch today.

Oh yes, Oh yes, Oh yes.... They both reached for the gun, the gun the gun ......fooooorrrrr the gunnn.

By the time the show opened that August, my baby was READY!! We were both nervous, I was nervous about the debut because I wanted everything to be perfect for him, I knew how much of himself he had poured into the role. Opening night was a success! Ticket sales were through the roof; everybody was calling to get seats. He ended up doing two shows a day most days except for Mondays, which are always dark on Broadway. I cooked some days and took care of our place. That was a really good period for us because we were able to have so much concentrated quality time together. He would literally eat breakfast, rehearse, perform, sleep, be on vocal rest, repeat. I went to about a dozen of the performances, sometimes just chilling in the dressing room. At some point I knew everyone's lines. This was for three months straight, and outside of going to dinner, there were no clubs or friends of his trying to get him to go out. I was relieved because most of them were still back in Atlanta and we were miles away in New York. Our circle that summer consisted of other Broadway actors, my boys some weeks, his road manager Terence Carter and his security guard Big Rob. It was a refreshing change from living in Atlanta and all of the negative distractions associated with that. We actually had dinner at his cast mates home, it was a sweet time. One night late, we got up and decided to ride the subway to Soho late at night. No security and no crew. We got off and just walked around for hours. Simple things. I liked living in New York and I think he did too.

Usher had his truck shipped and I learned my way around once the car arrived. I drove everywhere, shopping, poppin into museums, and exploring the city daily. Somedays I found myself out late, rushing back home before his shows were over.

In October, he ended up getting a severe case of strep throat while I was away in Los Angeles styling a Letoya Luckett job. I remember being so confused, thinking, *Now, how in da hell did you catch strep .... while I'm gone for a week?* Hmmm. He was sick as hell. He had fever, body aches, and was barely audible when he spoke. We talked to each other every night until we fell asleep on the phone. I missed him terribly. The production had a stand-in actor performing the shows for that week. He was on complete vocal rest. One night, while I was in my room at the Four Seasons Beverly Hills, I was on the phone with him. I was washing my face in the bathroom when suddenly I thought I heard something in the other room. I got real quiet and said "Hello?!!" I peeked out just as the door was opening. I was like, "Hello! Come back later...." thinking that it was housekeeping providing late turn-down services. It was him!! Usher had flown from New York to L.A to surprise me! He had a huge bouquet of flowers covering his face. I dropped the phone and ran to kiss him, strep throat and all! Aww. We had the best night ever. Mr. Flynn, "gave em the old Razzle Dazzle'… had a new meaning for me. LOL I was so in love and didn't care if my entire throat fell out the next day. Razzle Dazzle em.

CHAPTER 9

Rocket Love

❧

"Usher Frolics with Married Mother of Three"
"Usher set to Marry a Gold Digger!"

Mortified. That's the only word I can use to describe the way I felt when I saw my pictures — unflattering pictures at that — splashed all over the tabloids under negative and inaccurate headlines.

Usher and I went to St. Barth to celebrate my birthday and the impending New Year in December 2005. We rang in 2006 there. This was my favorite island and I had not been back in nearly five years. We partied for five days straight all over the island. We stayed at a private villa — a little beachfront bungalow along Flamands Beach. It was picturesque — alabaster white slipcovered Shabby Chic furniture with matching, billowy linen curtains, colossal white candles, sea salt weathered floors, a canopy bed, glass French doors, plantation shutters, and a huge wrap around terrace with hammock just along the white sand beach. It was the epitome of paradise. Our little chalet was like something from the movie "Beaches" yet the energy inside was very "9 ½ Weeks" minus the weird stuff.

The setting was so romantic, location exotic and we were blissfully into each other. There's nothing like that "canoodling in the ocean" kinda love. Something about feeling weightless, coupled with the warmth of your man's body, that is always so alluring and euphoric. It is said that cuddling boosts the immune system and releases the love hormone oxytocin, which we were absolutely reeking of. Our sexual chemistry was one for the books. Peanut butter and jelly. Undeniable and consistent. The thing about me is.... Well one of the things about me is that I am a flirt. He could see it in my eyes and the way I would move. When I wanted him, he knew it. We were a vibe, no we were a vibration. It didn't matter where we were or who was around. Our energy was unspoken yet clear between us. We rented a silver convertible Smart car and drove around, indulging in the best food and taking in the scenery. Nestled in the lap of luxury, the soundtrack to our escape was a solid playlist of Mary, Robin, Sade, Marvin, Stevie, Bublé, Sweetback, and Citizen Kane. We were literally *Livin' la vida loca*—didn't have a care in the world because we were blissfully in our own. Cues "Moments In Love", yes that was very much the energy. We dined then partied during the night, and then slept in most mornings. We ran into several other people that we knew while there, my buddy, the late great Shakir started calling me "Stella" permanently in reference to the movie "How Stella Got Her Groove Back". You gotta love Shakir with the one-line jokes, I appreciated him for not acting funny or treating me any different due to the break up with Ryan. We partied with Martha Stewart, LA Reid, Paul Allen, Lawrence Graff, Degrisigorno, and so many more, went on a few amazing megayachts and stayed out until dusk. On New Year's Eve,

Libyan leader Gaddafi's son gave a party at Nikki Beach and he gifted me a Chopard ring for my birthday. The experience in St. Barth was rarefied and surreal that is for sure. We felt that together we could conquer the world. This was until shit got weird.

One afternoon, as we hung out at the beach just outside our villa, Usher noticed someone taking photos of us.

"Don't turn around now," he said, "but there is a photographer at 9 o'clock." Truthfully, we thought we noticed him in time. But nope. We were way too late. I just wanted to crawl underwater, burrow through the sand, under the porch and dig a hole through the floor inside the house like a sand crab. I was sooo embarrassed and caught off guard. The point of traveling somewhere remote is to avoid the press, and not to care about edge control, back rolls, or forgetting to touch up my brows.

Side note: by the time you get a glimpse of the paparazzi they've already gotten the money shot…you can never get cute… not enough time. So, forget about posing, let alone shining up your ashy lips or elbows. The only time you get caught "looking photoshoot fresh" is when you call the paparazzi on yourself. I'm not calling anybody out, I'm just sayin' it's unrealistic.

The photos that were published of us were just awful. We didn't look our best, of course. We were in the middle of a lagoon…happy, wet and unbothered. We had been partying, convertible riding, and spoiling ourselves with the best food, gelato, and wine for days. The comments on the blogs were mean. "*She looks like a linebacker… Usher can do so much better…Oh my, he looks awful too—he's let himself go'.* I mean I wasn't thaaat damn out of shape, I probably could have been on the 'practice squad", but not a linebacker. Hell, he was on a much needed and rare work hiatus too. Sheesh. Can we live? Sucks teeth…Tuhhh.

The next day we started getting calls from our friends and family back home in the U.S. His publicist, mom, my sister Yolanda— *everyone*. And then came the tabloid stories. I was accused of creeping around on my husband, amongst other things. Usher was labeled a homewrecker… you know, for ruining my happy home (*slow eye roll!*). Oddly enough, my ex Ryan was also on vacation at the same time in the Bahamas with our boys and his new girlfriend. We had truly both moved on. My sons were up to speed and knew full well that we were separated. Only the public was late.

Nothing could prepare us for the backlash that we received in the weeks and months ahead. I had worked so hard for over a decade to build a career for myself behind the scenes. Now, here I was being tossed in the bullpen, stripped of my privacy, and being called manly, a gold-digger and unattractive. I was like "Dayuumm"(*Kevin Hart's voice) that's a lot to assume about a person based on a candid photo. I had always been a confident strong woman…never been called ugly. But once our relationship was out, people called me manipulative, evil, and blamed me for everything under the sun—global warming, any bad songs he made (past, present, and future), a wreck in Wisconsin… heck if he dropped his hat during a performance in middle school that was my fault too. They also said that I was the cause of his breakup with his famous ex, Chilli. Not true. He broke up with her in 2003. On top of that, I was not initially attracted to him, his attitude, style, age, and he was hard for me to work for so it was not ideal. Long before and into our relationship, these were my concerns. On top of that, he had several other notable trysts with models, dancers, mud ducks, and actresses before… and after we got together. People didn't stop to bother to think about or remember that. Furthermore, they never think of real timelines. Start and stop times are important little details. Stop "cancelling" people without full details.

Usher's mom, Jonnetta—who was also his manager at the time—had concerns about his brand. His image was that of a hot, single bachelor, and here he was dating a woman who was not yet legally divorced and had children. I understood her concerns. Any mother with a highly successful son is going to have raised eyebrows about any woman who comes around. Especially a woman that was seven years older and separated with children. I would express similar concerns about any one of my sons. But on the flip side, my feeling is that if one of my independent, adult sons came to me, maturely sat me down, and expressed his love for a person, I would at least hear them out and try to remain open minded. He literally did that, and she wasn't hearing any of it. I sincerely wish she would have handled things differently. Her anger towards the media reports soon turned towards me. I felt bad for Usher. Not only was he defending our love to the world; he was also dealing with fallout from his innermost circle. The relationship with his mother started to deteriorate. I got blamed for that too. Truth was they were already hanging on by a thread professionally for other reasons and her attitude toward the relationship pushed it over the edge. I was still polite and cordial toward her through it all. I smiled when I saw her and always bought great gifts for holidays and her birthdays. I could have held a webinar on "how to maintain a fake smile." Oddly enough, she gave us a huge baby shower for our first son Usher, at her house. There were at least 100 people in attendance and she was nice during the planning. It was always unpredictable. One day she would call and talk nicely and then the next stop speaking out the clear blue sky. I think they both were listening to far too many pessimistic people.

However, you can only maintain a stiff upper lip for so long. I didn't detest her, but I didn't like her cold attitude and it became harder to be nice while she was straight up nasty. I mean, here is a woman who has been through a divorce, a couple of baby daddies, and at the time, was dating a man named Eric, who was a former boxer and at least 18 years her junior. You would think she would have been a little less judgmental and far more compassionate. Love can find you at any time and come from anywhere. It is true, I was not yet legally divorced, but I was definitely fully separated and living apart. Divorce takes time. She should know that — rumor has it her beau was married as well, when they first got involved. I digress. The epitome of throwing stones while living in a large, delicate, extremely delicate... GLASS HOUSE. A crystal palace. An ice castle. Her boyfriend encouraged and supported us and expressed disappointment in her treatment of me. I'm pretty sure that her actions toward me were their coup de grace (no pun).

As Usher's manager, she was just not willing to work with us to devise a strategy to address the situation publicly. I felt a lot like Meghan Markle...Damn, Meka Markle. It felt like they were more worried about protecting his reputation, than quieting the fallacies about me. Instead, she told him to ignore the bad press, in hopes that it would go away. Well, it didn't. The appearance of a lack of support from his mother gave the erroneous stories legs and indirectly fanned the fires. I was roasted daily...they barbequed my ass every chance they got. I understood that this was unchartered waters for her— Usher had always been universally adored by the media and had never experienced a scandal, so to speak. I didn't have a publicist, agents, or a "team" to help me to navigate this new territory. I had zero support. I just wanted to hide; it was a very lonely place to be. The gossip mongers continued to spew their vitriol. Usher eventually released a statement to quiet the noise. It didn't stop the hate; but we kept living and initially the negativity actually brought us closer. My family and close friends were compassionate, but it wasn't enough. He became very defensive about me and angry that people didn't understand. Sometimes I wonder if her anger toward me was because we're similar in some ways, I think she felt that I was trying to turn her son against her or take her place. I am not the mousie, blend into the wallpaper type, I had my own career and money when I got with her son and I don't bend over backwards to be liked. That said, I was respectful, well put together and I loved her son. Maybe she thought I was trying to take her place as his manager. Oh, it couldn't be further from the truth. First of all, I'm a black woman, secondly I'm a mother of all sons, I am pro mother, and at that point in my life, I could barely *manage* to make a flight on time much less a superstar artist with contracts and an entourage. (She'd have to wait a few more years for his next wife to do that.) Besides, she and I were super cool before we got together. We would have dinner in her hotel room and have breakfast when we were on the road. Her sudden disdain for me never made much sense, because it was baseless and out of the blue. The funny part is Usher's father loved me to pieces. In fact I reunited them after being estranged for nearly 30 years. One day I was hanging at his mother's office (she wasn't there of course) and the receptionist called into Usher's office. She stated that a man was outside the office waiting to see him. He appeared to be a little irritated, so I asked who it was and he told me that it was his father. He and his father had been estranged for the majority of his life, because he was absent and perhaps he was only coming around because he needed something. I was excited and told him that he should at least hear him out and give him the chance to explain. I also told him that he never knows what his father was going through in his life. I also knew that his mother was a handful and hellllla challenging person to deal with, so I told him to certainly take that into account. I just felt that his father should have been given the opportunity to give his version. I told him "hey, you don't have to give him anything, but at least give him the time of day". Being nice is free. Sometimes adult relationships, the hurt, and breakups interfere with parenting. Thank God he listened to me, because his father came inside the lobby of the building, they talked, and hugged. His father was so happy that he literally had tears in his eyes. I felt so proud to be a part of their reunion. Eventually, we ended up seeing his father a lot. We called him "Urkie". I encouraged Usher to surprise him for Father's Day in 2007 by buying him a car, making sure that he had health insurance and a roof over his head. Basic necessities. Shit, I was pushing it, but hey what's the point of wealth if we don't share it with those that matter and I adored him. We also got acquainted with his Grandma Tina, cousins, his little sister Ushyra and Aunt Rena. They all attended our wedding, his little sister was the flower girl and got to know my family as well. Life is really short, because he got sick and hospitalized just two months after our wedding, the same month our son Usher V was born and passed away in January of 2008. I was so sad, yet proud that they had those two years together. He was kind, had a quiet speaking voice, played the piano and had a gentle spirit. He was my ally and I felt sad that he never got the chance to meet and love his grandsons. I have no regrets about encouraging that connection, but it may have made matters even worse between me and his Mom. Oh well life goes on, but we definitely felt like it was us against the world. He made that understood in more ways than one…

❧

In 2007, on a beautiful January night in New York, he made his love for me abundantly clear. Next level, crystal clear. He was already in the city recording for the *Here I Stand* album with his friend, Robin Thicke, and to attend the christening of our good friend, Mark Pitts' baby girl, Jaden. I flew in and we all went out to dinner at Tao where I got a little tipsy sipping on mai tais. I excused myself at some point to go to the ladies' room. When I got back, Usher had scrolled through my phone and had seen a text from a notable guy. This was someone we had discussed before. He was upset about it and confronted me later that night when we got back to Sony Studios. "You *still* talking to that dude? ... Wow," he said. I told him to leave it alone, and added, *"You still talking to all of your broads?"* He had just gotten in some hot water over being far too chummy with one of his tour dancers, so he didn't have room to ask me anything. His jealousy was kind of cute to me. So damn toxic, sighhhh.

We playfully went back and forth for a while as Robin dabbled around in the other room, playing and singing random songs on the piano. When we finally joined him in the main room, he began to play "The Stupid Things." Usher started singing and then turned to me, which embarrassed me to no end. *"All I want to do is please you... Please myself by living my life too... And all the stupid things I do, have absolutely no reflection on How I feel about you."*

He then asked everyone in the studio to come into the room where we were. His security, Big Rob, Terence Carter, and an engineer were present. Before I could say a word, he was telling everyone how much he loved me, and grabbed my hand before getting down on one knee. He said, *"I love you. I want you to be my wife and have my children. I want to spend the rest of my life being the I want you to marry me. Will you marry me?"* My eyes welled up with tears. It was unbelievable. He completely came from left field, best friends, confidants, now fiancé?

This was totally impromptu…so, he didn't have a ring on him. He ran around the studio and found a yellow string…some kind of fabric and tied it in a knot around my finger. Honestly, for me, he truly never had to replace that string. I was floating and my heart was so full I thought it would burst.

I remember wondering if he was drunk or something, but by the next morning, it was clear that his proposal was real. And me? I was already morphing into the seemingly perfect fiancée, asking what my husband-to-be needed. "*Can I iron anything? Are you hungry baby? What can I get you?*" We were both feeling giddy. By the time we got to the church for Jaden's christening, we couldn't stop giggling, holding hands, and smiling at nothing. It was like we were on a first date. Technically, we were—as fiancés. Mark finally asked, "What in the hell is wrong with you guys?" Usher told him that he had proposed, and Mark was thrilled for us—he gave us a big group hug. I wanted to shout out our love to the world. All I wanted was to be with him. I was anxious to share the news with my kids and family. However, we agreed that it was best not to tell everyone just yet. We certainly wanted to, though. It was a crazy happy moment—the kind you want to share with the world. It was January and cold, but everything inside me— inside us— felt warm like July.

By the second week of February 2007, we were back in New York. We were planning to stay for Valentine's Day, but were advised to return to Atlanta a day early due to an impending snowstorm. Usher was acting really nervous all that day, he kept rushing to the phone, running downstairs to the lobby and on the flight— all fidgety. He kept asking me if I wanted another drink until finally, I said, "What is up with you? What's going on?" He didn't answer me, but the restlessness continued. The plane landed at about 10 pm and we got home by 11 pm. There were flowers at the house, the night was chilly, and I was rushing to change for bed. At 11:58, he turned to me and handed me a box with an 11-carat Ascher cut diamond ring from Fred Leighton Jewelers. He wanted to present me with the replacement ring by the stroke of midnight on Valentine's Day. I was so surprised and I jumped all over him with joy! I think I slept 30 minutes that night, because I couldn't stop staring at my hand. This ring was radiant, ridiculously big and clear as day. I felt like a princess in a love story, but there was one little problem...my divorce had not been yet finalized. Oh, fugg! Details.

We got into a foolish fight the next day. I checked his cell phone— which I know is not cool— but my paranoia got the best of me. Way to kill the mood, right? I couldn't just sit my ass down and be content. I really should have been chilling! I was so accustomed to chaos and dysfunction in a relationship that I couldn't even relish in the great moment I was experiencing. Insecurity won.

I saw that he had called another one of the girls who used to dance for him. I flipped. He told me that he just wanted to tell her about our engagement. He said they'd been friends and I really didn't understand. I said, "That's bullshit. You don't owe her anything. She was never your woman and is never going to be. She was merely a broad you were f#&ing while you were on tour. One of many."

I was mad that he called her because I knew that they had a sexual past and that she didn't care about him being engaged to me. She wasn't exactly an advocate. We got into a big old, knock-down, drag-out fight. He got on the phone with one of my best friends, Nyeisha, and said, "This is why I can't fool with her!" meaning me. He was saying that I was ridiculous and crazy. "I just gave her a frigging ring!" he screamed.

It was senseless. We argued, slammed a few doors, and even broke a couple of things! I wasn't trying to control him, but our personal intimacy was sacred to me. Some called me territorial, but respect is not ownership — it's the one thing that we had that was to be just between us. When you're with a musician, you have to share so much of them with the world, because that's what the job entails. If you go out to lunch, people *will* walk up to the table and want an autograph; they ask to take pictures and say hello to their mother on an awaiting phone. When he's onstage, he has to open himself up, take some of his clothes off, bare his chest, and connect with his female fans. That's why the sex had to be just us. Plus, that shit was mine. I did not trust the idea of him maintaining close friendships with women that he previously slept with. Obviously, he did not agree. If you let him tell it, he was faithful. But I knew that it was not quite true. An affair of the heart or emotional cheating can be ten times worse. Anyway, the following morning after the spat, Mr. and Mrs. Dysfunction got up and caught our scheduled flight as planned. We were headed to All Star weekend in Las Vegas. Our quarrels didn't usually last long. If I'm a nonchalant girlfriend, worry, If I show you I care then you got me.

In March 2007, I got pregnant. It was two months after our engagement and although my divorce was now final, the ink was barely dry. I know, it was fast, but remember I had been separated since 2005. What can I say, I was speeding in the fast lane. Next stop, wedding planning. You can't make this shit up. I just knew that I didn't want to be big and pregnant at our nuptials, so we decided to set the date for sooner rather than later and agreed on July 28th. I would be early in my second trimester and not too far along for a couture gown. There was no true significance in the date for us, other than that it was the last Saturday in July and maybe for me, Jackie Onassis' birthday. We took a four-day trip to visit L.A. Reid and his wife Erica at their vacation home in the Hamptons on Long Island.

My oldest son Darrin went with us. One morning over breakfast L.A. said, "Where are you guys going to have the wedding?" I told him that I had no idea, which is when he said, "Why don't you guys do it here?" He continued, "We can have it in the yard," referring to his lush green grounds. I loved L.A.'s home. It had very clean-lined décor and divine artwork. And I loved the Hamptons. One day, while out on a walk in Montauk, we walked by a white on white convertible Volkswagen Beetle. I fell in love with it instantly. My fiancé surprised me and bought me an identical one with a big red bow. Usher was big on surprises. He was also warming up to the planning process once we hired our wedding planner Diann Valentine and designer Antony Todd, and even started to make décor suggestions, approved our invitations, and created his portion of the guest list. That part was really hard because we could only invite 70 people each and he had way more to include, so I gave up 30 of my 70 seats. Solid plans for our big day were underway. It was such a happy time for me.

A few weeks before the wedding, we flew to California to see my family in Oakland. My Grandma Estella was really sick and was in the hospital. I wanted to see her and I also wanted everyone to meet Usher. I was nervous as heck—worried that one of them would say or do some real hood shit. When we got to dinner, it was a little embarrassing because everyone was vying for his attention. I'd warned him beforehand, so he was cool about it, but I could tell he was uncomfortable. Valencia, my daddy's oldest daughter, who was sitting next to him, had her cell phone out. She was flipping through her whole family album, showing him relatives and in-laws that I didn't even know. There was her son's baby-mother's sister in one shot and a haircut she did for somebody in another (she's a hair stylist). You name it, she was showing it. *Woosah!* I could see that Usher was *not* relaxed; but he was being sweet, taking all kinds of pictures with whomever requested them. By then, everyone in the restaurant was starting to notice him and all I could think was: *Oh. My. God. Would these damn Klampetts, stop it!*

I wish that was the end of that story…but nope. We finished dinner and were about to order dessert, when another plate of food came out—a plate of jumbo prawns or something— and I spoke up, "Who ordered that?!" I mean, I'm the one paying for dinner! I turned to the waiter and said, *"Nobody ordered that food."* The two of us argued a bit and then he pointed to my niece and said, "She did ma'am."

I was pissed. That's super embarrassing. Someone takes you to dinner and at the end of the dinner when everybody's packed up their food and the plates are being cleared you whisper to the waiter to get more food? Really?

I said fine. I was so mad; it was solely about the principle at this point "Put it on a separate check then." Usher looked at me, shaking his head like, "No, don't say that." But I didn't care. She'd had a bit too much to drink anyway. When dinner was over, her Mom, my sister invited us to come over to her house. I told her we were busy, and she started playfully grilling me. "Busy doing what?" I rattled off a few things and we left. Usher told me I shouldn't have tripped off the food…we spoke about it a little in the car and eventually moved on. I thought that was that.

We were back in Atlanta and making wedding and baby plans when I got a call from my father. Your sister Valencia had a call from the *National Enquirer*.

"What?" I exclaimed "Why would they call *her*? They don't even know her. How would they get her number?" Valencia is 12 or 13 years older than me. We hardly even had a relationship, and rarely spoke beyond my childhood.

"I don't know," he explained, "but something happened at the restaurant. They called HER to ask something about a plate of food or something that was ordered. Something with you and some food…" I'm like what??? Nah, it doesn't work like that. I smelled a rat.

My father didn't have the details, except that my sister did talk to a reporter. I knew that something was fishy. How would the *National Enquirer* know to contact one of my dad's children? First of all, he has 16 or 17, and second, she wasn't a close family member. Granted, when I was in elementary school, I had gone to visit her and my niece and nephew during a few summer vacations for a few weeks. I mean, we spoke once or twice a year. She lived in Benicia, which is a tiny, remote part of Northern California. How would they find her?? None of this made sense. I suspected that if she did speak with them, she was the one to reach out to them. Wow! I smelled a rat. I was hurt— taken aback really— but I was too busy at the time to focus on it. I was planning my dream wedding for God's sake; I was also pregnant and in the process of moving into our new home. There was just so much going on during that time.

One week later the *National Enquirer* published a story saying that ***Usher doesn't know what he's getting into, he's set to marry a gold digger with a sordid past.*** Wait...what??! Me? I was mortified. The article accused me of welfare fraud which was completely annoying, it was so ratchet sounding. Besides, I was never a person to consistently request or receive public assistance, other than medical. Remember how much I hated them in 1990. I worked soon after my son was born and had a decent savings. I was angry with the magazine for not checking the facts. Their source was someone I hadn't been around in my entire adult life. Dinner was it! It was another bout of negative press to deal with. I was devastated and felt awful for my fiancé. They even had pictures of us from the dinner party that I surmised my si.... I mean the father's daughter had provided to them. I don't think she was initially taking pictures with the intention of sending them anywhere. I think she got mad when I mentioned the extra food her daughter ordered. She probably thought that I was being petty and that it was justified payback for embarrassing her daughter. She's the kind of vindictive person who'd physically tangle with the staff at the drive-through window of a Taco Bell. She'd throw food at restaurant employees over the smallest offenses. And when she argued with a former lover she'd say "That's why your mothe#*&ckin' daddy is dead!' ' She'd say and do the coldest things, many of which I witnessed. I knew she had a temper, but I never imagined that anyone in my family, especially a sibling, would do something like that. It was against the code. I was truly hurt. As a child I thought she was so beautiful—stunning actually— and she had this infectious laugh that made you forgive all her faults. When she was happy, she was fun to be around. I looked up to her. What's more, my mother loved her like a daughter. But when she was pissed...

Usher just said, "I thought you shouldn't have said anything about the food. I told you that night. I didn't see it going here and I'm sorry that this is happening to you, but people are a trip. I know that this is the way it goes...I've been in this business longer than you." He was right. Another notable actress said the same thing to me one day over lunch. She warned me about the price of fame and how family may betray you or sell you out. This was a lesson in learning to let things roll off of your back. I also realized that not everyone is meant to go with you on your life's journey. I was deeply wounded, however, and needless to say our familial relationship died then and there.

It was two days before the wedding. I was exuberantly running all over the city, grabbing last minute things. The night before, I stayed in a suite at the Mandarin Oriental in Manhattan with three of my bridesmaids. I had a total of five bridesmaids — my sister Yolanda, my lifelong friends LaNita and Nyeisha, and two newer friends Maya and Brea. I was having a few mild contractions that day, but my doctor attributed them to all of the excitement. Usher was still in Atlanta, where his close friend, Keith, wanted to give him a bachelor party. I didn't really love the idea, but I had a ton of things to get done, so my mind was happily pre-occupied. One of my bridesmaids still needed shoes, others needed earrings, and I had to visit my doctor. (I had a great backup OB in New York from our "Chicago" days.) Most importantly, I needed to find a better ring option for my husband-to-be, and I had to get all of this done quickly as we planned to leave for the Hamptons by midnight.

In the midst of running around, it suddenly dawned on me that I hadn't heard from Usher since that morning, so I called him. When he didn't answer I thought maybe he was just getting fitted for his tux. Then I wondered if he had even left Atlanta. I called Lila at Armani, who was providing all the suits, and asked, "Did Usher and the groomsmen come by for the fitting?" She said yes and that things went well. That's when my mind started playing tricks on me: *Is he really out creepin' on the day before our wedding?*

At about 9:00 pm I finally spoke to him. This time he called me at the hotel. He sounded somber; his voice was monotone. I ask him, "Where've you been, Baby? I've been looking for you since 4:00 pm. I've called everywhere. Are you OK? What's going on with you?"

"I need to talk to you for a minute," he said. "How old are you for real?"

"Huh? What in the fuck are you talking about?!!" I yelled. His tone and line of questioning was scaring me.

"I need you to be honest with me. How old are you? Are you 42 and born October 10th?" (Bear in mind, I was only 37 at the time.)

"Excuse me???"

"I'm just saying, I need to ask you this." He sounded really humdrum—too calm, almost like he was high,

"Are you 42? Were you born October 10, 1964?"

"You're kidding me, right? You're playing. My birthday is January 1, 1971. Call my mother, call my father, call Yoli, whoever."

"No, you're not. No, you're not. No, you're not." He was emphatic.

"Are you high? Have you been drinking? For real, you sound weird…where are you? Let me come to you. Where are you?" I was frantic but trying to be quiet. I didn't want the girls to hear me.

"I am in New York, but we're not going to be able to get married tomorrow. I've got a report here that says you were born October 1964. We're not going to be able to get married tomorrow." He was speaking in an incredibly calm and measured manner, using a lowered voice, as if someone was standing nearby.

My mind was spinning. I felt lightheaded, like my brain was levitating. He continued, "Did you live on Detroit Avenue in Concord?"

"Yes, I did. That was where I lived. That was my sister Yolanda's old address. What are you getting at? Are you checking my credit? Ayee, my credit is not great, so??… What are you looking at? Can I see what you see? Where are you???"

"Listen! Don't worry about it. I'm just saying I can't get married tomorrow!"

I slowly dropped the phone and started screaming loudly. I'm surprised the building didn't hit the ground, because it was that kind of hysterical shriek. My head was exploding. My three girlfriends who were in the living room of the suite, ran in and took the phone from me to find out what was wrong. I was having a full-blown meltdown, literally rocking back and forth. I felt dizzy, as if I was going to throw up. *Why would he do this?* I took the phone back from Maya and demanded to know if he was serious. He was... and sadly, it was Friday night at 9:15 pm. There was no way to disprove the falsehoods before the wedding. Hell, at this point I was really expecting Ashton Kutcher to come out of the closet and tell me that I was on next week's episode of *Punk'd*. This just couldn't have been happening. How?? Why now?

My friends struggled to get a grasp on what was happening, whilst also trying to console and calm me down. They attempted unsuccessfully to get him back on the phone. I couldn't stop sobbing and soon I was hyperventilating. I was a mess. Sidebar: I NEVER CRY! I always felt that it made me weak, so it takes a whole lot to unleash my salt rivers. Crying has always made me feel so vulnerable, especially in the presence of others. I have learned to repress my feelings. Yet on this night, there was no shame in my game. I fell asleep in my clothes and woke up on what was supposed to be the morning of my dream wedding in a puddle of tears. Somehow in my mind I was still hopeful that this was just a bad dream—that he would call and tell me everything was okay. But that was not the case.

The next few hours were actually pure comedy. This was like an outlandish wacky scene from *"Bridesmaids"* or a scene from *"Sex in the City."* Let's just call it: *"Bridesmaids in the City"*. My three bridesmaids were trying to devise a foolproof plan to sneak me out of the hotel without the paparazzi becoming aware. Paparazzi were always lurking outside of the Mandarin Oriental trying to get a shot of a famous person or a business tycoon staying there as a guest. Plus, they knew I was there. When you're in the midst of drama, it just feels like everyone knows and everyone is looking at you. We decided to split up. One friend carried the ginormous wedding dress, now semi-discreetly packed in a garment bag, through the main lobby of the hotel to an awaiting black SUV, while I exited through a service elevator that led to a side alley. This was a covert operation. We were going deep, deeeep undercover. Before all of this happened, we had reserved a helicopter to take us from a heliport on the Westside highway to the Hamptons. We raced in the SUV to the chopper and boarded anyway. I was determined to get to the Hamptons and look Usher in the face. I don't know how I knew he was there; I simply felt it. I figured that he would want to explain the circumstances or his version of them to L.A. My bridesmaids and I were playing Columbo trying to find him; it was all hands-on deck! Everybody was on their cell phones like it was a telethon. As it turns out, when he called me the night before, he was actually staying right across the street from the Mandarin, at the Trump Hotel. So close and yet so far apart.

At some point, I called my father, still crying, and I asked him when I was born. Yes, at this point I was second guessing everything! But he was already in the Hamptons, clearly taking full advantage of the open bar and was no damn help at all. Even my mom was scatterbrained when I called her, so I hung up. Nobody understood what was going on when I called. I'm sure I was speaking in tongues too. Screaming and rambling.

I was disgusted with everybody. I felt like I was in the daggone Twilight Zone. It was just crazy.

My girls and I got into the helicopter for what feels like the longest flight in the world. LaNita called and started threatening Usher, talking about how he was going to get his ass 'whupped'. "You don't know who you're fuckin with!!" she yelled. I guess that was his whole point. I had to calm her down. You gotta love that ride-or-die girlfriend who is as passionate about your pain as you are. Kick his ass sis!!

The pilot made a few announcements upon take off. Tears were silently rolling down my face. It was a bright, sunny day—not a cloud in sight...perfect for a wedding. We flew over the Hudson River. There were boats and barges below. I remember being virtually silent and exchanging forlorned looks with everyone for the entire flight. Upon arriving, the pilot said, "Welcome to Sag Harbor" and proceeded to tell us the weather. The helicopter made its descent into what looked like Area 51. It wasn't an official heliport, helipad, or anything—it was just a field of tall-ass weeds, dried grass, and a few downed tree logs. The nearest road was at least a mile away. Once we deplaned, the engine revved again and the rotors turned, creating quite the dust storm around us. A tumbleweed literally rolled by. We were so flustered leaving the hotel that we forgot to arrange for ground transportation. Can you imagine all of us with a big-ass Vera Wang wedding gown sitting on a huge piece of driftwood with absolutely no plan? (Another classic *I Love Lucy* moment!) Oh…and it was hot as Hades, and we had no cellphone service. It was like a sequence out of a dream—better yet, out of a nightmare. We sat there for a good hour trying to get someone's attention just to call us a taxi. Finally, some girls came by in a Jeep and helped us. I kept my head down…too embarrassed and afraid they might recognize me.

We got into a cab and headed to a pizzeria in Montauk. My first instinct was to call my play mom, Patti LaBelle. Once I got reception, my phone was ringing like crazy because some of my guests were still arriving and trying to figure out shuttle information, wedding details, and so forth. I didn't want to tell anyone else what was going on. I think I was still hopeful. I called Patti Webster, Usher's publicist. She said, "Tameka, it's strange because Russell Simmons' Art 4 Life event is going on in the Hamptons right now too, which is why I'm here. I didn't even pack clothes for your wedding because I felt in my spirit that it wasn't going to happen." I cried. Patti Webster's mom, an ordained pastor, was also in the Hamptons, so she came over to talk to me and pray with me at the restaurant. I never saw Usher that day. I don't even know how I got back to the city from the restaurant. I was that out of it.

By then everybody had been informed that the wedding was cancelled, so my phone was blowing up again. I wound up getting Usher to charter me a plane back home because there was no way I was having a *People Magazine* moment flying commercial. I was having premature contractions like you wouldn't believe, so I headed to Northside Hospital in Atlanta, where they admitted me right away.

Usher came to see me at the hospital on August 1ˢᵗ. He told me that he was wrong. I'm not sure where the false information on the report came from—maybe I fibbed about my age when I was younger to get a credit card, an apartment, or something else. When folks try and dig up rubbish on you in this world, they dig up *everything*. He believed me now, but it was too late. All of the money that we had spent on the wedding had gone to waste. We had planned for it to be catered by Jean Georges*, and* Sylvia's Restaurant in Harlem as something special for my family. Soul food was in ramekins. Flowers had been flown in from Brazil and Denmark. All of it was down the toilet, because he didn't believe that the woman he'd been best friends with, made love to, and made a child with, was who I said I was. Now, he was essentially saying "Oops I was wrong, let's do it!"

I wanted to hold out, make him sweat, and pout for a while, but then I couldn't. The next thing I knew, I was signing a 40-page prenup and finding someone to officiate the ceremony in a suite at a Marriott in downtown Atlanta. Judge Penny Brown Reynolds, an African-American judge, and her husband, Reverend Edward S. Reynolds, arrived to do the honors. Seven friends and family gathered on August 3rd, 2007 to witness Usher and I exchange vows. Sadly, his mother was not present.

❧

Can you imagine all of us with a big ass Vera Wang wedding gown sitting on a piece of driftwood with absolutely no plan?

❧

CHAPTER 10

Before I Met You

❧

After our intimate wedding ceremony in Atlanta, life kept moving. We had several calendar events scheduled. The first was a private birthday dinner with Senator Barack Obama. During the 2008 presidential campaign, then-Senator Obama was in town on his birthday. We received a call from his camp asking if Usher and I could come over to the hotel for a small surprise dinner since he couldn't be with the girls and Michelle that evening. I was at Neiman Marcus within two seconds of that phone call to find a dress! I was in my third trimester and felt frumpy, but I was so elated.

Senator Obama's birthday was August 4th—the day after Usher and I eloped. We had been married for one day, and I was so excited about my life at that point. Not only had I wed the man of my dreams, I had his baby in my womb—a boy who would soon bear the same name as my husband. *And* I was getting to meet Barack Obama! I knew the stars were aligned. My life's feng shui was on point! I was extremely happy. During the birthday celebration that night, we talked for at least four hours with the future president.

We talked about life, policies and what he was going to do if he were elected. He came in, and joked, *"I knew something was up! When we pulled up in the car and saw all of these people outside, I knew they were not all for me!"* There was actually another formal event going on in the hotel, which was the real cause of the traffic, Usher and I had slipped in practically unnoticed.

He was very easy going, down to Earth and a really big fan of Ushers'. He went on about how his girls were huge fans too and told us that his wife would be jealous that she was not there to meet him.

He and Usher huddled for a while and talked about Usher campaigning for him. He spoke about Michelle all the time. He was still smoking cigarettes during that period. I could smell the nicotine on his breath. He was so self-possessed, smooth as glass, and attractive. We stayed there for a few hours, enjoyed the conversation, huge dinner spread, and birthday cake that was delivered to the suite. His staffers did such a nice job setting it all up. I can proudly say that Usher and I were one of the first celebrity couples to support and spend time with our soon to be 44th President. It is such a proud memory for me.

Soon after that, I set the wheels in motion for a 'rescheduled' wedding reception. I felt adamant that we have a big celebration, because I was still being asked about the whole Hamptons debacle. Furthermore, I wanted to quiet the naysayers and hecklers. Of course, that's the wrong reason to have a big wedding, but I didn't care. I wanted it anyway. Diann, our planner was able to salvage some aspects of our original event. We decided to hold it sometime within the next three weeks! I was like, "Chop-friggin'-chop!!" *Two snaps and a circle.* We lost Robin Thicke's availability for our new date due to a scheduling conflict, but I was able to book Lalah Hathaway, my favorite female vocalist. We also secured Doug E Fresh as M.C., and my long-time friend, D-Nice, as DJ for the reception.

I decided on Chateau Elan Hotel and Winery for our "I" do-over," after scouting several local private residences and event spaces. Either the décor was too Southern Traditional, not secluded enough, or unreasonably expensive. Chateau Elan was great because our guests could stay there before and after the wedding. It was the perfect choice. Now enter Bridezilla: I was far more hands-on this time. I wanted every detail to be perfect. I began to obsess more and more as we neared the big day.

After our fairytale wedding, the magic really began...

Usher made me believe in magic—the kind that envelopes you, transforms you, and casts spells. Every day with him was an adventure. We would enter into the finest restaurants with the wine already chilled. When we arrived at the airport to embark upon another spontaneous journey, a greeter would meet us, escort us through security and back corridors. Before I could blink, we'd be whisked to an awaiting car that would drive us right up to the plane. And, if we flew private, the tarmac became our own red carpet. Sometimes, he would rent out an entire theater so we could be alone to watch the latest releases. We'd spend whole nights kissing, hugging, loving, and melting into each other. I was transfixed by the sensual way he moved, hypnotized by the life he offered me. It's like he waved a wand and placed the world at my feet, then showed me what other worlds were possible.

But Usher was different. If *"been there, done that"* were a person, it would be him. He was generally unfazed by random attention-seeking women, and ignored overt exhibitionists when we were out. He was very respectful in that regard. He seemed to enjoy flipping the camera lens around and focusing solely on me. When we were together, he was open to new life experiences, patient, and eager to please. His extravagant displays of affection would have been Instagram trending topics if IG were around then. From placing dozens of roses around our home to cutting heart-shaped butter for my Valentine's Day pancakes, surprising me with new cars, he made me feel loved and desired, as if I were *his* superstar. When I came home from the hospital after having Naviyd, I remember being met with tons of "push presents". There were purses, lingerie, post-pregnancy workout videos, exercise weights, sweet smelling candles. My husband was masterful at surprises. I was never sure, though, if all this doting—all these charming gestures, large and small, were real or if he was a master manipulator playing the hell out of me. The hopeless romantic in me believes it was all real, because the gift-giving and displays of love were mutual, I gifted cars, watches, clothing, time, and energy equally if not even more.

In the very first song on his amazingly underrated album, *Here I Stand*, which many people may not realize was inspired by and dedicated to me, he sings, "I always thought that I'd never find that one to make me feel forever young…together you and me will be forever young." In retrospect, maybe this wasn't a love song. Perhaps it was a warning: Proceed with caution. I didn't realize how much youth and relevance mattered to him. Not necessarily in terms of age, but in the ability to stop time and remain the young heartthrob that captured the hearts of millions around the world. In the ways that children often do, he reserved his worst behavior for me— the one standing in front of him offering unconditional love, because he knew that I'd never judge him and that I'd never leave. In return, he granted me access to the parts of him most people would never see. I remember the childlike delight in his eyes when he successfully managed to put

together a bookshelf, or how he loved to bake chocolate delectables from scratch, using recipes he learned from his grandmother. He told me that if he hadn't become a singer, he would have certainly been a confectioner. And, to me, that made perfect sense.

From an early age, his family called him "Big Time" and it's hard to put into words how deeply that impacted him. He was a teen, but he was also head of household, financially taking care of everyone around him. I thought I could nurture him in a way that he'd never been nurtured before—with no strings attached. I thought I could save him— heal the hurt in his eyes he thought no one saw. I believed I could mold him into the man I needed, but he was a case study in arrested development. He would shape-shift into whatever the people around him expected him to be because he'd never had to develop a personality outside of performing for a public who would scream his name but never know his heart. He was trapped in a Neverland of access and privilege, incapable of navigating adult relationships—let alone a marriage—because no one had ever expected or demanded more from him emotionally. It should not have taken me so long to realize that he was my Peter Pan and I was his Wendy.

For me, it felt as though, Usher had absolutely no concept of time and he didn't want to fully grow up. His friends called him "Boy Wonder" and more often than not, they would phone and say, "We're on an island! We're on *the* island!" It was a running joke describing how they'd begin the day in one part of the city and end up in another part of the world, all because Usher had a whim, a flight of fancy. And, really, it's part of what made him so beautiful. He's a god of youth, a myth, a defiant enigma, a sensual being aware of his power on the women around him and he uses it to his advantage. Still, I wanted to mother him, escape with him, make love to him, fly away with him, all at the same time. It's no wonder that we spent so much time in planes; it's like the ground couldn't hold him. Time itself couldn't control him. But I couldn't stay in Neverland.

Perhaps, the critics and naysayers were right; I was already too old for the games, regardless of how exhilarating they could be. Were they? Marriage and motherhood are what I wanted, and ultimately, I had to realize that it wasn't working— *we* weren't working— because our time together now wasn't rooted in anything real. I was the fantasy that was supposed to keep him forever young. Instead, I had the audacity to demand that he grow up… and now I know that I was asking for the impossible. I was asking him to be something other than true to himself, even if I never believed that he was quite sure who that was without applause and approval. Although I thought we had something special, I realized that while I was his Wendy, he also had a Tiger Lily, a Tinkerbell, and a few Ms. Darlings, too. He sweetly made them all believe they were the greatest thing, but even his main girl, Wendy, was interchangeable. Time soon would reveal this.

This was the most impulsive time in my life. 2007- 2008 was such a full year and busy beyond belief. We literally bought a house, got married, moved in, got a dog, had a baby, traveled frequently, finished an album, shot videos. I mean, we were both newlywed, overzealous, and perhaps far too ambitious. We had way too much on our plates for a first year of marriage. We needed to slow down and smell the flowers. Just decorating the mansion was a fulltime job. It was 12,544 square feet, located on four acres. Sprawling. It had a gated entry, 8 bedrooms, 9.5 custom baths, and included his & hers 2-story walk-in closets, grandiose fireplaces with huge 5-foot openings, a wood-paneled study, an audacious master suite, a large guest house, a chef's kitchen with a 15' foot island, Wolf and Subzero appliances, custom cabinets, yada yada yada… At first it was spectacular. But it amazes me to this day that something you once deemed to be your dream palace could so quickly turn into your fortress of despair. I was living there, cooking, showering, and doing everyday things, but somehow, I wasn't being myself. Although I have been blessed with so much abundance and access to opportunities and experiences in my life, I have never been much into the pursuit of material things. I was literally living every girl's dream life. I had everything: money, clothes, shoes, bags, diamonds, kids, cars, homes, and the husband. Goals, yes. But the truth is, material things never truly made me happy; they only satiated me temporarily. I learned this truth in my late 20's. The more I had, the more complicated things became and the emptier I felt. I kept replaying the lyrics in my mind..

"I've given you every bit of the man I am. I know at times it wasn't pretty, but it was all I had".

❧

The more I had,
the more complicated
things became and
the emptier I felt.

❧

CHAPTER 11

This Masquerade

❦

"Eu não sei quando ela vai acordar," I heard someone saying. The language was foreign, and I couldn't understand it. As my eyes struggled to open, I also heard the sounds of beeps and machines in play. *Where the hell am I?* I wondered.

"Nos a colocamos num coma medicamente induzido," the strange voice continued.

As my vision cleared, I saw that it was a doctor speaking. I suddenly remembered that I was in Brazil. The doctor, hospital robe, and the IV in my arm triggered my memory.

I had entered a medical facility in São Paulo. I was to undergo a routine cosmetic surgery procedure. But why then did I have a catheter inside me? *Something is wrong,* I thought.

"Oh my God! She is awake!" I heard my sister, Yolanda, scream. Why was she so surprised that I was conscious? She came with me to Brazil and I told her when I decided to go through with it after we

127

arrived. I was just having simple liposuction. I was told that in Brazil, getting lipo was like running to the corner Starbucks for a latte. No big deal.

Then my eyes turned toward the center of the room...

I saw him.

He was standing there, looking scruffily handsome, with a full five o'clock shadow that was always a delicious contradiction to his natural boyish looks. He was eyeing me with a mix of joy and confusion.

What's he doing here? I thought. *Wasn't he supposed to be in Las Vegas recording his album?* Then, I realized that something *was* terribly wrong. Why else would he have flown half-way across the world to be in the hospital with me? Hell, I couldn't even get him to come home to Atlanta on weekends. I knew he didn't approve of me going to Brazil in the first place. Wait a minute! He didn't know I was having surgery down here. My sister must have called him.

But why?

❖

Dreams are a tricky thing.

One type of dream can motivate you to achieve all that you desire. And the other can quickly turn into a nightmare, waking you in the middle of your sleep, disoriented, full of horror, and completely stressed out.

I know both firsthand.

I am a girl from Oakland, California, a town that while I was growing up had no real shopping malls. Yet, I worked relentlessly for well over a decade to become one of the most successful fashion stylists in the business. I created iconic looks with many superstars, including Patti Labelle, Lauryn Hill, Ciara, Jay-Z, Usher and Toni Braxton. And, I eventually married one of the biggest superstars in music. Usher was the love of my life. All of these were wonderful dreams come true. What I was sensing now, though, was that I was either awakening from a nightmare, about to enter one, or both.

As soon as I arrived at Sírio-Libanês hospital in São Paulo, it was apparent that my operation was anything but routine. The doctor, who had been speaking Portuguese earlier, was telling us that he had placed me into a medically-induced coma and was not sure when I would wake up. I'm laying there thinking *"What in the entire hell did my goofy ass do now???"* Fugggggg.

I could feel my husband staring at me. I had to look away. I was feeling horrible. I figured I must have looked even worse than I felt. I immediately sat up in bed and began to fix my hair. It was then that I noticed, with shock, that most of it was gone. I took great pride in making sure my hair always looked it's best. Yes, I kept a great weave, or something silky on deck when it was natural. Although, most people may be surprised to find out that Usher detested sew-in weaves, yet I still got them despite his objection. I am a bit headstrong at times, especially when I believe that something is right for me. I was keeping the weave. But, where in the hell had it gone while I was unconscious?

My eyes darted around looking for some lip-gloss. I know this sounds like the height of conceitedness, but umm my husband was in the room. I hated looking raggedy around him—or any person for that matter.

"How do you feel, Baby?" he asked me while caressing what was left of my hair. (Whoever cut my weave, also took some of my real hair!) We talked for a few minutes, before he raised the real question he was burning to ask.

"Why did you do this? Why?" he said, looking down at me while slowly shaking his head.

Unbeknownst to him, he was ultimately the reason that I flew off to Brazil. I was mad as hell at him and I was trying to rebel.

For months, he had been doing things that made me increasingly suspicious that he was cheating. I come from a long line of strong women. I grew up watching ladies that did not accept mistreatment or disrespect in relationships. I was not taught to turn a blind eye to your man's indiscretions. The actress, Jenifer Lewis, portrayed the mother of Tina Turner in the movie, *What's Love Got To Do With It*. According to the film, she told Tina (played by Angela Bassett) to ignore her husband Ike's obvious philandering. "Let a man be a man," she warned her. My mother *never* told me such things.

Each time I confronted Usher; he would always have the same response.

"You're trippin', woman," he would joke. And he was right. I was not really feeling 100 percent confident because I had two babies within 12 months. That's right, back-to-back babies! Any mother knows how pregnancy alters your body. While a little person is forming inside, you are physically becoming a different person too. Sometimes it's a buffalo, other times you feel like a walrus. I felt like a hybrid of both. I wasn't used to the blubber gut life coupled with being a public figure. Who knew paparazzi cameramen had time to zoom-into your third molar, ashy knuckle and blue undergarments? Hell yeah, I was shooketh boots. I suppose that my warped way of thinking was, if you can't change a man, you can just change yourself . I was dealing with some serious postpartum body image issues. I thought my appearance was apart of the problem. Talk about a mindfuck. I definitely had it all wrong. There are international beauties, women that are heralded as the world's most desirable and many end up alone, or lied to and cheated on. That most certainly wasn't it. No shit, Sherlock.

What I understand now is how incredibly amazing I was to be the vessel for five remarkable sons, wife to one of the worlds top performers at the height of his career, all the while perfectly imperfect. I was clearly doing something right. So what if my belly was a little loose?!! I was being foolish and played right into the hands of critics.

I remember listening to Mariah Carey talk about her weight struggles with Rosie O'Donnell when Rosie's show was on Oprah's OWN network. It was a few months after she gave birth to her adorable twins. She told Rosie, "I learned a lot…watching my body change. I didn't think I would ever be the same person." I could relate.

I had Irish twins — Usher V and Naviyd were born just a year and two weeks apart from each other. Post-pregnancy, my body felt like a marshmallow whenever I tried to squeeze into my favorite pair of skinny jeans! I felt totally out of whack. My boobs were the size of two huge grapefruits because I was nursing. I coulda gotten a sexpot billboard on La Cienega Blvd. I would always silently laugh at women with small frames and gigantic boobs before. Karma *is* a bitch. My stomach had a tiny, not major pouch. My arms were flabby because I had not worked out in a while. I was two months postpartum and I hadn't snapped back the way I did with my previous pregnancies. I was breastfeeding, just like I did with all of my boys. I thought that would cure my woes, but the weight was shedding so slowly. By eight weeks postpartum, I started wondering what went wrong. What I know now is that the experience with each child is different. The snapback culture is toxic.

On top of me thinking that he was cheating, I was struggling with body issues. He would butter me up with gifts. Satiate me with staff and pacify me with that sweet, calm register. In reply to my various accusations, he would say, "You're beautiful to me. I love you just the way you are." His words were comforting. He constantly told me that I was pretty. Every wife wants to hear that from her husband, especially after having two children. So, why was I still so anxious?

When Usher appeared on Oprah's *Next Chapter* in 2012, well after our divorce, she asked him what the main problem in our relationship was.

"Tameka did not know what it meant or what it was to be my wife," he said to Oprah.

With one sentence, he summed up our whirlwind romance, rocky union, and consequent split. That statement was so succinct. So painful. So true.

The reason his "you are so sexy to me" proclamations fell on deaf ears was because he was hardly ever home after our second son was born. He took off to Vegas to record what would eventually become *Raymond V. Raymond*—the album that served as an affirmation of our divorce. In complete contrast, *Here I Stand* in 2008 was a sweet love letter to me. Thematic and mature, the songs were a reflection of a man in transition—a man who was embracing personal growth and manhood. At the time it was written, he was a new husband, and while recording, he was an expectant father.

A pivotal moment in our relationship came that same year when he went on MTV's former video countdown show, *TRL*. He was there to premiere the video for his single, "Love In This Club." But, no one remembered the video after his segment.

While being interviewed, he abruptly grabbed the mic from the shook host and looked directly into the camera. "I hear y'all talking crazy out there," he said with anger. "She's a beautiful Black woman. Stop. Stop talking. And I love her. Stop it." He was riding for his woman and the relationship I respected it. Hey we were with the proverbial "shits". In love and sick of the haters, the lonely and the cynics.

Afterwards, people said *he* had gone crazy. "*Usher Has Meltdown on MTV*" some of the headlines in magazines, papers, and blogs declared. They even compared his appearance to when a barely dressed Mariah Carey appeared on the very same show doling out popsicles to the kids.

Since when is it crazy for a husband to defend his wife to those berating her? I wondered if it had been Brad Pitt telling people to stop harassing Angelina Jolie, how would he have been treated? I tend to think that he would have received a collective cheer from both the media and the public, not the flogging that my fiancé endured, as if he were Denzel's character in *Glory*. Where were all the "black girl magic" freedom fighters during my tenure? Nope… quiet. Most of my supporters and fans were total strangers that were fighting my battles in the break room at the water cooler and on social media. Sometimes it's the old friends that you got to watch, not many were very vocal in trying to protect us during that time. Silence is complicity. Grateful to those that spoke up and gave love a chance.

The blogs and tabloids were eviscerating our relationship—and me personally—so it felt great to hear my husband stand up to them. He tried y'all. Dead ass. But things changed after I became pregnant with Naviyd. We had always enjoyed a more than active and steamy sex life; I believe in keeping my man happy. But during my pregnancy, he sometimes did not want to be intimate. "*I don't want to hurt our baby,*" he would say. I knew that something was off, because that had never been a concern in the past.

Soon after having the second baby, he jetted off to Vegas to record, and he remained there for an extended period of time. One afternoon, he called me from Las Vegas at our home in Atlanta.

"Baby, I'm leaving the room now and we are going shopping," he shared. "Then we're going to be in the studio all night."

"That's cool. Have a great day. I love you," I said.

"Love you, too," he replied.

I went on with my day. Honestly, I was running ragged. I had a 1-year-old, Usher V (we call him Cinco), that was not yet potty trained, still in a diaper and just learning to walk. Naviyd was only two months old and still breastfeeding. It was a lot to juggle two infants. I do not know how women who don't have help or a spouse, do it. Thank God for nannies, hell I'll hold a rally! Mine really saved me.

Around eight hours passed, and I had not heard from my husband. I remembered him telling me that he would be recording, so I called the studio. Would calling his cell phone have been the ideal first step? Yes, but, the detective in me had already emerged, and before I knew it, I heard someone's voice on the other end of the receiver.

"*Yes, this is Tameka Raymond, Usher's wife. May I speak with him, please?*

"Oh, I am sorry, Mrs. Raymond. The session was cancelled. They were not in today. He has allowed other artists to use his session time," the unassuming young girl informed me. She was clueless about the consequences of her information. She was simply doing her job. In actuality, she set into motion a chain of events that eventually led to me separating from the then man of my dreams.

The next morning, after getting my two sons, Ryan and Kile off to school and then taking care of Cinco and Naviyd, I realized that I still had not heard from my husband. Strange.

I called his cell phone. Voicemail. I called his hotel suite. Voicemail again. Strangely, something told me to go online and check the blogs. I was no fan of them, trust me. But, since being thrust into the spotlight after dating and marrying a celebrity, and after becoming a constant target of theirs, I admittedly checked what was being written about me. That morning though, it was Usher's face that was splashed across the screen. Damn, never look for things you don't really want to find.

"Ocean's Five—Usher and Jermaine Dupri—Party in Vegas!" one popular blog blared on its homepage. It was all about how Jermaine and Usher were partying all night and how the girls who wanted to party with them were welcome, as long as they wanted to have fun. My "REDRUM" tricycle was warming up, I wasn't *feelin'* nary one of these gut ass feelings. MADASFUCK.edu.

Jermaine Dupri is a multi-platinum producer, hit maker, and was hugely responsible for the success of Usher's biggest album, *Confessions*. JD decided to form a little clique based on the popular *Ocean's Eleven* movies, starring George Clooney et al. Along with Dupri and my husband, there were also songwriters, Johntá Austin and Bryan Michael-Cox, and JD's assistant, Tyrone Davis. The clique eventually grew to become Ocean's Seven with the additions of rapper Nelly, and R&B cutie Trey Songz. Their idea was to be a new all-black version of Frank Sinatra's Rat Pack from the 1960s. Vegas was the perfect backdrop, right? Cool, but what they failed to consider was that one of the main members was married with children and a newborn at home. Jermaine was my homie for years, I knew him back in the L.A club days, I was just all around frustrated and mad at everybody there.

I sat staring at the computer for several minutes, which felt more like several hours. I could literally feel the outrage begin to swell inside. *So, wait-a-cotton-pickin' minute... he is off in Sin City straight kickin' it and we have a two-month-old baby and a 1-year-old?! No sir! Not on my watch!*

He promised me before he started this "traveling recording plan" that he would be in the studio Monday through Friday and be home on the weekends. "I'll jump on the red-eye Friday night, be home by 6 am, and you'll have me for the weekend," he said to me. But so far none of that was materializing. As I continued to think about the situation (getting angrier at him by the minute), it all started to make sense to me. I began to piece the puzzle together. They were pretty adamant about getting him out of Atlanta to record and I believe that they just wanted every memory of his fifth album "Here I Stand" forgotten. It was a great body of work, showing a young man evolving—coming into his own. He was ahead of his time— first to marry, have a complete family, and have the suit-and-tie image. They panicked, scrapped the promotion, and killed the project altogether. My position had been, *let the fans catch up. You cannot remain the teenage heartthrob forever. You have to grow up at some point.* Classic never trendy was my approach. He was definitely an outlier with that project. First of all he was an outlier overall. A total superstar, so I thought the forward transition and growth was healthy. Unfortunately, no one listened; I was told to stay in my lane. I felt that my husband's work was my lane or should have been. But I digress... it was like, anyway ma'am "Put together a few outfits for me, including some suits, and send them to me," as he requested of me weeks before.

"Why am I sending Tom Ford suits to Vegas for you to wear while you are holed up in the studio recording? What's really going on?" I asked. I was a little slow but never dumb.

When I saw the Ocean's Five clip, it all made sense. I was so disturbed. I read other blog posts and found out that a few of his celebrity friends and industry colleagues were also in Las Vegas, including a new R&B group comprised of females that were his former backup dancers during the 8701 & *Confessions* eras.

I worked with Usher during that period and I had heard that he had some sort of "relations" with one of the group members. I am not naïve or immature; I knew my then-husband had a past before we married (hell, so did I), but his alleged behavior in Vegas was not exactly helping me maintain a level head. Crazy thoughts of him frolicking with her again, as well other possible scenarios, played across my mind like the Times Square ticker. I was trying hard not to major in the minors. Meaning I had so much going on of major importance, why give energy to an unimportant thing? These lessons were coming to me slowly, my emotional intelligence score was about 90 (160 being the goal). The lowly caterpillar transforms into a lotis blue butterfly. I needed to lead with my head and not my heart as much.

When I think of his time in Vegas, I realize what he was doing. He was always viewed as the sexy, playboy singer. Now, he was married, with not one, but two kids and bonus sons. His fans were saying he was losing his appeal. His carrying on with Ocean's Five was a ploy to hold onto the image he had spent his entire career building. Admittedly, I can be very difficult at times. However, I am a reasonable person, though I can be also very emotional. I know now that I could have done a better job of understanding his position as a man whose entire life depends on the opinion and support of others. There is a reason that so many widely successful artists overextend themselves to their fans — they are a powerful bunch.

Back to Vegas— I also thought about the money that he was wasting by not using the studio time for his own purposes. When artists are recording, they "lock out" studio time by paying for the period up front. Since when do you relinquish your sessions for other artists to use the entire time? Especially when those sessions were being paid for with money from our budget? (We were married, so yes I thought of it as "our money") Typically, there are multiple artists in the studio at a time, walking in and out, working on their respective projects, but it was all in the name of his album. I was not his manager; I was his wife. And I saw that he was basically.... partying.

In addition to taking care of our family and home, I had put off my own flourishing career as a fashion stylist—when I married him— per his request. It was in writing too. Now, he was running around acting like he was single. So, I sacrificed for what? To basically be his "babies' momma"?

I had a big house and nice cars. But, none of that matters if your man is not there. And I missed my man. You can have the biggest, most ornate home with Schonbek chandeliers hanging throughout, but Luther Vandross was on point when he sang in his signature song, *"A house is not a home, when I climb the stairs and turn the key....'*

The funny thing about me is that as much as I like big homes, lavish vacations, opulent furnishings, and fine clothes, I'm really an urban hippie at heart. I could live in Birkenstocks, cut-off jeans shorts, and vintage t-shirts just as easily as in haute couture. Less is more and during this time all the material accoutrements couldn't fill the huge void, only he could do that. When you are going through your pain, none of your damn Birkin bags can talk to you or comfort you to make you feel that everything is going to be okay. Things are just things. Same thing I felt when my first marriage was on the brink. My stance hasn't changed on this ever. There's a difference in liking nice things and not being able to live without them. I just like them.

His honeyed words started to replay in my head. *"You are so beautiful."* Once comforting, they now sounded mechanical and laced with motive. If he really thought that, why weren't the kids and I in Vegas with him? I was not deaf, dumb, or blind. I had heard the rumors of him cheating with a bridesmaid from our wedding, who was also my closest friend at the time — the woman whom my sons looked at as a play aunt. I knew in my gut that the affair was real. All of that *and* he was not coming home on the weekends as promised. He had a serious lack of interest in being home at the time, and I decided to do something about it.

My decision cost me my marriage. And nearly my life.

My nanny, Diene, was with me the entire time Usher was working in Vegas and I was home in Atlanta with our two young boys. As the saying goes, she was my right hand. Coincidentally, she was just as sad as I was, but for another reason. Her kids were still in Brazil because they didn't have the proper immigration papers to be in the United States.

In my opinion, she was remarkably loyal and great with Naviyd and Cinco, Diene was taking care of my kids and not able to be with her own. I was crying along with her and for her. I was feeling sympathetic about her situation. I could not fathom having an ocean separate me from my own kids and not being able to see them.

So, one day, I noticed that she was extremely upset. I could tell that it was different than usual. I talked to her and found out that it was her son's birthday. She was distraught because she forgot to send him the present she had wrapped. Without hesitation, and on complete impulse, I looked at her and said, "Guess what?! You want to go to Brazil? Let's go."

I had a budget, so why not? In my mind, it was similar to a getaway with a girlfriend—or a girl's night out, but on steroids. It would be an adventure for me, plus, she would be able to see her children.

I bought tickets for myself, my sister Yolanda, my personal assistant Nicoma, and Diene. My sister applied for and got a rushed passport. Naviyd was only 2 months old, so I had to send his passport application to Usher for his signature of consent. He immediately tried to shut the trip down.

"What are you talking about?" he asked me. I could tell he was pissed. I remember him saying. "You are not going anywhere. Naviyd is too young."

I was not about to back down. He was having a great time in Vegas. He was supposed to be working, but was clearly partying like the pop star he was to his fans rather than the husband and father he needed to be for his wife and kids. Why couldn't I take a vacation and get away? Plus, I would be helping Diene. Sounded good to me.

"Well, the doctor cleared him, and he can totally fly," I told Usher over the phone. "He is past the one-month stage." Then, I decided to strike with the real reason for the trip. "And you don't want to bring your ass home, so we are going to Brazil," I snapped at him.

This trip would become a point of contention and fierce argument during our eventual custody battle. I thought I said, "Since you won't sign the papers for the boys to travel with me, I will send them to you in Vegas." But, when he and his lawyers brought the Brazil event up in an effort to prove that I was an unfit mother, they claimed that I packed the kids up and shipped them off to Sin City without his knowledge. To set the record straight I was forced to dig up the years-old emails between us from that time period. His emails actually proved that he asked for me to send our kids to Las Vegas to be with him while I was away. So, both of us were wrong and had rewritten history to some extent. All along, I had been thinking that I'd rightfully acted bitchy under the circumstances, and he thought that I had been spiteful because I sent the kids to him. The truth is, he asked for the children, so I sent them... and the emails made this clear.

So, after my sister's passport came, I brought on the backup nanny. I bought first class tickets for the kids, the nanny, and my other assistant Jasmine Ali.

Had Usher signed for the passport, I would have taken the kids with me. We had a nice suite and they would have been comfortable. I was planning to stay nearly a month in Brazil. My ex-husband had Ryan and Kile, and my oldest son, Darrin, was 18. But Usher was not having any of it, even though *he* had already been away from his kids for a month. In his mind, it was okay for him to be gone as long as he knew that we were at home. But God forbid I tried to do the same.

Admittedly, I was happy that he wanted the kids. They would be with their dad, whom they needed. Also, I thought that their presence would thwart all of the partying that was going on and derail his pseudo "Rat Pack" shit.

I could just imagine the Ocean's Five feeding babies and changing diapers. I was thinking, *Y'all better find some wet nurses to feed these children!* Honestly, I thought having to care for the kids would make him sit his ass down. Also, I wanted him to experience what I had been dealing with for the past month or so since he left us at home.

There were pictures of him hanging with rockstar illusionist Chris Angel, who was headlining a show at the time. I saw photos online of Chris with bottles of champagne in between dancers' legs. Usher was there with him. I was thinking *If you don't sit yo married-with-children behind down somewhere...*

Truly, there was one thought that kept running through my mind, while *you are out there partying and popping bottles and getting drunk in the club, here is your real responsibility that you have been slacking on.* I believe this was around the same time that Janet Jackson broke up with Jermaine Dupri as well. Janet was done. And I had similar feelings.

I was tired of being home alone with all the demands of raising babies. How could I show him that I can go have some fun too? Maybe meet a cute Brazilian guy... heck, two can play at that game. But how much fun was I really going to have with my sister, assistant, and my then 45-year-old nanny?

Diene would always talk about how things were less expensive in Brazil— from $1 Havaianas to great cosmetic surgery. I had been considering a little liposuction after having Naviyd. I wanted my body back. I decided to do it. After my second day in the country, I started meeting with doctors.

I did not tell Usher that I was going in for lipo, even though it was truly all for him. My plan was to get a Bain de Soleil tan, have the lipo to rid myself of that little post-pregnancy pouch, and be sexy for Valentine's Day. That was my entire objective. I wanted to be well-rested, tanned, get my hair done (a fresh new curly weave) and have a board-flat stomach again. It was a dummy mission from the outset.

Number 1. Never alter your appearance for a man. If you really want to change yourself make sure it's for you, not for the validation of anyone else.

Number 2. My pouch was not due to fat— my uterus was still enlarged. I should have stopped and remembered, *You just had a baby, numbnuts!!!*

Number 3. How was my tender tummy going to feel normal

by Valentine's Day?! Mission Impossible. My actions were too much about insecurity and Usher at the end of the day.

I left for Brazil to get his attention, but once there, the idea was to have the surgery, then return looking and feeling refreshed. It was all to surprise my husband and get my post-baby mojo back.

I entered the medical center on that ominous day excited and full of hope. Despite the obvious problems in my marriage, I was convinced that this procedure would be the first step in rekindling the passion that had brought us together years before.

Dressed in a generic, ecru colored gown, I was given a valium, and I laid on the operating table. I looked up at the anesthesiologist but couldn't see the details of his face because they were blurred by the bright overhead light. He injected my arm with a powerful potion. I remember taking note of his accent and watching his lips move as he spoke to me. It was as if he were lip-synching the directions, he wanted me to follow—directions that would ultimately change my life.

"Count backwards from ten," he said.

"10, 9, 8, 7, 6" I mumbled.

I woke up after what seemed like a few hours. In actuality, two weeks of my life had passed by, and the next few weeks were going to be some of the roughest of my life.

❧

I had an adverse reaction to the anesthesia. Either it was too old, administered in too high a dose, or it was not diluted enough. Maybe it was nail polish remover. Hell if I know. All I know is before the doctor could even enter the room to start the procedure, my heart went crazy. I went into full cardiac arrest on the table. When I woke up, I was dazed and disappointed. I remember asking, "Wait?? Ya'll, did NOT do the procedure!?" My thought was, *Oh damn. If I nearly died you should have at least made it worth the effort—I should be fine AF and looking right! Da hell?*

Due to the severity of my heart attack, the doctors put me into a medically-induced coma. They told my sister to call our family because they were not sure if I was going to pull out of it. They also told her that if I were to awaken, they could not guarantee that I would be the same person.

My sister called Usher.

"Oh My God! Noooooo!" he screamed at the top of his lungs. After calming him down, my sister told him that she needed to move me from the small annex medical facility to a full-fledged hospital.

I was in a small facility because liposuction is a short, minimally invasive procedure where the patient normally recovers within an hour. Typically, you are wrapped in an ace bandage, given pain meds, and are free to leave. I had just gone in for the lower abdomen. I was supposed to return to my hotel that night. The doctor said all I'd have to do is stay out of the sun and not drink alcohol. He assured me that I would be able to fly home within the next five days as scheduled. Although I was going to be a bit bruised and sore, I would be back in Atlanta by Valentine's Day. So much for that plan. Lucy strikes again.

Usher canceled his appearance that night at Clive Davis' annual Pre-Grammy party. Maybe it's just me, but that soiree seems to be a bit cursed at this point. The night Usher was supposed to perform was the same night of the Chris Brown/Rihanna incident. And in 2012, the beloved Whitney Houston died four flights up from the annual party in the Beverly Hilton Hotel.

I'm not sure how the media got a hold of my story, but it was making headlines at the same time as the Chris and Rihanna story broke.

Usher rushed to get an emergency visa because the LAX airport would not let him fly to Brazil without one. He was also arranging to fly a top neurologist with him.

I scanned the room, saw the infinite colors of the flowers that crowded the place, and then my eyes landed on him. I hugged him profusely. It was my first time seeing my husband in weeks.

I remember feeling super clingy in the hospital. I did not want him to leave, but he had to go back to the hotel to take a shower, make calls, and relax a bit. I complained to him later about his leaving. It was partly the medication talking and part battiness. I was looking like a war-torn wench. My sister told me that he came in with a pair of scissors and cut my weave out. I believe the doctors asked that he remove the artificial hair so they could do scans. They wanted to be sure that there was no neurological damage. So, my hair situation was unsalvageable for the moment. My skin was dry and my lips were badly parched. I didn't have my normal toiletries. To say I was a hot mess is an understatement.

I still felt overwhelmingly jealous, even as I lay in the hospital recovering from a near-death experience. The sad part is I still loved him so much—I still thought he was a fantastic man despite his shortcomings. He rushed to be by my side and he had a good heart when led by it.

Before all of this happened, I had been dealing with mixed emotions over a close friend whom I believed had gotten too close to my husband. I started to feel suspicious back in November 2008, when she went to Miami on my behalf to style Usher, because he was performing at the Victoria's Secret fashion show. He wasn't very happy with his performance, so his team all went out as a group to cheer him up, celebrate the show's overall success, and likely just hang out. I was 8.5 months pregnant, at home, and restricted from travel. My son, Usher V, also went to Miami with his nanny Porshia. The morning after the Victoria's Secret fashion show, she answered the phone in my husband's hotel room. I was given some lame excuse that everyone was partying, they all ate in the room, and she fell asleep there. I was convinced that the explanation was complete bullshit and I had a conniption fit. I literally had to close the bedroom curtains and lay in the dark to calm myself down. I called our therapist Sola and he tried to reason with me. Everyone made me feel like I was overreacting. They were "like brother and sister", she was one of my closest friends at the time, and of course they would *never* do anything like that. Stop being so insecure, I was told. She went back to Los Angeles and I had to refocus my energy, because I was pregnant and extremely busy as well. I gave birth to Naviyd on December 10th, he came two weeks ahead of schedule, healthy, but 2 pounds lighter than my other children. I ate much less with him. Stress while pregnant is a dangerous combination.

I came home from the hospital to amazing push- gifts, good food, and warm smiles. Three weeks later, Usher was scheduled to host a party at "The Bank" nightclub, located in the Bellagio Hotel. Maya, it appeared, was back in the picture. Together, they scrambled to hide the fact that they were planning a surprise party for me. They sent out invitations to a bunch of my friends and arranged to pay for their travel expenses so they could be at my birthday fete.

I had just given birth 21 days prior, but he convinced me that it would only be two days away from the baby. I left December 31 early, to return on a redeye on January 1.

When I got to Vegas, I was surprised to see so many of my friends at my dinner party at the Bellagio Hotel's Fix restaurant. There were approximately 25 people there—primarily couples. They included Nyeisha and Shon, Keith and Alana, Ryan and Claudette, Yolanda, cousin Dee Dee, Donyale, Maya, Jho, Fruity, BeBe, Jason, and others. After the dinner a huge custom cake made in the image of two Louis Vuitton trunks came out. It was beautiful.

Usher and I exited through one of the hotel's private corridors, which led to a freight elevator to the club. We often took alternate routes to avoid fans and being stopped for pictures—especially in a casino!! We stood for tons of photos at the club entrance and then were led to our VIP section. We rang in the New Year and everyone had fun.

The next day we shopped in the mall connected to the hotel. We also had lunch with half of the group. I think this was the biggest personal shopping spree I have ever been a part of. No expense was spared. My husband truly rolled out the red carpet and made my birthday fantastic. We then rushed to the airport for a red eye back to Atlanta. I had to get back to my babies at home.

Usher stayed home only a couple days to visit with the boys and pack additional clothing. He rushed back to Las Vegas, stating that he needed to be in the studio. I was not amused and questioned why he had to leave so fast. I was on the phone with Nyeisha recapping our Vegas NYE when she asked me out the clear blue, *"Where's Maya??"* Her tone sounded a little suspicious, and it dawned on me that I had not spoken to her since my birthday. This was odd because we were close and spoke nearly every day. It was weird not to hear from her after such a big occasion, I was a little concerned. I called her but she was not taking my calls. When Nyeisha got through to her, she told her that she was still in Vegas trying to make some money. This also seemed odd to me. None of this made any sense. When I finally spoke to her myself, she was vague about her whereabouts. She mentioned something about staying with a friend who danced in Las Vegas. The next thing I knew, she was hanging out at the studio with Usher and his friends. I didn't think much of it at the time, because she previously had a fling with one or *some* of his boys. I lost count. (Damn, I wish I could inset an emoji here.) A week later I had the instinct to fly back to Las Vegas (unannounced) because I truly missed my husband, but also because I had this nagging feeling that there was more going on in Vegas than just recording.

When I landed, Usher was a little confused, hella discombobulated, and said that he was away from the hotel at a meeting. My man sounded downright frazzled. I got my bag and headed straight there. I couldn't access the room immediately because there was no key for me at the front desk and apparently the alias had been changed. I felt a bit wary but remained calm. I didn't want to start off the visit with the wrong attitude. *A woman's intuition is a mutha...* Once I finally got into the suite, I noticed that it had been recently cleaned; the bed was made, there were no old towels, and everything was folded and in place. My private-eye instincts, however, were kicking into overdrive. I just couldn't help myself. Ughhh! I started overthinking and looking around. Side note: it's bad to do this, because all too often, when you look you shall find.

Yep, there they were— the infamous "stray hairs". Hey fellas, always tell housekeeping to thoroughly check for stray hairs... and ladies inspect the bathroom. There are always signs. The room was spotless, but I found a long strand in the bathtub and another on the hanging bathrobe. Dammit to hell!! Now I gotta act a complete ass! Though suspicious, I came with such great intentions and lingerie to boot. Oh well... *"Shit Show— Take Five... Action*!!" I ended up back in Atlanta the next night. That's when I started to replay things in my mind: the body language, the Miami hotel incident, Maya's new boobs, old text messages, the *Single White Female* vibes, it all began to click. They were having an affair. I was in denial about the physical intimacy part because I knew she had hooked up with his friends (plural). I figured that she was carefree but not careless. Something just wasn't clean in the milk. I was distraught and so broken-hearted. Most importantly, I wanted to fight. The Tameka of old was back and I promised her a good ol East Oakland ass whoopin', ghetto I know, but I didn't care and I had a pocket full of bail money. All logic went out of the window. I knew that my instincts were right. I was in denial for the longest time. What I've learned about denial is that it never invalidates the truth. Denial is a powerful thing. Turns out the hair in the bathtub and on the robe did belong to Maya . She was there and put on the robe because she was "cold". I was told the bathtub never happened. You see, in my lifetime I've known several types of women and I've had various levels of friendships. But I have NEVER understood the psyche of a woman who would sleep with or entertain her friend's man. It's the lowest point you can go. It's what I deem as "the mezzanine of desperation". Ground-zero low. I don't care how fine, rich, funny, or copious he may be: if he's the mate of my friend or kin, he's off limits. Period. In fact, he loses all attractiveness and sex appeal because I can envision him bumping uglies with the related person. Honestly, my rage turned into empathy. I felt sad for the person that would misappropriate my friendship. Maya became like a sister, present when my youngest boys were born, and she was one of the close friends that my husband charged with the responsibility of keeping us together during his wedding speech. She was my dog!! Even after she became a "person of interest" I allowed my boys to speak with her, because I never revealed to them what I felt about her. It wasn't a subject for the kids, nor was it their business. Maybe

I'm cut differently. During metamorphosis, even butterflies eat their friends at some point. Life comes full circle, you reap what you sow, whether you are religious or not. The seeds you plant can determine your harvest.

So, in an effort to reverse the roles a bit, I decided to take a week-long sabbatical and leave the responsibilities of parenting our two babies to Usher. My older sons were with their Dad at the time. It was a much better alternative than going to jail for manslaughter over another woman. I actually handled my new revelation with the propriety that only a queen in my position should. I acted with dignity, as opposed to the "can of whoop ass" that I doubtlessly promised. Brazil was far away, and it made great sense....

Even while Usher was in Brazil at my bedside, I was concerned that she might have flown there with him. At this point they were attached at the hip. And not because she and I were BFFs. I thought he was going back to the hotel to be with her. That was delusional, of course. He didn't bring her there, but don't forget I had just woken up from a coma and was disoriented. The mere thought of them together was too much for me to handle. I was outnumbered by hoes, wanton friends, and angry fans. I loved my husband and my lifestyle but was not about this life. There I was, still in Brazil on February 14th. So much for my grand plan to be super cute by V-Day. The media outlets loved to run the atrociously haggard picture of me leaving the hospital. I was looking beyond busted. They ran it every day online joyously. I had raccoon eyes, and my face was sunken. My hair was all chopped off and screwed up. The media seemed to prefer unflattering photos of me anyway; it went great with their narrative and snarky captions. Tearing folks down is a tough job, but hey someone's gotta do it. What they didn't realize is that the very stories they were running were, in part, why I was there in the first place. I'm just grateful that

I survived. The media is heartless. They will hound you with reckless abandon whether you are as beloved as Princess Diana or as hated on as I was. When they took her life, they ran with the story ... imagine what they would have done if I had actually given up my life.

This was one of the reasons why I was so resentful about Usher's Vegas party binge. I felt forgotten. I felt that he was trying to prove to his peers that he was still available. Furthermore, I just had a baby. Doctors discourage sex for at least six weeks. I understand that amount of time without intimacy can be hard—it was for me too, especially because he was away from home.

Then, I was looking at myself and thinking, *I have an egg-shaped body right now*. Truthfully, I wasn't that bad—in hindsight, I can see that. When I look at pictures from my New Year's Eve party in Vegas and snaps of me at Barack Obama's inauguration (I had lost 20 pounds that first month), Three months after giving birth your stomach naturally looks like the textured bumpy leather of a Dooney and Burke purse. Not to mention the overhang. I nursed all of my children, and had an abundance of milk production, so my boobs were the size of Dolly Parton's. They looked like ripe grapefruits with Oreo cookie nipples. Luckily, there was an upside—they were perky and all natural. I could barely sleep on them, yet I insisted on breastfeeding. My perception of my body at the time was just wrong. All wrong. I felt horrible, especially when my husband was working out every day and walking around with 12-pack abs while I was looking like a Big Gulp.

Regrettably, I continued reading the media stories and the blog posts while he was "working" in Las Vegas. Even worse, I read the comments. Note to self: Never read the comments. I knew better, yet I still succumbed to the urge.

"Oh, he is having a great time."

"Where is his wife? I know that she is mad."

"I know that she can't stand it."

I was reading the opinions of complete strangers and sadly, they were correct; I couldn't take it. This pushed me even more to have the lipo procedure. I was rebelling against Usher and compromising myself all at once. It was a dumb time for me.

⊷

Usher told me that he had a temporary visa and could only stay in Brazil for a short time, so he flew back to Atlanta a couple of days before me.

When I returned some 48 hours later, I was met by a greeter and an awaiting car service. As we drove into my subdivision and neared my home, I sensed that something was wrong. I opened the breezeway entrance gate to my house, entered the side door, walked down the long hallway towards the master bedroom, and instantly knew something was different. The place was cold. True, it was February in Atlanta, but this was a most peculiar chill. The energy was zapped. I suddenly realized the problem: things were missing, but more importantly the spirit was gone.

I did not arrive to a bevy of flowers or balloons. There was no special meal. No roaring fireplace. Instead, I came home to an empty house... His cars, clothes, and motorcycles were no longer there. Usher had completely moved out. He U-Hauled me. Dipped. Ghosted. When I spoke with him, he had no contrition, straight up poker faced attitude and showed zero remorse like Dr. Jekyll and Mr. Hyde.

Talking to him in Brazil, I knew he was happy that I had survived, but I could also tell that he was frustrated with me. He was embarrassed about the media reports and the criticisms. He was also mad that I still remembered to question him about Maya. I was like the relentless woman in the movie "Creepshow 2", who would never die, *"Thanks for the ride lady"*. Arriving back in the states, he likely stepped off the plane, walked through the airport, passed the newsstands and saw all the headlines of the weeklies blaring the news that his wife had nearly died while undergoing "massive" plastic surgery. It was embarrassing for me, so I knew that it was for him. The worst part was that I didn't even have anything done. It was undoubtedly rough to hear people ask, "Is your wife okay?" and know that it was not an accident that endangered her life—that she actually went into cardiac arrest because of elective surgery that went awry. It was not one of my best laid plans.

Remember, Kanye's mother Donda had just passed away from having elective surgery. I remember when I heard about that, I was so hurt by the news of her passing. *"Damn, why did she do that?"* I asked myself out loud. Then I followed right behind and did the same thing. Mine was such a selfish decision, all for vanity sake. I think this was the final straw for the relationship. I don't think it could have stood any more. Yet on the same token, I felt he was supposed to stand by me for better or worse. I would have been down for him until the wheels fell off no matter what outside people had to say.

I'm sure having his mother constantly in his ear, didn't help much either.

It was the beginning of the end.

"PRETTY FOR A DARK-SKINNED GIRL..."

After four years of public lashing and being criticized by other women (who looked just like me!), I decided to write a think piece for the *Huffington Post* on colorism, called "Pretty for a Dark-Skinned Girl".

The article was later picked up by several media outlets and I received praise from thousands of black women who had their own stories of struggling with self-love because they were deemed unworthy by our culture and community.

I had plenty of experiences to draw from. I was dragged and berated in the comment section of every blog for my appearance—especially my skin tone. These women should have been on the sidelines rooting for me. I had what they all dreamed of— a wildly successful, heartthrob-of-a-husband, with eight-pack abs and a healthy bank account. They should have been yelling *get it girl!* But instead, a lot of them were big mad and deeply envious. I sometimes would see "anonymous" comments that were likely from women I knew in Oakland. The attacks seemed much too personal to come from an internet troll. I'm not sure why people were so pressed by me.

In hindsight I shouldn't have cared. Half of the people talking trash on blogs don't have a pot to piss in. They're probably typing while standing next to their microwaves waiting for their hot pocket to warm—Heck, half of them probably don't even have teeth (side molars completely gone!). Yet, I let them get under my skin? I know better now.

I was thrilled my article got picked up. I thought maybe it could ignite change and encourage conversation. And it did; but of course, not without criticism. I was accused of plagiarism by an author I had never even heard of. She claimed that I had stolen content from her book, which had a similar title to the article I wrote. I was profoundly offended. These were my words and my thoughts. In fact, I spent a week writing and editing the piece because I wanted to ensure that it accurately reflected my experiences and that of other black women. Her accusations did not overshadow the powerful words I wrote.

I am proud of this piece and the truth that it represents for so many women like me.

Pretty for a Dark-Skinned Girl...

The deeply rooted intra-racial contempt that lies beneath this inane compliment is the reason I've chosen to spark dialogue surrounding the topic of self-hatred in African American culture.

I am a dark-skinned African American woman with features that reflect my ancestry. Debates regarding Light vs. Dark and other biases have plagued our race for years and continue to impact millions of Black women. The deeply rooted intra-racial contempt that lies beneath this inane "compliment" is the reason I've chosen to spark dialogue surrounding the topic of self-hatred in our culture. It saturates every aspect of our lives, dominating the perspectives of our generation as a whole. We culturally are so influential, at times inadvertently, that we affect all with the words we utter and the images we portray. It lends to the theory of systemic racism. I'm authoring this piece because I'm miffed by this reality and would like to share my views on these subjects.

It is a fact that many African Americans are often mixed with an array of other ethnicities (as am I), which allows for the spectrum of our features to be as distinctive and special as we are diverse. Why is it felt that the more diluted our traditionally African features become the more aesthetically acceptable we are considered? It was said in the 1960s and the sentiment seems to be forgotten, "Black is Beautiful." Wow, nearly 50 years later and is that now only meant for a specific shade? Nonetheless, I believe the beauty of our people and splendor of every individual is reflected in our varying features and hues.

Often dark-skinned women are considered mean, domineering and standoffish and it was these very labels that followed Michelle Obama during the campaign for her husband's presidency and which she has had to work tirelessly to combat. I was appalled when I heard a Black woman refer to Michelle Obama as unattractive. The conversation turned into why President Obama picked her as his mate. No one in the witch-hunt made reference to the possibility that Michelle Obama was smart, funny, caring, a good person, highly accomplished or brilliant. Nor did they mention that she previously was President Obama's supervisor. If she were fair skinned, petite with long straight or wavy hair, would the same opinions be linked to her? I seriously doubt it. It is believed that for the dark skinned, dreams are less obtainable.

In fact, I have read similar comments about myself that I am "dark, aggressive, bossy and bitchy." It has been stated that my husband should have been with a "younger, more beautiful" woman. Astoundingly, the majority of the remarks come from African American women and are mimicked by others. Sadly enough, I don't know, nor have I met 99 percent of those making these assertions. Funny, how we can judge another without having personally seen, interacted with, or experienced a person's character. Always love on people until they give you reason not to and create your own relationship big or small. Don't listen to others' evaluation solely about anyone, because their review is likely based on their personal vices with a person. Be it a rumor, they don't have good friendship chemistry, or a small political or religious view discrepancy, jealousy, a myriad of reasons could be factors. Experience things and humans yourself, they just might be YOUR vibe and your tribe. Haters will mess it up for you and the intended target.

As I began to delve into further research on this topic, and the more I read, I concluded that many (of our) people do not like what they see in the mirror. Seeing one's own reflection in another person and then dissecting it in an effort to destroy can only be the product of self-loathing. Why don't we celebrate dope assed people as opposed to hate and alienate?

There is an adage "hurt people hurt people". If this is true, then we must examine the root of negative words and judgments that are passed onto people. Unfortunately, we have internal stereotypes based off of skin color and facial features that stem from years of programming, dating back to the "Willie Lynch" method for creating a slave. In this infamous formula, one of the main factors in separating and creating division was placing the lighter skinned blacks in a higher position in the house, while those with darker skin were made to stay in the fields and deemed "less desirable". Much like the Caste System in India. No matter what strides we make as a people, these issues continue to plague and rot our souls, causing significant decay to a portion of our population and truly hindering our progress. Perhaps we show progress in our wallets and lifestyles but not in our mind set. Nowadays people care more about what's in the purses, than what's in their character. Are they really good people? Or is it their representative? Don't be fooled "representatives" come bearing gifts, tickets, dinners but can be evil inside and only there for self-serving reasons. Think outside of the box, is all I ask.

Reading magazines, social media sites, watching our music videos, and television shows feed our appetites for all things "beauty". Rarely, however, do I see depictions of grace and elegance in the form of dark-complexioned women. I Googled one of the more ethnic models, Alek Wek and I was saddened by the tone of what the bloggers wrote in reference to her complexion, features and hair texture. Ms. Wek's escape from Sudan, her journey, philanthropy, and groundbreaking success as a supermodel in America is not only beautiful, but it displays her tenacity and character. African Americans seemed to have lost their eye for character. These comments are evidence of the confusion that lies within many black people. It's the cruelty and prejudice that has spilled into the fabric of our everyday lives. It makes me wonder what have we collectively lost as a people? Our Minds.

I too have fallen prey, while on vacation in Brazil I decided to undergo tummy lipo surgery. After having an allergic reaction to the anesthesia, I went into cardiac arrest before the procedure ever began. I nearly lost my life over something as superficial as having a flatter midsection and trying to adapt to society's traditional definition of beauty. As I nursed my psychological wounds, I began to realize that trying to live up to the prototypes of external beauty paled in comparison to the fact that I have undergone labor, subsequently being blessed to raise five handsome, smart, healthy, intuitive, and happy children. I emerged from my ordeal realizing that my body is an amazing vessel that has given birth to life and that being healthy is what's important and nothing more.

It is my hope that our First Lady and others who share in this effort will continue to be the beacon to shine a light for those who toil on America's beauty totem pole. Now don't get me wrong or take my words out of context. I truly believe that everyone has a right to delineate what they deem is attractive, but we must not confuse perceived "attractiveness" with authentic "beauty." It is important for African Americans, especially, to realize that true beauty is a spiritual element that lies deep within an individual's spirit. It can neither be seen nor is it tangible. People tend to forget that beauty is not about looks and looks [are] not about beauty. One of my favorite quotes comes from the great poet Khalil Gibran who once wrote, "Beauty is not the face; beauty is a light in the heart."

CHAPTER 12

In Another Time

❧

Forgive us our trespasses

As we forgive those that trespass against us

Although them again we will never never never trust!

Them not know what them do

Big out to yi while I'm stickin' like glue

Fling skin grin while them plotting for you, true!

Forgive them father for they know not what they do

~Lauryn Hill Lyrics from Forgive Them Father

We all have such short attention spans. We pull people in only to push them away when we get tired of their shit. It's that urge to run— the fear of facing our own faults coupled with the uncomfortableness of having to deal with the shortcomings of others. I'd like to think that I'm different than the rest. But am I? I too walked away from my first marriage when things got hard. And then the same thing happened to me. It's the harsh truth. Some of this can be attributed to human nature, but most of it is because our generation truly doesn't appreciate people; we think of them as disposable. Our time is unlike the days of old when our parents and grandparents weathered every storm together.

There was a hollowness left behind when Usher moved out. I felt it deep in my soul. I knew we had problems in our marriage, but I always assumed that we would work things out. I felt confused. We had just celebrated the birth of our son, the holidays, brought in the New Year, and attended the inauguration of Barack Obama together. This literally happened in the span of two-months. There was a shift, but I didn't understand it at the time. I was deeply hurt, but I walked around like everything was okay— revealing no sadness or emotion to the outside world. Now, there *I* stood, back on solid ground after the rocket ship ride to my wildest dreams. Perhaps, I will never know what was real to him. I just know that I loved him deeply in a place where there was no space or time. We might not be lovers, but we're still friends and partners connected as parents to our boys. And, now, after years of healing, I can smile when he flies away.

You took me riding in your rocket, gave me a star....

We spoke regularly and he visited the house often, sometimes staying over. He had moved only two miles away, back to the original home he owned nearby. We decided that although we were living apart, we would work on our marriage— even seeking counseling. Were we broken? Yes. Fractured beyond repair? In my opinion, no. So, you can imagine my surprise, when I saw him on the blogs with another woman. Grace Miguel at that—a woman I had introduced him to less than a year before.

Usher and I attended The Grammy Awards in Los Angeles together on February 10th, 2008. I was excited to travel because I had been in Atlanta for a few months after our wedding. I was busy organizing looks for my husband and settling into our home. I had also enjoyed the huge baby shower Jonnetta gave me, and I had given birth to Usher V at the end of November. So, I bought myself a pretty silk mid-length dress with black beading designed by Matthew Williamson, and had my hair and makeup done. I looked and felt resplendent if I say so myself. We had a gorgeous suite at the Beverly Wilshire Hotel, and it was our baby's first time traveling so we brought our nanny Diene along. Usher's single "Love In This Club" from the *Here I Stand* album was soon to be released. It was full-on promotion time for him and this meant it was time for a few public appearances for me as well. I was always a bit uneasy when I was out with him publicly. Being in front of the photographers and fans, or simply walking to my seat felt intimating. It was a fun night though. We enjoyed the awards, and he comforted me, telling me that I looked stunning and that I should just relax. Alicia Keys opened the show, Beyoncé rocked the house alongside Tina Turner, and Rihanna performed with The Time. After the show, we mingled a bit and I went back to the hotel to feed the baby and pump because I was still nursing. I also wanted to change into more comfortable clothes. I switched it up into a casual look, wearing a Rick Owens white leather vest, white Thomas Whyle shirt, black Tom Ford tuxedo pants and heels. I rushed out to meet my husband at the*Entertainment Weekly* Grammy after party at STK, where Usher's mentor, L.A Reid, was being honored. The who's who of Hollywood were there— Janet Jackson, Kanye West, Chris Brown, Beyoncé, Serena Williams, and Owen Wilson to name a few. The party was blazing— great music, positive vibes and martinis were flowing. To keep the festivities going, L.A. Reid hosted a small private gathering in his bungalow at the historic Beverly Hills Hotel. We were having a nice time, grazing on finger food and hanging out. Usher played cuts from his new album...we listened to some new artists... My good friend, the late Shakir Stewart, and other Dej Jam execs were there too. Shakir always greeted me, arms outstretched, calling me *"STELLLLA"*— a reference to the movie, *How Stella Got Her Groove Back*. It was our little inside joke. I saw lots of familiar faces and caught up with former colleagues. By this time, I had worked with artists at every label. as well as most management firms and publishing companies. I knew a ton of industry people; some were like family.

It was there that I introduced my new husband to Grace Miguel. She walked in and we embraced. She was now a marketing exec at Def Jam Records. Years before, when she worked at Jive Records, she hired me to do image consulting for an artist, so we knew each other pretty well. She was kind to me and even once arranged for my son Ryan to travel with me to Chicago so that I could work and still continue my nursing schedule. We went way back and knew each other fairly well.

"Congratulations on everything," she said, "I know you got married and had another baby." She continued, "How are your older sons doing? I'm sure they're huge now." I told her Ryan, whom she had met as a baby (seven years prior) when I was hired to style a Syleena Johnson shoot, was "now eight years old." I thanked her for asking about the boys and then introduced her to Usher. She wished me all the best; I did the same, and we went on our way.

And that was that, or so I thought.

I was both stunned and confused when I subsequently saw the story about Grace and Usher on the internet. Talk about "shock and awe". *Why would he be photographed entering a hotel with Grace Miguel? Hiding their faces? The very SAME hotel where I introduced them a year earlier? Huh?! A woman he had only met once before, through me? She's not necessarily his type*, I thought to myself. I mean, she portrays herself as this holistic, hippie vibed, woke, non-materialistic naturalista—love, peace, and hair grease. Right? I saw it as a façade, because a truly 'enlightened' mind-body-and-spirit chick would never opt for the married, popular heartthrob or all the red carpets, flashing lights, designer shopping, and limos. Something didn't quite add up for me. The audio simply didn't match the video. But hey, if he liked it, I loved it… Nevertheless, she was a decent catch —a brilliant woman, clever, and highly calculated. I got it; she came into the relationship by portraying herself as the complete antithesis of me!! No weave. No makeup. Mild mannered. Seemingly pure and simple. The type to say, *"OH, these old thing*s." Yes, this was chess. A definite coup d'état was going down. Genius play. I saw exactly how Usher could fall for her. Urban legend has it that she inspired the Tribe Called Quest cult classic "Bonita Applebum". Clearly honey girl had *lived* and pollinated the industry long before my husband's first award show acceptance speech. For she had long been a muse to some of the founding fathers of hip hop. *"Honey check me out you got me mesmerized..."* Ok girl, I see you. Checkmate.

I asked Usher what was going on between them. He said that they were working together; she was helping him with a marketing strategy and reviving his brand. Apparently they got "reacquainted" during a chance run-in at Def Jam while he was there shopping a deal with a kid named Justin Bieber. Side note: Justin was a new, unknown YouTube sensation that his manager, Scooter Braun, brought to me to show my husband, who at the time was not very friendly with Scooter; however, I was. I fell in love with Justin's voice and immediately booked travel for him and his mother to come to Atlanta to audition for Usher. I literally called Delta myself because he was just that good. But I digress. Anyhoo, instinctively, I knew that wasn't the full truth, so I called her and tried to reason with her woman to woman. *"Hey Barbara, this is Shirley...the clothes on his back..."* She denied that anything was going on. Deep sigh. Perhaps this was the universe paying my karma for the men I had hurt in the past. Though I truly deemed my husband my soulmate. A soulmate is merely someone that is meant to be in your life. Perhaps not intimately, maybe not in the forever manner. Karma works in strange ways. Sometimes it is brought to us often so that we might teach or learn. Life is interesting—after all the wild years I spent in my 20s playing with hearts, here I was being played big time. Was this destiny? Breaking hearts and being heartbroken are always a catalyst for change. Maybe Usher was placed before me to be a mirror for some of my own past behaviors that needed to be addressed. All I know is that it didn't feel good and the streets were talking. Though she wasn't a close friend, I felt played... I was livid and had a bone to pick. So much for my theory about not being mad at the woman; shit changes when we're talking life-altering matters— marriages, small children, love, and divorce. Yeah, I was heated and that wasn't changing.

The internet went into overdrive after the photos leaked: *"Harpo who is that woman?"* one blog headline read, *"Is Usher cheating on Tameka?"* *"Whoa, looks like Usher is creeping on his bride!"* read another. He was back in the headlines, but this time it was for something related to *his mistakes*. I was always the center of internet scandal, always accused of manipulating and encouraging his decisions. This time it wasn't about me at all. He couldn't take the heat. He promptly filed for divorce. I was truly hurt. She had him in a trance. He changed; everyone saw it. He was so different. It was as if he underwent some kind of hypnotherapy. There were whisperings of crystals, incense, bongs, ayahuasca, and forgotten lyrics to songs while on stage. I definitely did not know the man that I had married just two years prior. Her influence changed him— whether it was for worse or for better was yet to be seen. My instincts considered her to be forbidden fruit and he had clearly taken a bite. They hid their relationship from the public for years, claiming to be business partners. I knew the truth and it was tough.

❧

Co-parenting after the divorce wasn't without its hiccups. He was used to having things his way, when he wanted them, and he did not want to compromise. I admit that I was challenging to deal with at times— yet everything I opposed or vetoed was in the best interests of the children. He grew frustrated with me. I kept telling him that this wasn't my first rodeo. I was an experienced mother who had a sharp intuition about my children. I knew what was right for them. All egos aside, a mother's intuition and attention to detail surpasses most. Sorry fellas.

December 2010, I planned a family getaway to my favorite island, St. Barth. I was taking all of my boys, my sister, niece and nephew, my trainer Shanay, and my friend Malika to celebrate my 40th birthday, which was also New Year's 2011. Usher had the boys for Christmas, so I purchased tickets for my nanny Diene and the boys to arrive from Atlanta on December 29h. I rented an ultra-cozy villa sitting on a verdant hillside overlooking L'Orient Bay. It was pure bliss. My older sons, the rest of the group, and I were already in St. Barth. On the morning of the 29th my nanny called me, sounding flustered. The boys were supposed to be dropped off with her at the airport by 8 am. for a 10 am. departure. She was there but they were not, and Usher wasn't answering her calls. Arghhh, here we go... See, when you are accustomed to doing whatever you want, you don't always adhere to parenting plans, schedules, a person's birthday... nothing. He finally answered after the flight's departure time. That flight had been the only one on Delta going out to St. Maarten that day. The tickets I had bought were wasted. What was more frustrating was that alternate flights were sold out. The charter from St. Maarten wouldn't refund our money. I was infuriated. So mad that I cried ... and I don't cry easily. I called my attorney from St. Barth, who then drafted a letter to his attorneys so they could discuss why he arbitrarily kept the boys instead of adhering to the arranged visitation schedule. We had talked about where they would be staying, and he had the villa contact and flight information. I was beyond HOT!! Any conversations or letters exchanged between lawyers' costs money. Sadly, he never sent the boys to be with me at any point during my entire birthday trip, and he offered no excuse, apology, or viable alternate plan. I was also disappointed in Grace. Whatever has passed between us, I thought *What kind of woman would sit idly by while her boyfriend's children were being kept from their mother?* Usher is the type of man to discuss almost everything with his woman, so I felt that she likely knew and was complicit in some way. This was my milestone birthday and I was spending it without two of my sons. I was beyond disappointed; my plans had been altered. I cried briefly on the morning of my birthday, but then pulled myself together and moved past it. I was blessed to be celebrating yet another year, healthy, and in one of the most beautiful places under the sun. All in all, I enjoyed my "40th trip around the sun" vacay and the rest of my family, but really missed having my youngest boys there. Men play this game well; I had dealt with this before and was all too familiar with my older boys. Usher knew how upset this made me from my previous break-up and was doing the same thing. Amazing. #FML

A few weeks later...In January 2011, he was about to embark on the European leg of his *OMG Tour* and wanted Usher V and Naviyd to join him on the road for two weeks. I was hesitant. He was already in Germany, so this meant that the boys would have to fly commercial with a nanny to meet him in Stuttgart. I wasn't comfortable having my two babies travel abroad with just their nanny. Plus, Bin Laden was still making threats and had not yet been captured. I told him that

I would fly with them personally and stay at a hotel elsewhere, while they spent time with him. These were my babies we're talking about; I didn't like the idea of them flying that far without me.

"Why do you need to come?!" he asked, "You're just being difficult." He wanted to see the boys, but only on his terms. His new "marketing person", Grace was there as well, and I knew that was the real issue. I didn't care much about that, although we were not supposed to have overnight guests of the opposite sex around the boys per our newly inked divorce agreement.

I maintained my position. "They are too young to travel that far with just your nanny. My preference is to accompany them on the trip." I had questions, "How will she go to the bathroom? Who will be watching them?" There had recently been an issue with them clearing immigration in Canada because they were traveling internationally without a parent. They were in customs for nearly two hours. I was adamant about not repeating this again in Germany.

"I am going to ask you one last time," he said, "Can the boys come to Germany with my nanny?!"

I didn't budge; I was serious about their safety. Heck, they were still in diapers!!

A couple days later, his attorney, called me: "Tameka, Usher would really like the boys to visit him in Europe. Let's meet in person to see if we can find a solution." She was cool, congenial, and exuded black girl magic so I agreed to meet. Besides, I knew her previously because we had met regarding my divorce from Ryan and had a few mutual friends. Although she was his lawyer, I figured that this was off-the-record and sista-to-sista. Wrong assumption.

I gave her the address to "Kangazoom"—one of three businesses that I'd recently established. I had received the settlement from the divorce and used a portion of the money to open a furniture store called Estella Home; a clothing store called Estella Boutique; and finally Kangazoom, a 11,500 square-feet indoor children's play center. I was doing the damn thing—working toward total independence and financial freedom. I wanted to prove myself to the world.

She is one of Atlanta's well-known black female attorneys. She is petite in stature, has a chiseled face and shoulder length brown hair. Poised, articulate and well-educated, she is a woman who appears demure at first, but that is certainly not the case! She walked into Kangazoom, looked around, complimented my business and chit-chatted with me like a girlfriend. Shortly after arriving, her phone rang. She said an associate of hers was meeting her to drop off a file that she had left behind.

When "said associate" arrived, he walked right over to me, handed me an envelope and said "Tameka, you have been served."

Wait, wutttt?? A process server?

I was speechless…*like huh?* The attorney, who had been friendly with me minutes before, abruptly made her exit, at which point, she realized that she had just pulled a fast one on a *bish* from East Oakland, California. I was completely gobsmacked. *Why would she drive all the way— 45 minutes to Alpharetta— to watch me get served?* Did she just want to see my reaction? She was clearly not coming to resolve any of our parenting issues, because she had to register the custody-suit filing in advance. You see, in order to be served, the paperwork HAD to be filed with the court prior. It absolutely made no sense. I guess she wanted absolute "proof of service". Wow, this was clearly personal.

I hurriedly opened the envelope and skimmed the document. Usher had indeed filed for sole physical custody of our boys!!! I was floored. My throat fell into my stomach. If that was her goal, she had succeeded. To this day, Usher swears he didn't know it was a sole- or full-custody filing. Somehow, I believe him. When you have so many 'handlers'—attorneys, managers, agents, PR people, accountants, and girlfriends running shit—you are frequently signing documents and oftentimes it's just the signature page that's being presented, with the rest being briefly "explained" by your advisor. People in Usher's position give out trust to these so-called professional people like it's a stick of gum. Especially lawyers. I've seen this done too many times with busy people, especially artists. They're always moving too fast. They also trust the wrong people and hurt the ones they should trust.

The court proceedings were ugly. I truly did not want to face my ex in court. I knew I was checking into Heartbreak hotel. He had the advantage— money, a flock of faithful sycophants, and the power of celebrity. But I couldn't imagine not contesting his filing to keep my babies. How could I live with myself if I didn't? What mother worth having the title would do that? I initially hired Atlanta based family lawyer, Randy Kessler. We had a few differences in strategy, thus the client-attorney relationship between us was short lived. I went on to hire an African American female attorney named Lisa YS West.

The days in court were long and the whole ordeal seemed surreal at times. Usher doubled down and as co-counsel to Ivory Brown he retained power attorney John Mayoue . The man I gave my whole heart to—the man I still loved and the same man who promised me forever— was now going head-to-head with me in what would be one of the greatest battles of my life. I needed to square up, but my loyalty to him wouldn't allow me to truly sling mud, especially in public. I was astonished at the readiness to vilify me and paint me as an unfit mother. My qualities as a loving mother were the very same attributes he married and celebrated me for. I was dumbfounded... and livid.

They pulled out all kinds of receipts—old ones, new ones, expired ones, irrelevant ones. You name it they brought it. His legal team made claims that I was mentally unstable, a welfare fraudster, had a volatile nature, and an unfettered desire to be in the limelight— all things that *so-called* prevented me from being a good mother and from creating a bond with my children. They were clever. They brought up things that they knew had been popularly-rumored headlines in the media, but that were also things he *knew* for a fact were untrue. My previous counsel had agreed to a psychiatric examination; at the time I didn't see an issue with it. There were questions such as: *"When you are in public, do you feel that people are staring at you?"* My answer was YES! (I was the ex-wife of a celebrity in a town—well nation—full of his fans and there was a new song in rotation called "Papers" annnnnd an album called "Raymond vs Raymond" Duhhh!?? Yes, they were staring.) *"At a social gathering are you more likely to sit alone or interact with strangers?"* My answer: SIT ALONE (and "keekee" about folks). I'm friendly, but not "walk up to complete and utter strangers in a party" friendly. I mean, I'm a girl from Oakland after all. There were hundreds of questions and my answers conformed to my life experiences, not the evaluator's general vision of normalcy. So, she deemed me to be something that I'm not. According to the opposition, I had a "narcissistic personality disorder." Oh, okay. *Confused.*

At times, I wondered just who in the hell they were talking about... the way they portrayed me could not have been farther from the truth. As I see it, there are two kinds of crazy women: You have those who are "Worthy of a Lifetime Movie" crazy, and then you have the "Street Girl— I'll buss yo ass" crazy. FYI, the "Street Girl" crazy has nothing to do with mental capacity. It takes an awful lot to bring her out. I wonder if I can get a SSI check, since I was "diagnosed" and all. I think not. Incidentally, people who have never been married are eight times more likely to be hospitalized in a psychiatric or mental-health facility than those who have been married. Funny, most of the women that were claiming that I was crazy were never married and didn't have a man in the first place. Even further, only 27% of Black women ever marry. I've been inducted into the first-wives club twice and have been proposed to another three times, so I think I beat the odds. Besides, I have always been a far cry from crazy—perhaps too sharp for my (and their) own good, but never crazy. Funny how people can trigger you and when you don't tolerate the disrespect, their favorite go-to line is "Crazy". Never mentioning the backstory or what prompted you to check them… His legal team also insinuated that I repeatedly left my children with virtual strangers. *Umm, never. Not ever.* The entire thing felt like a made for television movie. One where I had been cast in a horrible role...where I couldn't reach the director. Hell, it was a B-movie at that. With every court date was a shocking revelation. It was literally their job to make me look awful and character bad, because truthfully my parenting was never in question, I felt that this was a battle over ego and money.

I nearly fell out of my chair when they attempted to paint me as a relentless lush. They went so far as to pull out a two-year old Buffalo Wild Wings receipt from a business credit card statement. I had taken a group of my employees there to celebrate the completion of a demolition project. I'm practically a vegetarian. I *barely* eat wings (I'm a flats-only girl), much less drink 15 cocktails. They made it look as if I had taken all the drinks on the bill (however many they were) straight to the head, and then hurried off to bible study or something. Not the case— I probably had two drinks max that night. It's rather comical when I sit and think about it now... just the absurdity of it all.

Though, it totally wasn't funny at the time. Court is petty, costly, and the lawyers love it because they rack up bills belaboring moot points. We both probably bought our lawyers new condos and cars with the amount of hours we were billed, fighting essentially over an extra four days per month and tie-breaking decisions for toddlers who weren't even old enough to independently wipe their butts.

Of course, there was also the Saks Fifth Avenue Card debacle, which became a hot topic on the blogs and the news: ***"Tameka, Angry with Usher for closing Saks 5th Avenue Card."*** The press loves wild headlines and click bait and they rarely care about truths or who the casualties may be. Again, they portrayed me as some sort of gold digger, with low priorities at that. Let me explain: access to the Saks Card was one of the line items that we had agreed to in our actual divorce settlement. It was also not a basic credit card as the media outlets reported. It was a special VIP discount credit card that I got through the corporate office. I used it to purchase items for my clients and husband at a discounted rate. Usher, for whatever reason, removed my name from the card, which prevented me from using it, and then he closed the account altogether. Consequently, he was found to be in contempt of court and was ordered to reinstate it, which he never did. It really shouldn't have been as big of a deal as it was made out to be. But when you are living under a microscope, even the most minuscule things become sensationalized.

I was equally astonished when three former employees—most of whose salaries were paid by him (huge mistake) while they worked for me—came out of the woodwork to testify against me. His attorneys contacted anyone they could find phone numbers for. My former nanny, Diene Silva (yes, the same woman I had flown to Brazil to see her sons!) somehow wrote a lengthy statement, in perfect English, slandering me as a mother despite the fact that she barely spoke the language!!! Next up, they called a bombshell witness Linda White, an older lady that my older kids referred to as "Godmommy Linda". She got on the stand and testified that my kids liked her better than they did me and all kinds of other fables. No she's NOT my children's godmother, it was a term that they use out of respect, like Auntie or Miss. Ironically, she was someone that traveled with me to St. Barth after my son died and was a close family friend. My mother was most disappointed, because they were particularly cool. I'm still baffled at her choice to testify against me, when she was initially "Team Tameka" through it all. I was also astonished at the power of celebrity. Cash is king. So much so that I should have named this chapter of my life— C.R.E.A.M. (Cash Rules Everything Around Me). I had a few solid witnesses of my own, including my close friend Dee Dee Abdur-Rahim, my former long term nanny Porshia Williams, my sister Yolanda, and others including our joint therapist, Sola Winley. Sola risked a lot to speak on my behalf, because he was a therapist to both of us, yet he did so because he was abundantly clear on our issues and my character.

My attorney, Lisa West, stands about 5'6" tall, has a slender build and honey-colored sister locs, is well educated, and most importantly, is a black woman and a loving mother. She became passionate about my case and was truly outraged by the other side's attacks against me. Lisa wanted to drop grenades, exposing huge 'discoveries' too. She saw opportunities to fight on the level they were fighting on, but I just couldn't do it. In fact, I called a recess whenever I felt she was digging too deep into Usher's vices. I cared about him too much, honestly. In many ways, I likely sabotaged the outcome of the case. As a result, my counsel and I were often at odds and had heated side-bar discussions. I am blunt and brutally honest, but I'm not evil. I now realize that you need to be more callous than your opponent and an enormous bullshitter to win in court. Court Scheming 101. Duly noted.

I argued that his lifestyle as an entertainer was not conducive to raising small children and that his frequent travels, performances, and appearances made him inevitably an absentee father. This was my entire point. The crux of the case. Period. End of discussion. That said, while I tried not to expose or assassinate his character, I did have to answer their attacks and crushing accusations against me. At one point, he came to me and said "Let's just end this now. We can walk out of here holding hands and be amicable," ...BUT, in order to do that it was clear that I had to settle, agree to *his* terms and conditions, and sign a gag order. At that point it was too late to agree to a code of silence, my reputation had been slaughtered. Umm no, because I would essentially still lose the case only to save face. It would only be a win for him. Fuck that, I'm good boss.

None of this was my style. I credit my Bay Area roots for that. I'm ride or die –loyal to the end, even when it doesn't quite make any sense. The case dragged on through the winter holidays and beyond. On my son's 4th birthday, his dad brought him home a couple hours after the agreed upon drop-off time. When the security guard at the gate called, I went outside to greet them. Since it was the day after Thanksgiving, I had out-of-town guests and family inside. When the phone rang, I was eating a plate of leftovers – cornbread dressing, collard greens, smoked Honey Baked turkey slices, a Hawaiian Roll and all the fixings. (I am the Queen of the leftover "reheat") ... I stood under the porte cochere waiting for Usher to drive up the steep winding driveway. Instead, I saw them walking up, which I found odd, especially in November. I curiously said, "Why did you guys walk up? Are you hungry? Where's your car?" I was smiling and in a pleasant mood until it occurred to me that he must have had a reason to park at the bottom of the incline. He didn't respond, nor did he make eye contact before he started walking back down the driveway toward his car. My son heard the other kids' voices and ran into the backyard where his brothers and cousins were playing basketball.

I walked down the steep driveway behind him making small talk as he was rushing off. That's when I noticed a silhouette in the car. I said "Wait, I KNOW good and damn well you didn't bring that broad to my house?!!" Low and behold, it was her! Grace was in the front seat waiting for him. Chile, I set that plate down on a ledge and hauled ass to the passenger's side to have a 'lil pow wow. *Lord Jesus, Tameka Johnelle Foster, with the slick ponytail, from 90th and Olive in East Oakland had cometh back! Fix it Jesus.* I swung the door to the Range Rover open and tried to snatch her out of her seat with her seatbelt still buckled. *The Invasion of the Body Snatchers.* She had the strength of Job, because she wouldn't get her ass out. She was hella calm and exercised extreme, advanced, sensei like core strength to prevent herself from being drug out of the truck. Ol "Mrs. Miyagi" ass chick. I told you she was the antithesis of me. Her man was pulling me, and I was pulling her. I had blacked out and didn't even feel him trying to pry us apart. I just remember swinging. I hadn't been that mad in nearly a decade. I spat directly in her face because I wanted to disrespect her as badly as I felt she had disrespected me by being there with my ex husband that she had no business being with in the first place. She knew she had a bounty on her head with me. I previously told her over the phone that we had a problem. If "On site" had a face… It was just a matter of time. How dare she show her ass up at my house? She should have waited at the gate, the corner or at a nearby Waffle House. I had become undone because I was outdone. I have always struggled with being strategic, because I'm hella transparent. I show too much emotion and I wear my feelings on my sleeve. This was a definite chink in my armor. As it happened, this incident served as a massive strike against me and it was, of course, mentioned in court. My lawyer was so mad at me for falling for this ploy. She believed that it was an intentional land mine set up to evoke a negative reaction and make me look insane. It's a move also known as "gaslighting". Gaslighting allows the opposition to gain power, and it is all about control and manipulation. Hell, I was never good at chess, especially when my heart is involved. I especially didn't care for her because I never felt that she looked out for me, given the circumstance. I live by a different 'code', I feel that if I nabbed someone's dude and ended up with her whole family. The least I could do would be to totally look out for the ex and make sure she and the kids were 200% straight. No room for selfishness or triviality because the code was broken in how you got him in the first effing place. We all know how you get them is how you lose them. I guess ex-wives pose aExes can be allies, if you play your cards right. Particularly, ex wives.

I also hated the court drama and thought what woman would allow her man to do this to the mother of his only children. Yeah nahhh, I didn't care for her get down too much, to put it frankly.

We went through the ringer in court for 19 months to be exact. It was a daytime soap opera — deception, betrayal, infidelity, fame and a whole lot of melodramatics. The media ate it up. My ex-husband, American pop-royalty vs. me, the Wicked Witch. There was also talk of me being evicted from the marital home. Not true. Our home was always to be sold as part of the divorce agreement. It took two years of it being on the market before it sold. I benefited from the sale and moved to a manse on the very same street. Although, I thought selling the house the kids grew up in was a bad decision and poor judgment. There was no real love loss in regard to that.

In the middle of all that, there was tragedy too. My entire adult life taught me about grief. However, there are levels and layers to stress that no one can ever prepare you for. You simply have to experience them to understand. It's like trying to teach someone how to be on fire. You can't. When the flames hit, all you know is that you want relief. You want out. While it's said that time heals all wounds, there are many that never fully heal.

During the break in the custody case, I endured something that no parent should ever have to endure. My beloved son, Kile Glover, died in a horrible accident. His passing began a period of soulful mourning that still persists. The case was naturally postponed for a while. During that time, I stayed out of the spotlight as much as possible, sought the solace of friends and family, watched sunsets, and tried to reestablish some level of tranquility and normalcy for myself and my other boys. I just attempted to pull myself together as well as I could.

I hoped that Usher would drop the case, surely, he didn't have the energy, and I most certainly didn't. However, he wanted to keep the battle going, I'm sure with much urging from his lawyers. I learned during this process just how much lawyers like to put a battery in your back to keep you hyped up. He was sensitive enough to offer an option to delay the proceedings so that I could take time away to grieve. It was thoughtful of him, but I insisted we move forward. This might seem crazy to some, but it's the way I deal with things — head on. I was already at my lowest point and if I was going to take another blow, I wanted to take it then and there… so we pressed on. Low key I was more insulted about the fact that he wanted to proceed at all.

I recall how in the beginning of the trial, there were days when Usher and I acknowledged each other in court, exchanging warm smiles. But I think that the days when he knew his lawyers were about to attempt to tarnish my character, he never made eye contact. He became a different person. Looking at him, I could see no trace of the man I once knew. They say that humans have three faces— the one that the world sees, the one your friends and family see and one that's just for you. I think it's so funny that you truly don't know a person until you break up with them. Beneath all of the shiny parts, the reality of who we are always shines through especially in times of adversity.

Still, I didn't hate him…my heart was filled with sweetness from the memories of who he once was…who we were.

Chapter 13

I Was Here

❧

Meke, come home immediately. Kile was in an accident.
He has a cut on his head.

July 6, 2012, 3:18 pm. That was the day and time that would forever change my life. My instincts kicked in the way only a mother's instincts can. I had just arrived in Anguilla on holiday when I initially got the call, hundreds of miles away from my son. We were separated by distance, but I felt Kile's pain. I knew my baby was hurting. I thought he wouldn't be calling me if it were just a cut. Let's go back a bit...

July 4, 2012

Since separating, Ryan and I were sharing custody and time with our boys. They were going to be spending the week with their dad and I was going to be traveling. It was the 4th of July and I was scheduled to fly out for a friend's wedding. The part of this that haunts me is that it was my turn to have the kids, but I opted to switch due to the wedding invite.

That morning, I woke up in a bit of haste because I had overslept a little. I was supposed to be out the door at 5 am to catch my flight. I still had to pack my bags, shower, get ready, and make it to the airport on time. Once I was dressed, I scrambled to get everything into my suitcase. As a mother of five, I was a self-proclaimed master at packing bags. I rushed around grabbing clothes out of drawers, off hangers and out of the pile of washed clothes in the laundry basket. Beachwear – check. Pajamas – check. Toiletries – check. Casuals – check. Evening wear – check. I had been invited to Evelyn Lozada and Chad Johnson's wedding. I was a friend of Evelyn's, and as it happened, Diann Valentine, who planned my nuptials, was planning Evelyn and Chad's too. I wasn't sure about leaving the boys, but Diann convinced me. "You really should come, Tameka. It's in St. Maarten and it will be really nice," she said. Since the boys were able to be with their father for the 4th of July weekend, I thought I'd join the wedding group in St. Maarten and then fly over to Anguilla for a couple more days.

I got all my things together and headed out to the airport, but it wasn't until I arrived there that I realized I had brought the wrong passport. In my haste, I picked up my old expired passport. I called home. Kile answered and said, "Hello." *"Hey, Kile. Baby, please go to Mommy's closet and find my other passport. I'm at the airport and I brought the wrong one. And please wake up Noonie so he can bring it."*

"Noonie's got to rush it to me Baby. I'm in a hurry." "Okay, Mom. Hold on. Let me check…" I could hear him rummaging through my stuff. A few minutes later, he came back on the phone and said, "Mom I got it! I found it!" "Oh, my sweetie pie, thank you! You are a genius. I love you boobie. Thank you so much." Kile replied "You're welcome

Mom!" That was the last conversation I had with Kile. With those final words, I flew out of town to join my friend's wedding celebration and the boys joined their father for the weekend and some holiday fun at Lake Lanier.

July 6, 2012, early morning

My friend Tia and I woke up in St. Maarten. We had a good time at Chad and Evelyn's wedding two nights before. The entire group stayed a few extra winks in the islands... The day after the wedding Tia and I hopped over to Saint Barth for a day trip on a 12 minute, tiny, puddle jumper flight. The following day, July 6th, we had planned to leave St. Martin—the French side—to go and stay a couple days at the Viceroy Hotel in Anguilla. I loved to stay in swank boutique hotels and this was a Kelly Wearstler design, so I was excited to visit again. We had scheduled to travel to Anguilla by ferry. While waiting at the terminal, I popped into a tiny boutique and purchased a pair of blue cotton harem pants and a yellow Diesel tank that said the words "Lost" for myself and a plaid button-down shirt for Kile. Who knew how profound those quick purchases would end up being? Lost?... Ironically, I didn't buy souvenirs that day for any of my other boys. I would usually buy trinkets for the younger boys when I traveled. Kile was specifically on my mind. I didn't know at the time. This very shirt is what I would end up dressing him in for his funeral.

When Ryan called a few hours later, he told me that there had been an accident. Kile was out in the water with the other kids. He was tubing with Jordan, a girl four years older than him. Jeff, an associate of his, was on a jet ski and had accidentally ran into them. The children were both immediately airlifted to the hospital. I had to think quickly. How was I going to get back home? There were no more commercial flights that I could get out on, so my next option was to fly private. I just remember running and screaming through the hotel.

My friend Tia worked to keep me calm and make arrangements with the accountant to get me a plane fast. We ended up meeting a kind woman named Rose Hodge at the airport and her husband Kirby was a pilot, had a plane and agreed to fly me to Atlanta. He was awesome and did his best to get me there quickly. We encountered a difficult red-neck immigrations agent in Florida while refueling and clearing customs. Captain Hodge was extremely professional and remained calm. Thank goodness for their kindness and availability.

It took me close to nine hours to get to Atlanta. When I arrived at the hospital, I remember weaving through people to find the room my baby was in. I had so many questions regarding what happened—important questions like: *Will he make it?! Who rode with him on the helicopter? Who's the top neurosurgeon in the country? Is a craniotomy possible? Wow, did this really happen? Why this hospital? Who in the hell was in charge??* And *"Why did I ever leave him?"* I was horrified. Every part of my body hurt. I went from being gutted to feeling violated. Kile was made in my likeness down to his nail beds. I carried him for over nine months, and to see him lying there lifeless was excruciating. Everything seemed convoluted; my vision was blurry; I just didn't get it!! The room had a distinct odor—that medicinal hospital stench. And there was a cacophony of elevator dings, monitor beeps, and ventilator wheezes too. I was powerless. As a mother, anger wasn't my first thought. I just wanted to do something to fix it all. I knew I had to make it through this. Kile was lying there motionless. He had suffered a traumatic brain injury also known as a T.B.I. The odd thing is, he had no other visible injuries—no broken bones. He was practically unscathed physically. There was only that "small cut" on his head, which turned out to be a significant cerebral laceration. My beloved Kile had suffered severe head trauma and he never regained consciousness. They declared him brain dead from the outset. I debated both the meaning and the implications of that term and was adamant that only "life" would be spoken about in his room. We made a pact with the chief of staff and a head physician at the hospital, Dr. Fortenberry, that they wouldn't enter the room speaking about his prognosis, nor would there be any talk of removing him from lifesaving equipment. I simply wasn't having it, and I didn't care if it meant sitting in his room for the next eleven years or going straight "John Q" on folks. I even went so far as to demand that the hospital staff start hydrating and feeding him intravenously, which also stirred an acrimonious debate. They weren't feeding or medicating my boy because they didn't want to use any additional resources on him, and I was not here for it. The staff had given up, but I hadn't. They were merely trying to appease me and I knew it. By the end the doctors were knocking before entering, because I wanted the energy a certain way. I was so sincere about this.

Tensions ran high between his dad, stepmom and I at times; there were a lot of opinions that I didn't care to hear. My only goal was to save my baby's life. I had a theory: When I first found out that I was pregnant, I heard my child's strong heartbeat; I heard nothing then about brain activity. As we sat with him in the hospital now, his heartbeat was strong and his vitals were good, so in my mind he could survive this. Meanwhile there's so much about the human brain, its capabilities, and functions we still don't know. I feel like doctors that practice medicine oftentimes are doing just that—practicing.

For fifteen straight days, I fasted, prayed, didn't socialize in the visiting areas, didn't comb my hair or return home. We ended up having so many visitors, it resulted in an overflow \ on the floor below us. Restaurants graciously donated full catered meals for our guests. I only left the room to go to the chapel to pray. I never left him alone or unsupervised. I washed him, sang to him, prayed over him, played his favorite music and movies. His father read the bible to him every day. I had a friend bring holistic books, an aloe Vera plant, and coconut and grapeseed oils to rub on his wounds. They told me that the ICU did not allow live plants on his floor, so our aloe plant had to be smuggled in. I was determined to bring as much soothing to Kile as I could. I wanted all of his favorite things and people around him. Even if they were not mine. It was a selfless time.

I spoke life into him as much as I could. My ultimate goal was to make him comfortable and connect with him in order to understand how he felt. Two of his closest friends, Marc and Craig, came to visit with him, and he received hundreds of letters from friends, teachers, and strangers. The entire room was covered with cards, banners, and signs. Even his favorite Disney crush, China Anne McClain sent him a voice message singing his favorite song "Dynamite" and saying, "Kile wake up. Kile wake up. We gotta hang out…" I always spoke to him as if he could hear me. I believe that words have power and that he was cognizant of them.

Around days ten and eleven, I was advised separately by both a psychic and a Christian pastor to let Kile know that it was okay for him to go— that the decision was ultimately his to make. They told me to "release" him. I don't think I've ever been faced with a harder truth, and certainly have never been charged with such a difficult responsibility. They say that God gives his toughest battles to his strongest soldiers. My faith was being tested. *Why God?!* More than two weeks of prayer vigils, massages, visitors, positive affirmations, acupuncturists, Bible passages and spiritual readings, hospital meetings, fasting, miracle research, homeopathic remedies, Boiron Arnica pellets, and calls into prayer lines, I came to the realization that my son did indeed have to choose whether to come back to us or fully cross over. I wholeheartedly believe that the decision was his to make.

I also truly believe that on July 06, 2012, Kile had seen the other side; he merely gave us time to process what was happening. It's obvious that the grass was greener, and he was ready for his new home. On the morning of July 21, 2012, his Dad called and asked that my friend LaNita quickly bring our son Ryan to the neighboring hotel where he was staying; a barber had come to cut their hair. Literally 3 minutes after they walked out of the door, Kile's heartbeat began to slow. Dr. Fortenberry knocked and poked his head in the door and I abruptly yelled, "I know!! Please leave" I sat with Kile, holding his hand, begging him to stay. I said, "No Kile, NO!!!" "Please baby... wait". I cried and begged. At 9:32 am, my beloved boy's heart stopped beating...and just like that, he was gone. I had lost my sweet angel. The thing that boggles my mind the most is that with all the days of visitors, family, and friends, Kile waited for the very moment when he and I were there alone to take his final bow.

The days following Kile's death, I had to begin planning his funeral. I was laser focused on having the details right, I think I gave myself "busywork" in order to cope. From going down to the mortuary with his father to make arrangements. I took it from there, planning details, making sure that his hair was freshly lined, that they concealed his scars with the right shade of make up, and being certain that he had on the perfect outfit with a pair of my favorite sneakers. (They were a pair of multicolored Missoni Converse that he had been asking for the longest time) I also worked with DL Warfield to design his obituary. I wanted it to be like a mini magazine that shared so many of his most pivotal moments, art, and family photos. On the day of the service I remember seeing droves of people outside of the Wieuca Road Baptist Church. Once I arrived, I was led into the family waiting room in the church. I asked the funeral director to quickly take me into the chapel to see my son one final time before opening the doors to the public. Alone, I looked at him and said a few important words to him. I turned to the Director and said "You can let them in now."

As a parent, you never fathom that you will have to bury your own child. You hope that your time will come before your children, but God had a different plan for me. He took my son and left me with the most magnificently vivid and positive memories of him. Kile was unlike anyone I have ever met. He had a unique spirit — so pure, loving, and wise beyond his years. Looking back, I realized that I had an angel on earth.

My solace is that I love Kile, and all of my children, every day as if it were their last day on earth. We had the kind of relationship where we were not afraid, shy, or too busy to express our love to each other. I constantly told him that I loved him, and he always told me that he loved me too. I am grateful that I don't have any real regrets. It would've broken my heart if I hadn't told my son that I loved him in the last conversation that we had together. In fact, I always told him.

My wish for all mothers and fathers around the world is that they *show* their kids every day that they love them, not just through words or material things, but by spending quality time with them. Love is a verb— an action word. I have countless memories of simply talking and listening to Kile, cooking with him, enjoying music together, going on a Saturday nature walk, a field trip, dancing in the living room or my office and being silly. We had so many fond moments together. Don't assume there will be a tomorrow, because nothing is guaranteed. Use the time you have with your children to love them, celebrate them, and teach them as many lessons as possible while you can, because you don't know when your last day with them will be. I'm so thankful to God for the eleven years that He gave me with Kile, and the quality time that we as a family got to spend with him.

My children show their sorrow in different ways. They get sad at random times, triggered by a thought or visual memory of their brother. They have such a pure recollection of Kile, remembering everything about him. Each of them grieves the loss of their brother in their own way, and I give them the space to reflect as they feel is best for them. My role as their mother is to listen to them when they come to me — no judgment, no advice, no holding back.

My fourth son, Usher , and my youngest, Naviyd, will sometimes cry out of the blue. One day Nav came home from school wanting a picture of Kile. "Mom, Mom. I need a picture of Kile so I can create something for Day of the Dead." They were learning about Dias de la Muerte in his Spanish class and he wanted to honor Kile. The boys miss their brother and remember him so clearly even though they were only three and four years old when Kile passed away. It amazes me how clearly they remember him. I think they felt Kile's spirit – it was one that everyone from young to old felt.

I mourned my son's death in private. I took about a year off and I stayed low, healing on my own. I mourned, and mourned, then mourned some more, unsure of how to process what happened. I kind of stared at a wall until around Kile's birthday in March. For eight months, I pretty much sat still, unable to face any outside scrutiny. I didn't want to make any public appearances or go anywhere for that matter. I feared being judged, avoided being criticized, and I didn't want to give anyone the opportunity to look at me and say, "What's her reaction?" "Hmmmp, She don't even look sad". I wanted to grieve on my own, free of judgment. By the way, what does "sad" look like? People are crazy, trying to measure one's pain based off outward appearance. I was broken but I didn't cry every moment of every day. I took time off, but I also understood that I had to continue on with life. I would be stopped in my tracks some days, overcome with memories of Kile, but I would carry on making memories with my other four children.

To this day, Kile's death comes to me in sharp waves. I can talk about him now, but sometimes the slightest thing will remind me of him, and I'll just lose it and break down crying. I often think of Kile in the morning as I rise for the day. I'll use that time as a quiet moment, allowing my tears to flow freely. In other instances, I need more time, so I'll stay in bed for a couple of extra hours to weep. There are days when I feel like I've completely processed his death, and other days when I am still in disbelief, having difficulty making sense of it all. Why? I don't understand. Why did it have to be my child? Am I being punished for something? What did I do to deserve this? It causes me to think back on the entirety of my life and reflect on everything I have done.

Healing has been an ongoing process for me, and I have learned to trust it as it unfolds. I allow it to take its course because there's no right or wrong way to grieve the loss of a loved one. Everyone has to grieve at their own pace, and I believe everyone has to mourn and express their emotions. When you have the urge to cry, don't hold back. Allow yourself to share your emotions. Never put on a façade because you think you have to be strong for yourself and those around you. When my children ask me about how I am handling Kile's death, I tell them the truth. I want them to know it's okay to not be okay sometimes. I want to show them how I grieve while letting them know that they are free to grieve in the way that they feel is best for them. At the end of the day, your life has been irrevocably altered. Lifehack: It's only when you allow yourself to grieve completely— allowing your tears to rock your mind, body, and soul— that you give rise to space for gratitude to take over.

To this day, I choose not to put away photographs of him or other little keepsakes that remind me of him. I see pictures of Kile multiple times a day. It is one of the ways that I honor my son. There is nothing in this world that is more final than death. When we laid Kile to rest at his burial, I knew there was no going back. I knew my life would never be the same again, but I also knew that I had to persevere.

Then, on a day during the first week in August of 2013, something happened that reversed much of the emotional progress I had made. I was sitting in my dentist's chair for a routine check-up and filling. My mouth was full of cotton, and the dentist's bib was attached when I got a call from Usher. At this point he and I weren't on super-friendly terms, so this wasn't a call I was going to ignore.

"Hello," I answered, talking even though the dental exam was still in progress. "Where are you?" he asked.

"I'm at the dentist in Alpharetta," I responded. His tone worried me. It was a tone that was all too familiar.

"You need to get to Children's Hospital—now."

It was like being hit by a bolt of lightning. I was shaking at this point. I had snatched the bib off and was rushing out of the office with my jacket and purse swinging around me as I made my way to the car. I felt powerless, terrified, and more vulnerable than I'd ever been before. I'd lost one child already. Losing another wasn't an option. *Not again*, was all I could think.

Usher V, who was four years old at the time, had been playing at his father's house near the pool when his little brother Naviyd threw a tiny toy car into the water for his brother to retrieve. The tiny car slipped toward the middle of the pool and as Cinco jumped in to get it, it rolled into the drain. Apparently, the drain had no cover. Cinco reached his little hand into the opening to grab the car, but the suction was so strong it was as if the drain grabbed him instead. His arm was caught and held there so tightly he couldn't free himself no matter how much he tried. The nanny, who happened to be Usher's Aunt Rena, dove into the pool after him and attempted to release him but she couldn't. My younger son, Naviyd, jumped in too. Naviyd has always been fiercely protective of his older brother. It took nearly *five minutes* to rescue Cinco from the pool and I don't know how much longer to revive him with CPR.

I arrived at the hospital to find my son slipping in and out of consciousness. The prognosis was bleak. The doctors believed that my son would likely have cognitive disabilities and would never be the same again. They also feared that he was developing pneumonia. Cinco was quiet. He stared blankly into my eyes, and just as I did for his brother, I laid with him and prayed over him. My world was rocked, and I was at my most desperate. Forget a man. Forget my career. Forget everything. My children are my heartbeats. I'm a mother before anything. The idea of losing another child was unimaginable and equally unbearable. *Faith, by Vanessa Bell Armstrong,* one of my favorite gospel songs, came to mind. Faith in God was all I had at that moment.

The entire ordeal was stressful and per our custody agreement my son would be required to return to his father's care once released from the hospital; I wanted both boys back at home with me, so I filed an emergency custody hearing for temporary primary custody. I also wanted to exercise the *Right of First Refusal* clause, which meant that when their father was not present, the children would come home to me, rather than stay in the care of nannies. Oy vey! Another day of mud-slinging and high temperatures in the courtroom. The 911 recording from the accident was played (I, of course lost my composure!); untruths and exaggerations flew; and yet again I was painted as the wicked witch in pursuit of fame and money. The ruling did not go in my favor, no surprise there. In a made for TV moment, my ex walked over and embraced me as we exited the courtroom — an obligatory hug for all to see. I was unfazed. In actuality, I was more so concerned about him squeezing me too tight and ripping off my DIY struggle ponytail (that thing was holding on by the "hairs of my chinny chin chin"). Back in the headlines we went — this time he as the doting dad trying to make peace; me as the crazy ex-wife with a "moderately severe mental disorder." Wait, moderate, and severe?! Dang, make it make sense.

I am thankful that my son pulled through with only a minor scrape on his temple and an injury to his forearm that serves as a lasting memento of the incident. Today, my boy has very little recollection of the unpleasant occurrence, but he now has Type 1 diabetes as a result. This diagnosis came six months after the pool mishap and is believed to have been precipitated by the shock of the event. Between losing his big brother and being stuck at the bottom of a pool for five minutes, it is ONLY by the grace of God that he is alive, and very likely the cause of his illness. For those of you who don't believe in God, please explain how a child with small lungs could be trapped underwater for nearly five minutes and still survive as he did. That was definitely God and the work of his guardian angel.

Cut from the Same Cloth

Losing a child is an experience that my Grandma Estella and I share. It's funny how life works out. She was like a pistol. I was always taken aback by her strength. She was poker-faced— never really showed any emotion. I don't know if that was just her exterior in front of people or if she was truly free of emotion in private as well. She took the tough love approach with everyone in her life, and the delivery of her advice was always pretty matter of fact. This tough exterior is what she showcased when she lost her own child as well. Grandma Estella lost her son, my Uncle Melvin, to ill health even before Kile was born. When she learned of his passing, and while at his burial, she did not shed a single tear. I don't remember seeing her cry once throughout that entire experience. Unlike her, I was very emotional. I cried many times mourning Uncle Melvin's death—even a few times while I was sitting next to my grandmother. She seemed unphased by the tears of others, never compelled to join in the sadness. "God was ready for Melvin and I never question the Lord. He gave me this child and it's His position to take him away," was all she would say to others.

At the time, I didn't understand my grandmother's approach. I thought she was wrong. I was hurt that she didn't mourn Uncle Melvin. I questioned whether she loved him or not. She didn't react the way I thought she should. I was young and only knew one way of grieving, and that was my own. Looking back, I realize that bearing a hardened shell *was* her way of coping. In her own way, she grieved and healed by trusting God. Her faith was her foundation and she used it as an anchor through all of her experiences, including tragedy. She taught me that life is unpredictable, and we must trust the plan that God has for us.

I have repeated my grandmother's words many times in my mind after Kile passed away. God was ready for Kile and I never question the Lord. That stance gets hard. I come from an inquisitive era, we wanna know why, how, why again, who and what. Much different than my grandma's generational mindset.

Those words gave me strength at a time in my life when I needed it the most. It calmed me and helped me feel more at peace with where Kile was. Kile is in heaven with God. He gave me this child and it's his position to take him away. My son was an angel on earth, and he remains an angel in spirit. I am grateful to have learned about trusting the process — both creation and death — from my grandmother before her own passing.

I lost my Granny Lou and my aunt Angie over two decades ago. I received the news when I was in New York City for the annual Island Def Jam Music Group's Christmas party. I was alone, and I didn't know how to react. At that time, I used to feel embarrassed to grieve — seeing it as a sign of weakness. I didn't want others to see me cry or feel compelled to console me. I sobbed alone in my hotel room, then pulled myself together and got ready. I went to the party and worked to hold my sorrow in. It wasn't until I flew back home to California that I really processed what had happened.

My grandmother had been a believer in natural and holistic medicine her entire life. Even when she was diagnosed with cancer, she chose alternative medicine as opposed to chemotherapy. She underwent advanced natural treatment in Mexico. Although she had lived on her own before the treatment and was in remission afterward, she needed a full-time caregiver upon returning to the U.S. My aunt Angie—my dad's sister—moved in with her to provide that care.

One day in December 1995, while my Aunt Angie was asleep in the back bedroom of the house, my grandmother was in the kitchen making lunch. She inadvertently started a fire, which quickly spread into other areas of the kitchen. My grandmother was 73 years old and fragile from her vigorous cancer battle. She did her best to walk down the hallway to get my aunt up, yelling "Angie! Angie!" but my Aunt Angie was sound asleep. By the time my grandmother made it to the back bedroom, she couldn't breathe. She had succumbed to smoke inhalation. My family was devastated; the hardest hit was my father. He was inconsolable. How does one lose both his mother and sibling abruptly? It was so tragic.

My father also took Kile's death really hard, drawing parallels to losing his mother, sister, and daughter. My youngest sister Venus died in a car accident when I was 30. I was told that a couple of boys from her neighborhood stopped by the house and picked her up, possibly in a stolen car. While they were driving, they thought the police were following them, so they took off. They sped down the road, driving fast and recklessly, eventually getting into an accident. The car was wrecked, the boys were unharmed, but Venus was dead. It was another senseless death. She was only eighteen years old when she died. My father had an affinity for her. I was twelve when she was born, and although we weren't very close, I loved her and was shocked when she passed. He relived tragedy and heartbreak all over again with Kile.

By the time my mother passed away in June of 2015, I was finally able to stop resisting death. With each person's passing, things did not get easier, but I was able to find more peace in their exit from this life. Burying Kile was so unnatural. Children aren't supposed to precede you in death. So, losing Kile before I lost my mom, helped prepare me for my mom's departure.

I was in Anguilla again when I learned of my mother's death. Her birthday was June 19th and I had spoken to her on the phone prior to that day. My sister Yolanda was in Oakland visiting friends and since we hadn't seen our mom for her birthday, she was going to go pay her a visit. "I'm going to Momma's house. I'm going to help her organize and re-decorate her place as her birthday gift." She was going to buy her some new towels, linens, a few decorative pieces, and help her put it all together. My mother loved to keep *everrrythang*; we always jokingly called her a "Hoarder-in-training".

"Oh, that's really good," I said. "Momma's a total packrat, and she's got so much stuff in that house. Help her get organized. Help her get rid of some of that junk."

Two days later, my sister called with worry in her voice. "Girl, have you talked to Momma?? I've been calling her for the past two days and she's not answering the phone. It's weird. I got into her building, and I can hear her television on. I'm banging on the door, but she's not answering."

I thought it was weird. It was normal for our mom to have the television on 24/7, but it was so unlike her to not answer the phone. She stayed on the phone (usually with us). Finally, my sister called the building maintenance for help and within minutes the firefighters came to break open the locks. Inside they discovered that our Mom had passed away. The coroner determined that she had died of a heart attack three days before she was found. With that, I had again laid another loved one to rest.

Broken Heart Syndrome

As a society, we are socially conditioned to view death negatively. It is something that is resisted even though it is inevitable. Our physical lives are temporary, but we seldom remember that. Death, in its own way, serves a meaningful purpose. It is a reminder to not take life and time on earth for granted. Somehow, I feel that Kile knew this.

Kile was a brilliant young man who was always full of life. He laughed, sang, danced in the rain, created, and loved others without holding back. In his eleven years on earth, he showed me what it is like to live life to the fullest every single day. There wasn't a person who met Kile who wasn't impacted by him. He was loved, and he loved in return with no expectations. Deep down I know that he was prepared for death, having been content with the life he led, even if those of us around him weren't yet ready for him to go. My children are like my heartbeat — they are my soul. So, when Kile passed away, it was like one of the ventricles of my heart had closed. It was like I had lost a portion of my heart. From my own experience, I can see how people could die of Takotsubo, also known as "Broken Heart Syndrome", after such loss.

Nobody is perfect or immune to obstacles and tragedies in life. The human experience includes engaging in wars, bleeding from cuts, and healing wounds. Life happens to us whether we are ready or not, and all we can do is accept it and powerfully tackle it head-on. It is not about becoming immune to tragedy, shame, and heartbreak, but rather, it's about having unlimited power, freedom, and happiness in the face of it all. We often talk about those who are afraid of death, but there are just as many people who are afraid of living after the death of their loved one. What I do know is that you owe it to your beloved to live a bigger, bolder life and to do it with excellence. It would behoove me to live fully for the both of us. I would be misrepresenting our time to go dark and wither away, I feel inclined to flourish and carry on his legacy. This is just what works for me. There is no correct or wrong way to grieve and heal.

Don't judge yourself for how much time, space, or support you need as you deal with heartbreak and tragedy. Likewise, don't accept other people's judgments about how you deal with the greatest difficulties in your life.

Is there a way to get over losing a loved one? I don't know how, and I don't know if one truly ever does overcome it. However, I do know that I take it one day at a time. I try to live my life beautifully because tomorrow is not promised to any of us. I was cautioned that sometimes the message is in the reflection and not necessarily the storm. Oh life. No two days are alike and not one is promised to us. Our dreams may be ahead of us, but we never actually know what the next day may bring. I have come to terms with the notion that there truly is no reason to stress over tomorrow; tomorrow will stress over itself. Do not fret about what tomorrow may bring. We have to take this thing one day at a time.

The late great make-up aritst Roxanna Floyd and Lauryn Hill.

Kingston, Jamaica 1998

Lauryn Hill, Kingston, Jamaica, Miseducation Album shoot.

1998

We decided to make a splash at the Grammy's—Toni Braxton.

February 2001

Jerry + Jermaine + In our own world.

New York City 2006

Welcome to Atlanta…

1997

First custom home- Before
landscaping was complete.

1999

Christmas time in the Bay (before
our marriage or sons).   *1997*

I have always explained
the importance of
giving back to my kids.
Christmas time outside
a homeless shelter for
mothers and children.
Downtown-Atlanta.

Christmas Eve 2011

Kile and I—Mother and Son dance.

2011

Madre will always be a favorite!

Beach wedding/ my 30th birthday celebration January 1, 2001- Negril Jamaica Linen was the theme, I designed my gown and the groom wore Ralph Lauren. We had a ball with our friends & family.

Fun fact: This was shot in Atlanta At my home. Mi casa su casa.

I personally decorated our first home and it was featured in a magazine. Not bad for a fashion gal.

2002

Clownin' around backstage. Always fun with Patti LaBelle.

Honey Magazine cover shoot with Ms. Lauryn Hill. Shot by Jonathan Mannion I styled nearly 70 magazines, award shows and music videos with Lauryn, she was a great long term client.

Justin was a part of our family in the early days.

As a girl, I aspired to be like Oprah, this letter meant the world to me. Handwritten at that!! I was in Heaven!!

2003

Fade 2 Black Madison Square Garden. Huge project, phenomenal experience. When Jay decided to "Change Clothes" I was honored to be a part of the process.

November 2003

Special day!! President Barack Obama was Inaugurated into office. I styled Usher for the perfrmance and my boys met the First family! (FYI: the coldest day I've ever felt.)

January 20ᵗʰ 2009

The day after my elopement wedding, we had dinner with Barack Obama on his birthday.

August 4, 2007

Always working… Daddy
looked great in his Armani tux.

The Dress—Vera Wang classic.

Every once in awhile, right in the middle
of nowhere, love gives us a fairytale.

September 2007

Gayle King and I chatting at my
reception dinner.

September 1, 2007

Aunt Sadie is definite goals!!
At 84 she danced the night away!

September 1, 2007

The first of three Estella Boutiques- Roswell Georgia - the décor was shabby chic meets Little House on the Praire but the fashions were trendy and sustainable.

2010

KangaZoom Alpharetta

I owned and operated the cleanest indoor kids facility ever.

2010-2013

Kile as the Scarecrow.
The Wiz 2011

Naviyd at age 3.
2011

Ryan and Kile at home.
Photographed by
Robert Ector
2010

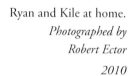

Filming for
Atlanta Exes-
Dress: Tom Ford.
2014

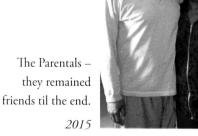

The Parentals –
they remained
friends til the end.
2015

Paris, France
2015

Mom and I at "Top Dog"
hotdogs in Oakland.
2015

Happy Place –
Italy
2013

Paris, France
It was 9:57pm!!! Warm and bright!
July 2019

The Great Wall
of China
June 2013

Marrakesh,
Morocco
July 2019

Saint Barth, Absolutely love Rihanna!

January 2015

Chennai, India

July 2019

Dubai Desert

June 2021

Jumping for Joy!

Rosebank,
Johannesburg

South Africa 2018

Peace in Porto Cervo!! Sardinia, Italy owes me
nothing! I've been four times and I love it here.

July 2011

Shanghai China, Shanghai World Financial Center (Second tallest building in the world).
March 2019

Co Parents- Burj Khalifa.
August 2019

Sitting at the top of the world with my boys.
The Burj Khalifa 2019

My son Ryan scoring at UPenn football game.
2018

Accra Ghana Kile's World Foundation presents Ryan M Glover football Clinic.
Shot by Grahl Photography
May 22, 2021

Arzachena, Sardinia, Italy
"Living my BEST life."

2011

Kile's forever Girlfriend - Love to
"Queen Bey"always!

Los Angeles 2013

Behind the scenes.
Atlanta Exes
promo shoot.

Los Angeles 2013

Grown, Unattached, and Unbothered.

At Home 2015

They are not just sons to me. They are my life, my soul, my heart, and most of all, the reason for my existence.

My Four Heartbeats.

Shot by Robert Ector.
May 2019

Having fun with the kids in Ghana.

May 22, 2021

CHAPTER 14

Mad at God

❧

F olks are serious about God. How serious? Put it like this: in a club a DJ will stop the music just long enough to check you or have bouncers remove you if you say the wrong thing about God. It's complicated. In the Black community and many others, opinions on God and religion are set in stone. No matter the new evidence, we prefer to stick with our 'ol time religion'. The fact that you've gotten this far into a chapter called "Mad at God" is encouraging. It tells me that maybe— just maybe—you have felt mad at Him too. Big mad.

We don't believe in questioning God, much less getting *mad* at Him. In fact, growing up if I even uttered the words "I'm mad at God" there was a good chance my Momma or Grandma would have sent a hot skillet, airborne from across the room, straight to my forehead. We just don't play with God and questioning him was out of the question. Think about it.

So, let me say at the outset, I am a woman of faith. Even with my flaws and areas of my life that are still under construction, I still believe in God. This chapter is not a contradiction of my faith, but rather an outgrowth of it. I believe God is good. I believe God is great. Yet I, like you, have had times of confusion when I try to reconcile what I see around me every day. It hurts me when I see people of God suffer immeasurable harm. I get discouraged when a missionary who has dedicated her life to providing aid to others is murdered by those she seeks to help, or when a sick child deteriorates from a rare disease while criminals walk around strong and wrong but still healthy. It is with this spirit that I decided to write this chapter — to challenge long-held assumptions in an effort to arrive at a place of clarity about the mysterious ways of a loving God. Go with me as I delve into sensitive, unchartered territory. I ask for your patience, and that you hear me out before you shut me down.

Picking a fight with God is admittedly a bad idea. Well, the first problem is, you can't win — or can you? I once read a story of a man named Jacob. Turns out, this man challenged God to a fight ...and won. I know, crazy right? I found it in the Old Testament. In short, Jacob wrestled with God all night. When the sun rose, God was leaving, but Jacob wouldn't let him go. He was holding so tight that God broke his hip to get away from him. But that's not even the fascinating part. As a result of Jacob's testicular fortitude (aka big enough balls to challenge God!), God changed Jacob's name to Israel and blessed his descendants forever. Yes, that's where the name Israel comes from. The name means, "He struggled with God."

I, like Jacob, have struggled with God. I don't believe questioning God about the misfortunes we see around us is a sign of unfaithfulness or unbelief; I believe it's just the opposite. I question Him because I believe. But certain things are beyond my understanding. Some things make me mad. Let's take my dear grandmother Louise, a devout

Jehovah's Witness, hands down one of the most gentle and God-fearing people known to man. She won and went into remission after holistically battling cancer, later to succumb to smoke inhalation due to a house fire where she and my aunt Angie perished. In the blink of an eye my precious Granny Lou and Aunt were gone.... how possibly could this be His will? I have a dear friend who did everything right. She and her husband remained celibate until they were married. They were the most loving, faithful couple you would ever want to meet. After five years of marriage, they were ready for their dream to come true—the dream of having a child. They got pregnant. They had an elaborate baby shower. Everything was absolutely wonderful. Their monthly baby-wellness checkups were going beautifully, and then on the day of the baby's birth she was stillborn. I was just mystified and heartbroken for my friend. I know of 14 and 15-year-old girls who just pop babies out like Pop Tarts—girls who have had zero prenatal care or a clear intent to become mothers. It just boggles the mind.

I'm sure you remember several years back, just thirteen days before Christmas in 2012, parents of young children attending Sandy Hook Elementary School in Newtown, Connecticut layered their kids with warm clothes, packed lunches, and kissed their foreheads for the day. Everything was normal. Soon nothing would be. Only a few hours later, 20 of these children and 6 of the school's staff members would be shot dead. The killer was a demented 20-year old who also murdered his mother in her home before leaving to end innocent lives at that school. And for what reason did God allow this?

I also think about the amazing people in my own life who have suffered tremendously as a result of loss. People like my Aunt Cassandra, my uncle Melvin's wife. She is the family glue— a pure and virtuous woman with a jovial laugh. In the 80s she lost Uncle Melvin, who died of organ failure. Five years later she lost her only son, my cousin Dwayne, to a senseless death. Shortly after that she lost her one remaining child, my cousin Dawn. Her entire family was completely ripped away from her. I can't understand it. God, what did Aunt Cassandra do to you? Why has she been dealt such a terrible hand? I think of my friend April Daniels, who lost her husband LaShawn, nicknamed Shiz, in a car accident. Again, he was another amazing soul... a man of God…a great father and a loving husband. It just makes no sense to me.

I think of our superhero, Chadwick Boseman, who inspired a generation both on and off-screen, especially boys of color. I cannot wrap my mind around his death. I am in awe of how he pushed through adversity. He gave us so much of himself; but left us in the dark about his illness — never taking the attention away from his craft, not allowing anyone for a second to pity him, pray for him or offer preferential treatment. He remained committed to inspiring us by portraying icons of our past like Jackie Robinson and James Brown; and benevolent superheroes, like King T'Challa, who represented our hope for the future. In his short tenure as an actor he took on solid roles that were poignant and meaningful. He was strategic in building his legacy. His death sent our community into instant mourning. It hit different. Chadwick was our Black Panther — our gentle, unpretentious, unassuming warrior. So much grace, so much humility; yet taken from us in his early 40s, while at the height of his career. Why?

My darling Kim Porter, one of the most beautiful brown girl representatives ever born. I last saw her at a birthday party, we hugged, danced a little bit and giggled. She looked beautiful as always, yet one week later she was gone. She was one of the smoothest, most even-tempered and zen people I know. And I will always miss her, but I can't help but ask, why God?

The world has been plagued with a pandemic. Covid-19 has claimed the lives of innocent people. I lost my dear uncle Bruce and another friend. Scientists and doctors can't seem to find a cure. Is it a pandemic or plan-demic? Because now it turns out even the vaccinated are not immune.

The only reason we call unforeseen events, "Acts of God," is because we realize He can see them in advance. He is the only one who can. He's the only one with the power to prevent the pain before it arrives.

It's so predictable. After every personal or national tragedy, we hear a familiar cliché. It goes something like this: "God's trying to teach us a lesson and we learn best from pain and sorrow." Really? If this were true, then the world would be at the peak of enlightenment given the amount of pain and sorrow we experience every single day. I'm going to say it: I'm mad at God, and presumably He's mad with me.

When we question authority, it points towards unmet expectations. Why else would we expect more love from God, unless we knew he was capable of giving us more? If you think this is about religion or atheism, you have terribly missed the point. This is not about religion. This isn't about Christianity, Judaism, Buddhism, Islam or any of the other multitudes of belief systems. Ironically, no matter what you believe, life is fair in one aspect— it punishes us all.

So how should we view our relationship with an all-wise, all-powerful God when we're met with unnecessary pain? No matter how you look at it, God holds all the cards. It makes sense to at least try to understand what makes Him tick – and better yet, what ticks Him off. Why? Because we can't extend our lives by even one second longer than God wants us here. Our money, political connections, intellect, or beauty is worth less than beetle dung when God calls your name. As much as we love our children, we can't redirect a tornado from heading to their school. Again, God holds all the cards. And that brings me to my next point.

There's a time-tested question that's never received a good answer. I'm sure you've heard it before: "Why do bad things happen to good people?"

In my estimation, a much better question is this: "Why do good things happen to bad people?" I've never been able to reconcile the number of mean, evil, backbiting people I've met who have wonderfully successful lives, healthy children, and fulfilling careers. How does that happen? We tend to want to make bad people seem like they live miserably when a lot of them do not. Many are having the time of their life being rich, traveling the world, and enjoying or screwing over their families. It's so confusing. If you think about it too long, it will upset you. On the flip side, I know some of the kindest, most loving, gentle people on earth who are either broke or sick or both. Why does God allow this? We're told God takes the good ones because He needs "another angel." So, I mean, how many angels does Heaven have right about now? Several million? How many do they need up there? I think it's time for God, please kind Sir, to let some of the good one's stay down here…and I wish He would have started with my son.

I remember arriving at the hospital in Atlanta the day of Kile's accident and feeling so outraged and angry at everyone. I had so many questions that I wanted to ask God — mainly "How could you let this happen to *my* baby?" and "Why *my baby*?"

I prayed and cried, prayed and cried, and then prayed again. Surely my God— the God I serve— would not allow this, right? It was impossible. I mean, He made the sun, moon and stars. Certainly, he can save my son. Kile was a little celebrant. He was going to touch the entire world with his art, his beautiful voice, his love, his heart. I never doubted God for a second. Even after the doctors told me he wouldn't make it, I told them I knew the master physician. I told them I was a woman of faith. I told them I'd appeal to a higher court, and I believed this with every fiber of my being. When my Kile took his last breath, his heart simply stopped beating and it felt like mine did too. It seemed God showed up, but only to watch my son die. I was so mad at God. You see, I have always deemed God my father—my *heavenly* father. Just like the times when I would sit on the sofa looking out the window, waiting for my daddy to show up to take me out for a movie, and he would be a no-show, there was deep disappointment. This is no different. Why can't I question my father? We talk about everything else!

There is a pain beyond tears. There is despair beyond words. There is a brokenness that goes far beyond consolation. Over and over I replayed that weekend. It thought about how many small things could have made a big difference. How many other places could Kile have gone that day? He could have spent the afternoon at Hobby Lobby, a craft shop he loved, or maybe the Apple store. Maybe if he'd stopped by Wendy's for his favorite 'Baconator' sandwich for just five minutes that would have been enough to miss the crash. I could have perhaps not traveled, skipped the wedding in St. Maarten so he would have been with me instead. Everything had to go perfectly wrong for him to die. One nudge here or one nudge there and my son would still be alive.

I remember the look on everyone's face when they arrived at the hospital after he had been pronounced dead. It's forever etched in my mind, along with the antiseptic smell of his room, the sound of curtains being pulled, the chill of the hallways, the rude noises of machines constantly inhaling and exhaling...and the silence when everything was over. I wouldn't wish that on my worst enemy. For something that was supposed to make me stronger, I'm feeling conflicted every day. My sorrow is a relentless pain insatiably eating at me, to put it lightly.

I'm eternally grateful for the time I had with Kile. I'm also grateful for the two weeks in the hospital before his heart stopped. He was my absolute favorite eleven year old in the world. But every once in a while, I'll sit up at night looking for answers in the sky or the pages of my Grandma's bible. Before I know it, the pages are soaked in mucous and tears. There are mornings I wake up and I just scream in disbelief, begging to know. "Why me? There's so many people with children that live until they're 100. Why me, God?" I want to believe without doubting. I want to know what it is I'm missing. Befuddlement would be a fair description of my mind on this. How could my Father let me down?

Have you ever gone through something that made you question everything you've been taught to believe? What do you do when you love God, but silently question whether He really loves you? And how do you express ideas like these without sounding sacrilegious?

Have you ever been mad at God?

CHAPTER 15

Love Under New Management

❧

Find what it is that energizes you, what makes you tick, what sets your soul on fire, and run with it. Let the rest peter out—the distractions that create cyclones in your brain, the negativity, the betrayal—all of it.

My children are my focus. They are what drive me. In many ways my life and my legacy is dedicated to them.

Creating a lasting memory of Kile is now my greatest passion. I have a new purpose. Everything that I thought was important before has become trivial. Losing him wasn't a choice, but I do get to choose how I honor him. I choose to focus on celebrating his life, and in this way, I will keep his spirit alive until my last breath.

During the months after he passed, I was too grief stricken to move. My family and my closest friends, including LaNita, Nyeisha, Dee Dee, and Aaliyah, came in from out of town and stayed by my side for the first few weeks. But then they left, and things got silent.

That's one of the hardest parts about dealing with the death of a loved one. People rally around you immediately after and then understandably, they have to go back to their lives. Back to work, back to their husbands and their families. You aren't upset with them for moving on, but things for you become extremely lonely… you are frozen in time, paralyzed in your angst, and unable to move some days. Simple things become difficult, like getting out of bed, putting one foot in front of the other, or preparing a meal.

Time seemed to crawl. Alone with my thoughts, every memory of Kile played over and over in my head, for what seemed like an eternity. The silence became deafening.

Few things brought me joy. I even hated the sunlight. These were dark times.

Leaving home was a rarity. My local girlfriends would call me up and say, "Girl, you need to get out of the house. Let's go for dinner." I went sometimes, but mostly I opted to stay in. I didn't want to be out in public because I feared being criticized. I had been so heavily scrutinized over the prior few years that I didn't want the court of public opinion to put my grief on trial and judge that too. *No, ma'am this was much too personal.*

I knew I needed to claw my way out of the depths of the unimaginable pain I was feeling. I had four remaining children who deserved a *whole* mother and I had a legacy to build for my new angel. With my knees buckling and a perpetual emptiness in my heart, I dried the salty tears from my face and got up.

In January 2013, two months before what would have been Kile's

12th birthday, I started thinking of ways that I could honor him. I couldn't have his death be in vain; I wanted him to have a lasting impact on the world.

❧

KILE'S WORLD FOUNDATION

A budding virtuoso, Kile displayed feats of skill well beyond his years in singing, dancing, acting, and visual arts. He starred in stage productions; wrote, produced and performed songs; painted abstract art; and designed CD covers for his own music that he created.

Determined to make it in the world of acting, he had his eyes set on having his own show on Nickelodeon and stayed on top of audition dates.

"Mom," he would say. *"Nickelodeon is auditioning kids! We need to go to Orlando. If I could just audition, I know they would choose me."*

We never quite made it to those auditions, but he became a fan-favorite at his school— even securing the part as the sweet-tempered scarecrow in their production of "The Wiz" two years in a row. I recreated Michael Jackson's exact costume in the play for him to wear, complete with a little curly wig, popcorn-cup hat, and a Reese's wrapper for his nose. Boy, could he act, and his voice was amazing!!

I wanted to build a charity that was a reflection of Kile's spirit and artistic abilities, with an emphasis on giving young artists the opportunity to explore their creative interests with the guidance and support of mentors.

I reached out to Ryan to partner on this initiative. Honoring Kile was something I felt that we could and should do collectively. Having lived in Atlanta for many years, Ryan had more of a footing there. He had a large social circle and was well connected. Some of his closest friends were politicians, executives at Fortune 500 corporations, and successful entrepreneurs. With my additional connections in entertainment and the world of fashion, I thought we could work together to garner the right kind of support and funding to push the charity forward, but Ryan didn't want to do that. He preferred that we honor Kile separately in our own ways. I was flustered and deeply disappointed, of course, but I was determined to press on with the planning and launch of *Kile's World* anyway.

On the evening of March 29, 2013—Kile's 12th birthday—I stood in front of a packed room of friends, family and supporters and launched the Kile's World Foundation at the Woodruff Arts Center in Atlanta. Dozens showed up to celebrate Kile's infinite love of the arts and to inaugurate his charity. I was moved by the support and vowed before the gathered crowd that I would fulfill his legacy by using the foundation to further art education through art-based camps and eventually through a magnet school specializing in the arts for children. By that summer we were running four month long programs in dance, theatre, vocal, and visual arts. I had the camp set up so that the attendees were required to choose a Major and a Minor, we literally put together full productions, and on the final day of camp we did a finale performance for all the parents and supporters to come watch the performance. This enabled parents to see what their children had been working on and make come to fruition in just one month. We turned it into a real production and the kids have from day one of camp, through the duration, to learn the performance material and present their art. I ran a tight ship, from morning drop off, to handling lunches, disciplinary action and participation. I was like a cross between Principal Joe Clark and Debbie Allen's character "Lydia Grant" in Fame. I take my camps very seriously, number one Kile's name was on it and number two my name was on it.

Parents we're always amazed to see how much we took their children out of their comfort zones and taught them performance art. So many extremely timid children ended up being incredible performers and artists. The camps are always a great success.

❧

SENATE BILL 136

My angel, Kile, also has a senate bill with his name on it. He would be so proud.

Kasim Reed, the 59th Mayor of Atlanta and a close friend of Ryan's, set the wheels in motion for the establishment of a boating education and safety law in Kile's name. This was something Ryan and I had briefly touched on while Kile was in the hospital. I became very committed to seeing it through and I am happy that this goal became a reality.

My lobbying efforts started with meeting Georgia State Senator Butch Miller, whom I was introduced to by my attorney Ashley Bell. Senator Miller arranged for me to speak before the state senate because he's the leader who represents Lake Lanier. I was super nervous, but I was clear about my concerns and adamant about my position. In that meeting, I shared how our lives were irrevocably changed by the sudden and untimely loss of our son, and how having proper boating laws could help prevent other accidents in the future. As it was, Lake Lanier had a horrible reputation as a death trap. There is a documented record of it being the deadliest lake in Georgia. The Law Enforcement Division of the Georgia Department of Natural Resources reported more than 150 drownings and 57 boating incidents from 1999-2019. Why has no one successfully sued them? Annually so many lives are lost.

I couldn't understand why the strict rules and regulations for operating a vehicle on land did not apply on water. In the state of Georgia, the waterways were a free-for-all in every sense. There was no requirement for a license or for boating education, and no penalties or repercussions of any kind for being under the influence of alcohol while operating a watercraft. I fought hard for change — I went to the state capital building, attended the hearings, and spoke before the house.

We were successful in our collective endeavor. On the morning of April 23, 2013, I got dressed in a white t-shirt bearing the logo of the *Kile's World Foundation* and drove to Lake Lanier to attend the signing of Senate Bill 136 — the Kile Glover Boat Education Law and the Jake and Griffin Prince BUI Law. Jake and Griffin Prince were two precious brothers who lost their lives when a drunken boater collided with their family's pontoon. On the day of the bill signing, I met their mother Tara Prince. There is an ineffable bond between parents who have lost their children. Inspired by her courage and tenacity, I held her tightly— I felt and knew her pain all too well.

The bill SB136 increases the age requirement for wearing a personal flotation device from 10 to 13 years old; reduces the legal blood alcohol limit from 0.10 to 0.08; increases the penalties for hunting or boating while under the influence; and requires individuals to complete a boating education course prior to operating personal watercraft.

I'm grateful to Ryan and Kasim for taking initial steps to get things off the ground; and to the several others who all had a hand in bringing this important legislation to fruition, including Georgia Governor, Nathan Deal, my attorney Ashley Bell, and Senator Butch Miller.

The day was bittersweet. Being on the banks of Lake Lanier for the first time ever was grim and was further confirmation as to why I never took anyone up on their invitations to go there; it made my stomach turn. Even before Kile's accident, I personally did not care for man made lakes and vowed never to step foot anywhere near those ensorcelled and damned waters. History has proven that *Lake Sidney Lanier* is an artificial lake that was built on land the government bought to complete a water project in order to answer local water supply issues along the Chattahoochee River. It's very foundation was rotten to the core. Oscarville was the name, it's residents were a part of a black community that was thriving. It has been said that more than 250 people drowned as they filled the lake and there are existing small houses, farms, buildings, businesses, and even gas station structures submerged. Sunken livelihoods. To say the least, it was gratifying that my first and only time there was for the greater good--though, I still wished it was drained and gone forever. So much loss has occurred there... so many lives disrupted.

❖

SEEKING JUSTICE

I'm not the vengeful, sue-happy type, but I believe in holding people accountable for their actions.

In Fall 2012, I initiated a lawsuit against the company that owned the jet skis. At the time of the accident, Kile was floating in an inner tube that was being towed by the watercraft. I was awarded a $500,000 payment from the suit and intended to use the funds to further *The Kile's World Foundation* and other initiatives. Ryan, who had initially refused to be involved with the litigation, telling me to "leave it alone" sued me for half of the settlement. My lawyer encouraged me to fight back, but this would have put the settlement before a judge in probate court and I couldn't bother. I paid up and carried on. I had had enough of court dealings with my custody battle and I didn't want this to be yet another spectacle. I should have fought, but it wasn't worth the price of my peace.

While I can't make excuses for anyone, I will say this: It was a trying time for us all. We were in the midst of coping with the ultimate tragedy, battling grief so complicated that it's difficult to put it into words. Ryan and I both acted emotionally and sometimes illogically during this time. I also recognize the devastation he must feel having been there that day and experiencing the tragedy firsthand. I never negate the hurt that he must be carrying. There were other moments when we came together for our other son Ryan after Kile's accident. I hold no grudge.

ATLANTA EXES

It was also around this time that I was approached by producers, Vernon Lynch and Jeff Dyson, to be considered for a reality television series. To be honest, reality television had never been my thing. I watched a few shows from time to time but had never actually considered being on a show. Catfights and concocted drama is not for me. I had been approached a couple times by the *Real Housewives of Atlanta* brand and I graciously declined. However, the production company promised me that the experience would be much different than any of the other shows on the air, so it piqued my interest. *Why not?* I thought. *Showing a sisterhood of black women supporting one another and sharing how we have overcome adversity sounds good to me.*

I also saw this as an opportunity to nationally promote my businesses and collect a check. I figured that being on television would be like a free advertisement for them. I was thinking strategically. I may have great taste and look well put-together, but remember, I had an ironclad prenup with Usher and left the marriage with under a million dollars and bunches of expenses. I needed to recoup some of the money I'd spent between legal (custody) fees, and the hefty investment of my own personal money into my businesses KangaZoom, Estella Home, and Estella Boutique. Quite naturally, after our home sold in Roswell I wanted to make sure that we continued to live in something comparable and safe. Yes, I needed the money and thought the exposure would make good business sense.

After a few conference calls, the producers arranged for me to fly to Santa Monica to meet with the heads of VH1. I suggested a few more ladies whom I thought would be a good fit for the show. They ran some additional names by me as well ... and voila! The prospective cast was flown to Los Angeles for the preliminary meeting. Initially the group included Christina Johnson, Monica Ambrose, Sheree Buchanan, Kim Elba, and me. They eliminated a couple of ladies, and Monyetta Shaw and Torrei Hart were later added.

Kim Elba and I got off to the best start. Then I mentioned that I, like so many other women in the world, had a major crush on Idris, she wasn't quite feeling it. Understood, it's awkward. Semi-jokingly, I told her that no matter where I saw her ex-husband, he was going to get a kiss from me— yep, I had plans of laying a wet-one on him. Kim laughed it off, but I could tell that she wasn't amused. Ha Ha hell. Hey, at least I was Transparent-Annie. In my defense, he was single then and she and I were not yet friends. We met for the first time at the meeting. When I learned that she didn't make it onto the show, I was kind of relieved. If the slob fest ever went down with Idris, I wouldn't feel like a snake. Spoiler Alert: The thing about me is, if you're my friend, I won't even as much as make eye contact with your man or your ex. Nahhhh, I understand boundaries and I also understand unspoken insecurities. There's nothing worse than a bish lusting after your man and all up in your face. I wish others had the same regard for me. But that's a whole other story.

The show was greenlit and the preparation for filming began. The first episode was shot at my house. I kind of think that I was the leader of the pack although that was not my intention. My personality is colorful. I say things with my chest, I don't beat around the bush, and I'm not phony. The producers ate it up. They decided to make me the antagonist, so nearly every scenario was something about me and what I said or didn't say. I made one joke and it turned into a whole "you think you're better than everybody saga." I think another three episodes were dedicated to a "white bras" comment. It was blown up so much that I decided to write a book about it, called *White Bras and 101+ Other Style Faux Pas.*

The editing on these shows is masterful. It allows producers to portray a person in any way that they want. They can place facial expressions that were made in the beginning of a scene in a completely different portion of the scene. I am super expressive with my face so I gave them a lot to work with. They had a field day with my eye rolls, my side eyes, and my itty-bitty, perched lips. The fans were none the wiser and took to social media to read me for filth. Every week. They really let me have it, often calling me an awful friend and saying that I was stuck up, all while vocalizing how much they loved the other characters on the show. I was like, "I could give a rats ass." I went on social media blocking sprees. The block was HOT. I had fun with it because I couldn't believe just how naive television watchers were.

We only did one season because there ended up being some kind of lawsuit drama with our production company. There were claims that the concept had been stolen and I heard that another woman came out the woodwork. I don't know what really happened, but the

"Exes" franchise had high ratings and the show was a total hit. I hated that we didn't get a second season to highlight more of our business dealings, our true personalities, sisterhood, and our varied lifestyles. Our introductory season was rough, but I was happy that I was able to spotlight my work for my son's foundation and moments from his trial. I'm not a fan of showing such vulnerable and personal moments on television, but it was something that I was dealing with head-on at the time. This was my reality and you can't authentically show the good shiny moments without the bad. It's all part of the yin and yang of life.

Not only was I dealing with the bitter aftershock of losing my child, I was forced to replay that day over and over again as I sat in court for the trial of Jeffrey Hubbard, the man responsible for the collision on Lake Lanier that took Kile's life. Hearing the painstaking details of the accident was difficult, but I felt that I needed to be there. Besides, no one had ever given me the exact play-by-play of what happened that fateful day. Coming to grips with the carelessness of the Department of Natural Resources was especially hard. What came across loud and clear was that the DNR was negligent for not citing Jeffrey when they should have, and that the accident was totally preventable. My poor son was having a great time playing on his iPad and only volunteered to ride with a friend so that she didn't have to ride alone.

The trial ran for eight days. On the last day, Ryan's wife Marsha, who Kile affectionately referred to as his second mom, testified about the accident and the chaotic moments following it. I was not present in court that day. I imagine it would have been gut-wrenching for me to hear her testimony first-hand. She gave an account of the reckless manner in which Jeff was operating his jet ski, calling his behavior "crazy" and "erratic"; and she detailed her failed attempts at getting him to stop.

I oftentimes wonder if things would have been different had I been at the lake that day. I know I would have been a force to be reckoned with because my presence is always felt, my words are not minced, and I mean what I say especially as it relates to my children. I tell myself that Jeff definitely would have stopped the horseplay on the jet ski. He would have heard the tone of my voice and straightened up quick. Lord help me, I don't know what I would have done had I been there to react with all my might and the results had still been the same. I am a staunch believer in pre-destiny, however, I also believe in energy. I just don't know what in the hell happened . Nevertheless, I can't imagine how in shock they must have all been that day. I think about the trauma often. As much as I'd want to have been there, I'm glad I wasn't. I'd probably never sleep again.

On February 24, 2014, following 90-minutes of deliberation, the jury found Jeffrey Hubbard guilty on all charges. On March 5, 2014, he was sentenced to four years in prison. Was I satisfied? It's hard to say. Content that justice was served, yes. But no penalty is just for the death of your child. No one wins in these situations. Jeffrey is a decent man—one who acted foolishly and negligently, but a kind man and a father. He loved Kile and I can only imagine that he is still haunted by the tragedy. I forgive him. It wasn't intentional.

In 2018, Ryan launched *Kile's Beautiful Mind Foundation*. Its mission—not too dissimilar from the mission of the *Kile's World Foundation* I had founded— is to honor Kile's creativity by supporting underprivileged children who are passionate about the arts. The foundation held a large fundraising gala in late 2019. I was thrilled when I heard that they raised a large sum of money in support of these children, but I was also confused by the similarities between our organizations.

To add to my confusion, many of Atlanta's elite residents were invited to celebrate my son's life and legacy and yet somehow, I did not make the formal invite list despite being Kile's mother. Neither did my children. This was both hurtful and distasteful. I was told that an evite was sent. I never received it. A phone call, a text... something more personal would have been appreciated—basically, the same courtesy that I extended for each of my events in honor of Kile, though they never responded, showed up for or supported those events.

The similar mission, name, and purpose of the foundation puzzled many donors, including some who were supporters of my charity. Later, several people asked why I wasn't at the event because they assumed it was a joint collaboration between us. As mentioned earlier, I proposed that we join forces on several occasions prior to the launch of his competing foundation. My position was that there was strength in numbers and that together we would have more influence than we would have separately. Furthermore, no one would be in a quandary about which effort to support. The two foundations put some of our donors in an uncomfortable position. Creating separate organizations with essentially the same mission was futile. At some point you have to let bygones be bygones. My position is that if I am willing to let unpleasant feelings from the past be forgotten, so should he. When you lose a child together all of the other issues should become so minuscule and irrelevant. None of this is about our personal feelings, it should be about celebrating, exalting and uplifting Kile. But why separate non-profits with a comparable mission? It just made zero sense to me. Our children always remained the ties that bound us even after we divorced. Maybe grief tied a knot in that bond too tight for us to untangle. I was willing to try, but as it stands we continue with our separate efforts to commemorate Kile's life.

I thought about throwing in the towel and closing my foundation after this, even having a few quiet conversations with my angel Kile: *Baby, I tried. But Mom is tired.*

Instead, I pivoted, shifted focus, and changed the mission of Kile's World Foundation to celebrate young people who transform their thoughts into action or "E-Motion", thus helping others and imploring the world to do the same.

We are now focused on rewarding "acts of kindness" amongst children. The idea came to me when I read the story of eight-year-old Keoni Ching in Battle Ground, Washington, who made 300 handmade key chains and sold them to raise money to pay off the lunch debt of the students at his school. I was brought to tears by his compassion. It reminded me of Kile's generous spirit. I thought to myself, *Children like these deserve to be recognized and celebrated.* My revived mission has ignited a new fire in me. I am keen to move it forward. Our first endeavor was a trip to Ghana after my son Ryan's college graduation in May 2021. We initially planned Ghana as another one of our annual Mother and son trips, but this time with a give back component. The first time that I went to Africa, it was to South Africa, visiting both Capetown and Johannesburg during the Global Citizen Festival in December 2018. While there I visited an orphanage with Usher and his entourage, I was moved to tears when we got there and the children ran out to greet our big group. I remember having to stay back a bit, because I was crying so hard, because I didn't have anything to give them. They came out smiling and excited, some with no shoes, hair unkempt, small clothing, nevertheless jubilant. This time I vowed to go equipped with goodies and necessities to give. My son Ryan and I thought it would be great to teach American football to the youth in Ghana. He just wanted to do something simple, like find a park and gather a few boys to play. But of course, me being me, the idea wasn't epic enough. I then decided to make it an event in honor of Kile. So I began researching locations, parks and fields in Accra. I first reached out to a couple of Ghanian celebrities in the US, to no avail. A friend connected me with a local American woman in Ghana, a lifesaver named Danielle who was an integral part in seeing this camp to fruition. She was my boots on the ground person, who visited various locations, ordered signage, paid vendors on my behalf, organized the lunches and transportation for the kids. We had several 3 and 4am conversations, text exchanges and *voilá* ......

Kile's World Foundation presents: The Ryan M. Glover Football Clinic was born. The free clinic had about 100 boys aged 5-19 in attendance, although ages 5-15 was the original target, it was well organized and well received. We also had the pleasure of collaborating with the American Football Association in Ghana, who played a fundamental part in bringing in a portion of the boys as well. Proud is an understatement, the football clinic was seamless, the kids were happy, and we gave away over 120 balls, toothbrushes, toothpaste, socks, tshirts, masks, totes, and backpacks... and tons of candy treats. It was time and money well spent. Kile's World is a 501(c)3 organization yet we rarely raise money or get much support, I think it is because the perception is that I'm this gazillionaire due to my ex husband, an inheritance or some secret lottery winnings. Hell if I know, I just know that I pay for 80% of Kile's World Foundation events out of my personal money. With little or no support from anyone, exes, consistent donors or otherwise.

Something magical happened while I was there. It's indescribable. While we were setting up for the camp, there was an adorably bashful boy who was keeping to himself. I was drawn to him immediately and realized he wasn't wearing sneakers. He actually had some yellow rubber slides. I offered him a pair of socks which he put to use, but throughout the day I noticed he kept clinging to me. There were several dozen kids there but for some reason we were drawn to one another. I ended up posting a photo of the two of us on social media. The next thing I knew, friends were commenting on how they thought the child in the photo was Kile. I honestly didn't see it at first but now it all made sense. I can see the slight resemblance to Kile that my friends saw but for me it was his energy and his sweet spirit. I later found out that he was born in the summer of 2012 which was the same summer that I lost Kile. Sometimes God works in mysterious ways to send us comfort.

I am also working on an 8-episode, 3-D animated series called **"The Odd Life of Kile Lyles,"** centered around a young boy with superpowers, who lives a normal life by day and saves the world by night. Ironically, before his death, Chadwick Boseman's work in "Black Panther" influenced my decision to give Kile superpowers in my animation series. I'm more motivated than ever to complete the series now, to pay homage to them both. I have self-funded the project entirely, which has been challenging. Everything from the cost of character design, illustrators, character registration, animation, script writing and illustrations have come from my pocket. I have meticulously detailed the characters' physical appearances- facial structures, movements, and bodily frames. Their personalities, habits, and style choices are all a part of the intricate personas I created. Be it as it may, I am determined to have Kile star in his own show. It was his dream, after all, and I plan to make sure it comes to fruition.

I operate from a deeper place now. Most everything I do is purpose filled and intended to benefit my children. This renewed sense of self has given me the strength to overcome the deepest hurt and most painful obstacles. It has allowed me to forgive and function from a place of love.

I think it is fair to say that I have found my "North Star". I've come to realize that once you're accurately anchored, your ship is truly stable, only then can you be of service and help others. Those are my growth goals. I now find happiness in small things and the light in even the darkest of moments. I find joy in being with my boys, in the work that I am doing for Kile, and in traveling, especially to places where I can find comfort in beautiful sunsets. My life is richer and more meaningful now, not despite my loss but because of it.

I've come to realize
that once you're
accurately anchored,
your ship is truly
stable, only then can
you be of service
and help others.

CHAPTER 16

Muses

❦

H istory is chock-full of prepossessing muses, who have inspired some of the world's most brilliant works of art. Described by the Merriam Webster Dictionary as a "source of inspiration" or "guiding genius", the word "muse" can refer to anyone or anything that influences a creative visionary.

Picasso had Dora Maar. She inspired much of his work in the 30s and 40s, including the *Portrait of Dora Maar, The Weeping Woman,* and *The Woman Dressing Her Hair*. Elizabeth (Lizzie) Siddal was John Everett Millais' muse and inspired his most famous painting, *Ophelia*. And of course, we have plenty of designer-muse relationships in the world of fashion, such as Grace Jones and Azzedine Alaïa; Madonna and Jean Paul Gaultier; and Audrey Hepburn and Hubert de Givenchy, Lauryn Hill and John Galliano.

For me, my precious Aunt Sadie is right up there with these icons.

Sadie Mae Carter-Williams, 97— talk about a lady with standards and staying power. A timeless beauty — I mean svelte frame, squinty eyes, sharp prominent cheekbones and chestnut skin. She is the younger sister of my grandmother Louise, "Granny Lou", making her my great aunt. Since my grandmother's untimely passing, she has become my family's royal matriarch and she happens to be my spirit animal. She is a woman after my own heart. Plato's theory has it that it's possible for a soul to split in half and land in two different bodies. Twin flames are said to have an even deeper connection than soul mates. The soul mate connection is based on energy— but twin flames are said to be mirrored souls, the other half of you, so to speak. A twin flame can be a friend, lover, or in my case, a family member. Deep, right? Now, I'm not a philosopher, but this concept certainly makes sense when I think about myself and Aunt Sadie.

If there ever were a gem in my life, it's Aunt Sadie. Born in 1924 in Houston, Texas, Aunt Sadie has lived a sheltered life. Her parents didn't allow her or her sister to go out too much— they were fiercely protective, and even placed a swing set and a slide in their backyard to prevent them from playing in the neighborhood park. They were exposed to the arts, though. They attended opera and theater productions, entering through the back door, as was required in their time, and sitting in the balcony. Aunt Sadie attributes her sequestered upbringing to her present love of being around people. "The more, the merrier," she always says. She also recounts the times that she and my grandmother Louise went shopping with their mother at Sakowitz and Foley Brothers, both upscale Houston-based department stores. They would make purchases that had to be delivered, because blacks were not allowed to carry packages out of the store for fear that white customers would no longer want to shop somewhere blacks had shopped. Funny how the proprietors of the stores saw no color when it came to the "green" money their black patrons spent in their establishments.

Today, at 97.5 years old, Aunt Sadie is well traveled, cultured, dignified, feisty, and clever. She is a trailblazer, full of class, and always dressed in full regalia. She makes it a priority to remain slim given her petite frame, never allowing herself to weigh more than 148 pounds.

"I love to be held in arms," she says. "And it's hard to cuddle if I get too big."

If she notices the scale creeping up, she will fast for a couple days to get her weight back down to where she thinks it should be. Health is wealth to her—she eats sensibly, exercises three times per week, and does strength training. Let that sink in. At 97 years old she gets up and works out three times per week. She's doing something right, as she has been able to remain virtually free of medication for years. She only takes two pills per day— a single blood pressure pill and Vitamin D. She puts me to shame, entirely.

Sadie is also incredibly organized. For years, she has pre-selected her outfits, complete with the accessories, and places the full look in garment bags. I have photos of her from her earlier years elegantly dressed in richly embroidered ball gowns, with just the right amount of cinch at the waist and a string of beautiful pearls adorning her neckline. Before cutting it short, her hair was always tightly curled or neatly pinned back. She is the perfect model of an upright woman who carries herself with complete sartorial elegance—the black Queen Elizabeth.

In her heyday she was a business owner and member of a social club—*The Twilight 12*. It was through big upscale gatherings and hobnobbing with other power players and lords of industry that she established some of her more long-term wealth. I learned this year that she and Granny Lou hailed from a rather well-to-do family of upper middle-class Blacks. Sadie came up during the Great-Depression, and yet her family never stood in the face of poverty. Her father owned a restaurant by the waterfront where a lot of sailors docked. My great-grandfather, Logan Carter, was a restaurateur at the Anderson Clayton ship channel during a time when blacks didn't own businesses. Theirs were the only spot that served Blacks back then. Because my great grandfather monopolized the market, they didn't feel the economic strain of the depression the way others did.

Nothing Aunt Sadie did was arbitrary; her every move was well thought out. In 1970, she married Cleophas Williams, whom I lovingly called Uncle Bill. He was her deceased husband's co-worker— albeit a little further up the totem pole. He would eventually become the first Black President of the ILWU local 10 Union—the Longshoreman Union in San Francisco.

Bill spoke at her deceased husband's funeral. At the end of the service, while waiting in her limo to drive off, Aunt Sadie saw Uncle Bill and stopped his car to thank him for his kind words. A year later he became her second husband. *She's a bad mama jama!*

Bill was a man of achievement and distinction — the kind of man Aunt Sadie gravitated towards. I remember visiting their home and seeing Uncle Bill sitting studiously at his desk, writing notes with his calligraphy pen and inkpot. I have never seen a man with better penmanship— he wrote big beautiful letters. Uncle Bill was a leader in a time when you didn't see Black men in positions of power in America. He was the lone person of color in all-white rooms. Aunt Sadie and Uncle Bill were married for 50 years until he died in 2016. To this day, she credits him for "taking care of her for the rest of her life."

"Never have physical intimacy with a man that is not in a position to take care of you," These are pearls of wisdom she has echoed to me throughout my adult years. Another of her gems is, "Drinking. Shopping. Men. Eating. Whatever. You can do anything in moderation,"

Full of advice, she shared with me that she once left Bill for a short while, moved back into her mother's home, and converted to Islam. She said that early in their marriage, Bill had somewhat of a temper and would speak to her rather curtly from time to time. Given her upbringing, she was not used to being spoken to in this manner. So, while he was at work one day, she packed up her *clothing* and her full-length mirror and walked out on him, leaving everything else behind. She said she didn't care about the furniture, but she wanted her favorite mirror to see her full looks. Remind you of someone?

This moment would serve as an incentive for change and a turning point in her marriage and her life.

When she arrived at her mother's home, she noticed that there was a Mosque across the street. Intrigued, she parked her belongings and went to take a look at what was going on in the building. She met the Imam—the head of the Mosque— on the steps before entering, and after striking up a conversation with him, she began regularly visiting the place of worship, which led to her converting to Islam. She studied the Quran and eventually became a teacher to some of the younger women at the Mosque. The Captain of the MGT was her title. All of this was short-lived though, because soon thereafter Bill came back to get his lady. I mean, do you blame him? She was *it*. He knew he would lose her if he didn't act quickly. Men gravitated towards Aunt Sadie. She speaks of being lavished with expensive gifts from suitors before getting married. One gentleman even bought her a brand-new Thunderbird!

"I am not prepared to live without you," Bill pleaded.

She went home with him and things in their marriage changed drastically after that. Bill realized that he was, in fact, married to a queen and started to treat her as such. Together, they visited every continent, over 100 countries, many states and went on several cruises. Aunt Sadie says the cruises numbered at least 16. She loved traveling the seas and would take a photo in front of each ship to capture her outfit. "I wanted to make sure I never wore the same thing twice on any boat, *Honey*," she told me. Through her travels, she accumulated exquisite pieces for her wardrobe—custom silk kimonos from Japan and bespoke alpaca wool suits from New Zealand. Uncle Bill amassed a custom wardrobe as well, including tailored, cocoon-pina silk Barong shirts from the Philippines and European suiting. They definitely loved the in-life.

Aunt Sadie was an *it girl* before being an *it girl* was a thing. So much of who I am as a woman and tastemaker is influenced by her. She gave me my first job in her clothing boutique. I fell in love with fashion because of her. I credit my love of the best of the best to her as well. As a young girl, I remember walking into her dressing room and being in awe of her pristine white-mirrored vanity table, playing with her powder puff, and gazing at the beautiful dangling jewels from her mannequin. I wanted to be just like her.

I was enamored with her grace and elegance as a child; however, it took until I was in my mid-30s to fully realize what a true gem— a national treasure—she is. I had always loved her, but never quite realized what an enigma she is. I should have been attached to her hip, watching her every move well before then. Back then I viewed her just as an annoying relative that loved to snap far too many photos. Boy, was I wrong. I'm making up for lost time now. I call her frequently and try to see her as often as I can. I want her to feel the importance that she is in my life and for her to know the impact that she has had on me.

She's my role model, voice of reason, and life coach. I consider myself so blessed to have her. While her physical body has aged, her mind is brilliant, and she is as fiery as ever. And of course, she is still dropping knowledge every chance she gets. She always tells me to focus on being a good person and the rest will fall into place.

"I have lived a glorious life," Aunt Sadie has said with pride.

She has done life right. I remember asking her if she has ever had cancer. She responded matter-of-factly, "Yes I had it," as if it were no big deal... had it, beat it, and moved on with life. That is just her attitude and mindset about everything. Don't dwell on things, focus on the positive, and keep going. In March of 2020, she lost her only son—my cousin Dan. She cries often, misses him terribly, but gets up every day and keeps going. If only we could all be so buoyant. Seeing how she has dealt with losing her child, gives me strength.

I aspire to her level of greatness— to be in my late 90s, still have my wits about me, and be able to confidently assert, "I have lived a glorious life." This really is all that I could hope for.

Sadie poured much of herself into me. So much so that I'm not sure who I would be without her influence. As I sit here writing this, I'm having an epiphany about just how acutely similar our lives have been. Though she didn't birth me, I can easily say that Aunt Sadie is my spiritual mother and I her child.

I've certainly learned from her that happiness is not something that you postpone for the future, but rather it's something you design in the present. Lifehack: Be sure to listen to the oldest person at the table. The information you can glean from them is invaluable. It's to your benefit to hear from the wise people who have lived life. I've certainly learned from such these conversations that happiness is not something you postpone for the future, but rather something that you design in the present

❧

I cannot complete a chapter on muses, without talking about my Five Heartbeats™—the center of my universe. I coined the term "five heartbeats" in 2009 when speaking of them.

My boys are all pieces of art, hand painted by the Most High, and brought into the world by me (a humble vessel) — what an honor. It is said that women who are dominant in behavior and are in good condition, are more likely to have male children. The studies got the dominant behavior part right, and I must be in pretty good condition, because I gave birth to five of them jokers. I actually tried three times for a girl and got boys each time. I feel so blessed to be a mom to boys and can't imagine it being any other way. They inspire my life, in more ways than one, each holding the key to my heart in a different capacity. I am absolutely smitten by them and often find myself amazed by their genius.

Thank you, God, for each of my sons. I love them so much. I'm absolutely enamored by their existence and cannot imagine living my life without them. I realize that I was only the tender age of 19 when I decided to have my first child. It was a sensibly tough, yet a wise and necessary decision. Everyone told me I was not ready to be a mother, yet I entered into this journey of Motherhood anyway. Armed with youth, a brave heart, an iron-will, and admittedly a degree of naiveté, I proceeded into what I have sometimes likened to a gang initiation. It's a harsh analogy, I know. But being a mom really is like being thrust blindly into a scary abyss. You have to be sure-footed, quick-witted, and committed with every fiber of your being to survive for the sake of your new tribe member—this blood you've pledged to protect at all costs. Nobody told me what to expect, nor could they prepare me for what was to come. None of my girlfriends, younger sisters, or cousins were parents at the time.

My first-born, Darrin Lorenzo, led me into motherhood. I am grateful to him for transforming me from a saucy, know-it-all teenage girl into a full-blown woman. He inspired me at a time when I didn't even know myself, let alone know how to be someone's mother. When I got pregnant at 18, everyone reminded me of that fact. The questions came flying: You do realize that you aren't ready to be a mother, right? How do you plan to raise this child? What do you know about being a parent? You know it's hard work, right? Still, with much fortitude, I made the decision to bring him into the world. No regrets at all. He is pure perfection.

I jumped into the role without a lot of foresight. It wouldn't have mattered anyway, because nothing could have prepared me for the demanding, action-packed, tiring world of motherhood. Exhaustion consumed me, but I fought the good fight and kept a brave face. My mother, grandmother and community were watching, and I wanted to prove to them all that I could do it.

Darrin was always a calm and well-mannered child. As a teenager he was thoughtful, respectful, and exceptionally mature. Even at the age of 16, as the stepson of a global superstar, he remained balanced and down-to-earth. He was completely unbothered by it all. Lord knows, I would not have been that way had it been me in his shoes.

Today, at 30 years old, he remains laid back, unaffected, and modest—he's just plain cool, like his father was. He's a singer-songwriter who marches to the beat of his own drum. Trends don't interest him and neither does keeping up with the pulse of pop culture.

He is a music and black history historian, who is far more interested in the greats — Otis Redding is one of his all-time favorites. He has the spirit of a hippie. I joke that he belongs in the Woodstock era. He is such an old, evolved soul, wise and rich in values. There is nothing flashy or pretentious about him. He lives simply and humbly. He has never been problematic; Darrin is and will forever be my day one. I thank God for such a blessing and a game changer in my life.

Nine years after I brought Darrin into the world, along came my sweet, gregarious, highly intelligent, and athletically inclined, Ryan "Mekai". I was much more prepared for his arrival. I knew what to expect this time around and was ready to conquer motherhood. Ryan, who just graduated from the University of Pennsylvania where he was the only Black quarterback on the football team of this Ivy League school, teaches me so much about discipline, hard work, and the importance of being a team player. Currently he is receiving a masters in law at the University of Pennsylvania while also attending the Haas School of Business and quarterback at UC Berkeley. He also has the biggest and most beautiful heart— always making me pause to think about people and current events. He has seen and experienced devastating loss in his life, yet he remains humble and kind. Like Darrin, he has witnessed me go through two divorces, and has dealt with the unfortunate death of his younger sibling, with whom he had an unbreakable bond. Watching how he has managed these difficult moments as an impressionable young boy has inspired me.

Throughout the many differences that his father and I have had over the years, he has always remained diplomatic and never seems to choose sides. I am proud of his character; and have the utmost respect for him. I get choked up talking about him because he is that special to me. He is going to bring so much greatness into this world — he already does. I get goosebumps thinking about the husband, father, and changemaker that he is on course to be and will ultimately become.

Kile Ishmael—my angel and artisan, so uniquely and wonderfully made. Picture the likes of Andy Warhol, Steve Jobs, Emeril Lagasse, and Justin Bieber fused into one human being. Yep, that was my Kile. The pain I endured during labor with Kile was unlike anything I had ever experienced; it took my threshold for pain to new heights. I joked in the delivery room that I was secretly being filmed for the pilot of "Fear Factor." It's either that or I was on an episode of "Punk'd" because this was some serious pain. It makes sense now— I was birthing a heavenly messenger into the world. If I knew then the life that he would ultimately live and the legacy that he would leave behind, I would have better understood the pain. After delivering him, I got an Arabic tattoo that read "To defy with courage." At 11 years old, before transitioning to Heaven, he was already a computer 'techie', a musical prodigy, budding chef, and a young Rousseau. I realize that he was an angel from the start. It all makes sense now. Who knew a boy could make such a lasting impact in eleven short years? Well, Kile Ishmael Glover sure did, and it's an impact that will forever be.

In 2007, six years after Kile was born, I was blessed with yet another son, Usher "Cinco" V. He is the epitome of fearlessness and exudes charismatic charm. He is always the most likeable guy in the room. People are drawn to his carefree and happy spirit. As a toddler, he taught himself to swim with no formal instruction. He learned simply by watching his older brothers, Ryan and Kile. He is a brave boy. I don't think I have ever met a young person with his energy.

At the age of 5, he endured a near-death experience in a swimming pool. It was a complete freak-accident that could have ended tragically, but thankfully, my strong, resilient boy bounced back from the incident with no broken bones or damage to his brain. I am forever indebted to the men who acted quickly to administer CPR to save his life, and to the doctors at the hospital.

Ironically, today he still loves the water and is an ardent swimmer (a future Olympian if he so chooses), an avid gamer, mathematician, amateur lawyer and great debater. Of course, he is still an adventurer— loves to play, climb trees, and swim in lakes. What I'm most proud of though, is his heart. He is incredibly giving and would offer the clothes off his back to a complete stranger in need.

Naviyd Ely —my youngest born, whose name is Persian for "God's Gift" or "Good news", was born during a time of great uncertainty in my life. His name emphasizes what he is to me. He has brought me sweet joy. He may be the youngest, but he has the oldest soul (and has even had grey hair since the age of three). He is constantly worried about everything and everyone around him. He's a very precocious child, who has striking similarities and personality traits to those of my beloved Kile. He still speaks of Kile almost daily and remembers him well. He is a book lover and aspires to be a singer like his brother Kile, and of course, like his dad. Fortunately, he's had many fine influences in this regard.

As a baby, his rosy face and innocent eyes reminded me of a Cherub's, straight out of a Renaissance painting. He smiled nonstop and has two dimples on one of his cheeks. Unbeknownst to him, on days when I was down or feeling glum, his energy lifted me. He was my peace in the midst of a rather stormy time in my life. He continues to be my peace. Today at 12 years old, his spirit is still just as sweet and pure. He is my little protector, always thinking of his mom—even promising to build me a spa *to retire in.*

My boys are my most treasured jewels. They are by far the greatest deed that I could have ever done.

I would not trade them for anything in the world. They are and will forever be, my greatest sources of light, love, insight, and motivation. Each of their fathers are wonderful men in their own right, and while I like to think that I had a hand in some of their formidable successes, the kingmaker in me has always been actively engaged in elevating my boys and my men and seeing their dreams come to fruition too.

❧

*My boys are my
most treasured jewels.
They are by far the
greatest deed that I
could have ever done.*

❧

CHAPTER 17

Dizzy World

❧

Dizzy World my mind is in a daze, plastic smiles mixed up with phony ways, we can find peace of mind for every will there is a way.

-John Foster - (song Dizzy World)

I have hundreds of friends. Scratch that — I know a lot of people. Correction: I have met a lot of people. A lot of "industry folk". But few are actually friends. "Friend" is a word that has been diluted and used far too loosely... as is the term "*sis*". But once you realize that every person you encounter along the way is a teacher, you will learn how to better compartmentalize these associates. Especially living in Los Angeles, one of the more superficially glib towns in the country and a place where haughty narcissism and vaingloriousness is the norm. A city where, it's all about who you are connected to and who those people are connected to, rather than about having and cultivating real genuine connections. It's only in LA that you'll coincidentally find a pack of gorgeous, highly successful "friends", hanging out as besties that they "spiritually connected" with errr… met less than 15 days ago (all in the same industry). Oh okay. Wow what a coinkydink? Sis, where are your pre-industry friends though?

When my second marriage ended many of those friendships also ended. I was left behind because, for the most part it was my ex they all want to be in the good books with. I no longer mattered to them. It became, "Wow girl, I'm so sorry you're going through that… Can you possibly get me some tickets or passes to the concert?" It's laughable and it still happens.

The separation was hard. The divorce proceedings were brutal, but the impact of former "friends" and supporters not calling me back was truly disappointing. We had once gleefully laughed together, broke bread, slept at each other's homes, swapped stories, celebrated some of life's greatest milestones, and were closer than close. I have and still hold some of their secrets. Then the music stopped playing — the keys changed, the tempo slowed, and regular conversation turned to awkward hellos. It's almost as if these wonderful friendships never existed. Perhaps they did not. Yep, I still know what you did last summer.

There are so many people I've referred, supported, advised, connected, and introduced over the years who didn't show the same courtesy to me on my projects. Hell, most didn't even show me gratitude at the time I helped them.

The industry can be quite deceiving. Few celebrities show their authentic selves. Many are broken (and some broke!), although they'll never admit it. There is a constant façade of success and of having it all together. The "others" (those who enjoy celebrity by proxy) love to be around people they deem as "hot". Many of them wear a mask to conceal their unhappiness. Behind the mask often rests self-doubt, loneliness, and an overwhelming lack of identity. If you peered deep into the window of their souls…oh, the things you would see.

I have several acquaintances who make six-figures or better. Some are even millionaires, and they all have more than they need. I have helped them expand their network time and time again. Yet, when I reached out for support of my various efforts — whether it was to attend an event, make a donation to my philanthropic efforts — they were silent.

There aren't a lot of Black females in the world of animation. Since I started embarking on this new endeavor, I often feel like an oddity. Plenty of acquaintances could have helped move my project along, if not for me personally, then at least for the culture. Getting ahold of some of these associates, however, was well-nigh impossible. I heard nothing but crickets.

The same was held true in other areas of my life. I was a prominent and successful image consultant and fashion stylist for over two decades—certainly long before meeting, styling, and eventually marrying Usher. I could pull looks in my sleep. Once again, my friends—some of whom were in executive positions for global brands and who employed stylists for projects all the time — never offered me work when I needed it most. They preferred to hire newcomers with less experience. Of course, it had nothing to do with talent or capability. I can explain it to you, but I can't understand it for you.

Let's play devil's advocate for a minute: Maybe they assumed I didn't need the money, or perhaps unbeknownst to me, I had rubbed them in the wrong way, committed a social suicide of sorts, or more than likely, they were cautious about being affiliated with me post-divorce. The cancel culture is real. In their minds, I was no longer running in their "A-list circle," so why stand by me and risk other connections. There is a good ol' boys club in the entertainment biz — not everyone is privy. They remind me of' my white friends who only post #BLM as opposed to using the entire phrase "Black Lives Matter" because they don't want to be in full support. #BLM is just close enough when it is convenient or beneficial to them.

It shouldn't be this way, but that's the downside of this "crab in a barrel" business — it's every man for himself. In the "crab in the barrel" analogy, a crab can escape alone, but with others crawling around in the same bucket pulling each other down, it's hard to move up. It smacks of an "I don't mind if you succeed, just not faster or further than me" mindset.

Some industry people only fraternize with other industry people who are able to help them. The latest hot girl is conveniently their new "sis" du jour. The minute you are no longer hot, no one will check for you. If loyalty can change based on ones status or money, it was never true loyalty or real. Even further, this industry will chew you up and spit you out. When you're UP everybody loves you. Otherwise, you could be off the scene, missing in action for six months and not have any of these so-called friends even check on you to see if you're breathing. Cold world. I have never been that way, unless I was busy giving birth or going through some other major life change. I love to brag about others' success. I am always excited and applaud when my friends take steps forward or reach new plateaus. My attitude has always been, "Wherever I can take you, you're coming with me". If there is a door to access that I can help you kick down, say no more. I'm just not a hater. I've been afforded opportunities, experienced many amazing things, and have had true abundance in my lifetime. Because I believe there is enough to go around, I have *always* taken my friends along. And when I didn't take my friends along, it was because they didn't want to come—not because they weren't invited. They most certainly were. From the White House and the Grammys to the gorgeous beaches and serene temples of Indonesia, I have asked friends to join me. I even took some in the midst of their betrayal! Why not? For me, life is all about experiences and those experiences are far better when shared. Things are just that—things.

Beyond friendship – if there is something that I can do to help another person, especially another black woman, I am game — each one teach one. I believe in paying it forward, and I always root for the underdog. I have been a cheerleader, an armchair adviser, and a 'plug' connecting people to resources that could help further their endeavors whenever possible.

I've encountered some people with this same mentality, but there are many who don't live by this sentiment at all. As such, I don't always receive what I give — invites get *lost* in the mail.

Women, in particular, are mercurial. I have come to realize that when some of them feel threatened, insecure, or they simply dislike another woman, they can engage such damaging behavior as backstabbing, gossiping, sabotaging another's reputation, credit hogging, and purposely excluding or outright pushing someone out of their social circle. The gag is chicks like this help you to develop a thick skin and sharpen your trust radar. But when you are initially starting on your journey to success, you cannot afford to be around such harmful people. What you need is supportive and inspiring company. The wrong energy around you will effectively deplete your will and stifle your passion, creativity, confidence, and everything else you possess.

I'm certain that you have some envious people in your life who either ghost you when things aren't going especially well, or who scoff at your happiness and success when you're on the rise. You know the kind—the ones who are quiet during your wins, yet give standing ovations to others in the same careers. It makes you wonder if they're mad at you or mad it's you?? As soon as I identify relationships that are at hatred's helm, I either cut them off with the scissors they handed me or I keep those "friends" around to observe how they move, always remembering to serve them from a long-handled spoon. I overstand the depth of the wisdom in the trite-as-hell advice, "Keep your friends close, but your enemies closer". It's a practice that keeps you on your toes. We learn the most from our worst experiences. Frenemies teach us who to trust and who *not* to trust. It's character-building. Learn to forgive them—doing so robs them of any power over you, contains the situation rather than exacerbates it, and puts you one step ahead in the game. The whole time they're looking at you like competition, while you're looking at them as a friend. End of the day we all deserve to have people in our lives who think we are a big deal! No competition, no envy, no comparison, no hate, just "I love you and there's no one else like you" type energy.

Some thought that when I got married my demeanor changed, I was standoffish. They were probably right, my life had drastically changed, I was in a very fast-moving life, I couldn't always stop for the small talk or the same simple banter as before. Other times I may have just not seen them while rushing around with a million other things on my mind. I was under immense pressure in that life; I may not have always been all smiles. People who really know me would attest that no circumstances changed who I truly was. Only those looking for reasons to find fault.

I play my enemies like a game of chess, where I rest, no stress....

~Lauryn Hill

Aside from friends and acquaintances disappointing me, some in my inner circle did as well. One thing that many of the people close to me haven't always acknowledged is my vulnerability. There were people who didn't rally around as much as I would have expected during my darker times, particularly when I'd lost my son, and before then, during my painful divorce. When a family splits, you have to understand that a kingdom is being torn asunder. My world became smaller and much lonelier during those times.

What put the icing on the cold-hearted cake after the loss of my boy, was the lack of emotional support from my ex-husbands. Granted, as Kile's parents, Ryan and I were equal in grief as he was *our* son. However, I felt very isolated. I carried that child. I gave birth to him. I needed more than a pat on the back. Because I have a very tough exterior, I think people, including those who know me well enough to know better, overestimated my strength at that time. Even sturdy trees are felled by storms.

The strong person is usually the one bleeding in silence.

Then, some time later, even one of my idols let me down. I can't tell you how heartbroken I was when Oprah interviewed Usher in 2012 and raised the subject of how many people were opposed to our marriage. She implied that maybe he should have listened to them or to his instincts. Why did she insinuate that I was the faulty party? *How Sway?* She's been bringing us relationship insights for almost 35 years. She knows there are two sides to every story and then there's the truth. We corresponded once, long before then, and she wrote that she felt my heart through the pages. I have that letter framed in my home office. Well, I pray she's feeling my heart through these pages. I still love her, but it was rough and I was disappointed. I think women should stick together before siding with the most popular or the taking the man's side automatically. I felt defeated by that interview.

Of course, people had other misperceptions about me too. A common assumption, especially during the bleak years, was that I was richer than I was. Truth is, I'd gone broke; Yes, broke broke. I was still embroiled in a custody battle; I had also recently launched a series of new businesses; I had lost my son; and I didn't work for almost a year after he passed. I still had business overhead and personal bills mounting up. I was literally borrowing money just to maintain. On one occasion, I borrowed $500 from a blogger that I didn't previously get along with just to pay a bill. We became friends after many years of negative blog stories, she ended up closely following my custody trial and learning who I really was. We remain in touch to this day. Some friends and family thought I was just being cheap. They didn't know that I had hit a financial rough patch. In some ways it's my fault for not telling them, but I had my pride. They always saw me as wealthy even when I didn't have money. I guess that's the definition of "not looking like what you're going through." I can personally attest to the fact that the strong ones are the last to be checked on and the last ones we pray for. After losing Kile, I got quiet and people who were supposed to be *my people* got even quieter. I was strong because I had to be for myself and for my kids. One of my many gifts is the ability to put on a brave face contrary to broken feelings. I did it alone.

I'm not really a "wear my heart on my sleeve" type of woman. I suppose I proved it then more than ever. I hid how I felt. I spent a lot of nights by myself, grieving. I cried for the baby I had lost *and* for the pieces of my life that lay in shambles around me. I cried for all the relationships that ended and for the way the world seemed to hate me for not being good enough for Usher, a man they didn't know or completely understand. What I have come to learn and accept is that no matter how much you extend yourself, the love and friendship you offer other people is not always reciprocated.

Even after I gained new insight, replenished my energies and engaged in new projects, I still frequently felt alone. The truth is some people cannot bear your light. Sometimes your spirit is too much, so they don't invite you into certain spaces out of fear that you will steal a moment. When you radiate a vibrancy that comes from knowing yourself *and* your self-worth, not everyone can handle it. As it happens, character cannot be developed in ease and quiet. Only through experience of trial and suffering can the soul be reinforced, ambition ignited, and success achieved. Never let your obstacles become more important than your goal. In all things, be fruitful and multiply. The world is filled with people, who no matter what you do, will point blank not like you. But it's also filled with those who will love you. You will not be for everyone and that's quite alright. Focus on those who can see and hear you. Don't waste your time trying to convince people of your value; they won't ever want what you're selling, there is no persuading them to stand beside you or support you. You're not for everyone, and they're not for you. Realize that you are the prize, and don't reduce your gift or diminish your energy for people who are dead set on misunderstanding you. Did you know that a hippopotamus can outrun a full-grown man? This fact alone tells me that no matter how heavy your load, you can win the race despite trials and tribulation. There are people out there who will say I'm mean or insensitive, there are others out there who may say that I'm too direct but one thing you won't hear is that I'm fake. Although, due to my mouth, I have been told that I need a delay like an award show. I get it, I will start taking more "pregnancy pauses" in respect of those who don't like hearing the real deal. Fact is, I live with no filter, so I don't have much of one when I speak. People that use heavy filters when they speak are often bullshitters. See the thing that pisses people off the most is when you're telling the truth. Folks can't stand the truth, they'd really rather you bullshit them. I'm just not very good at that. I see that a lot. Perhaps sometimes my crowd reading skills need sharpening. Hey I'm just being authentically me. What you see is what you get.

"A Woman in harmony with her spirit

is like a river flowing.

She goes where she will without pretense and arrives at her destination

prepared to be herself

and only herself."

— *Maya Angelou*

It took me some years to reach this level of understanding; I get it now. I am not looking for a million fake friends. I am grateful for my small but mighty tribe. They answer when I call; support me on a whim…and I will go to the ends of the earth for them.

I don't desire to be in rooms filled with huge egos, fake personas, superficial laughs, and awkward Pan Am smiles. I realize that people, especially women are envious of shit you can't control, like your vibe, the way you light up a room when you enter, the way that others love you and the way you bounce back every time. The biggest scams going are women's empowerment brunches and retreats hosted by popular mean girls. They are the main ones screaming *"Girl Power"* and *"Black Girl Magic"* but truly elitist as hell . You're only invited or their friend based on your affiliation, or if you have a ladder that they can climb. It's all a farce, disingenuous, It's not for me. Life is too short … days pass by as quick as light, and I know all too well that tomorrow is not promised. My need for peace outweighs all things, and so, I've learned that alienation is actually protection. I am most certainly not willing to sell *my* soul in the name of cool.

Dating after marriage and over age 40 has also been an interesting journey for me. All too often, men are intimidated by my ex-husband's successes and have expectations about my expectations. Strange as it may seem, I'm not looking for my ex-husbands in anyone else. I meet men who say things like, "Oh I'm sorry, I don't sing or dance, but I make a mean pot of gumbo." Others make even more than a passing reference to them, actually talking to me about their successes. That is the world's biggest turn off for me, because they show that they are intimidated. I want a guy who is willing to stand on his own laurels— someone who is striving towards his own greatness apart from anyone else. The goal is for the independent, intelligent, strong, both God loving and fearing man to find me and not be intimidated by my past or exes. I have dated since being married and I love the notion of being in love. I *embody* love. I know it when I see it... and how it feels when I truly have it.

❧

The truth is some people
cannot bear your light......

.....People that use heavy
filters when they speak are
often bullshitters.

❧

CHAPTER 18

Alright

❧

M y life is so much simpler now. I have peace of mind. A few years of embarrassment, heartbreak, and tragedy has allowed me to shed all that does not matter. I have removed the coat of armor that once weighed me down and appreciate the ability to have only genuine connections now. I still have moments where I have the urge to cry and I do not hold the tears back. I allow myself to grieve in the way that feels most natural to me.

I have learned that living life is about being your authentic self. As my grandmother would say, "God makes no mistakes. You were born exactly as you should be. You were perfect at birth and you will be perfect in death." Looking back, I realize that I never fully got away from my true self. I am still the outspoken, sassy, fun-loving, down-to-earth girl from Oakland. I may have slightly strayed at times, but I have always come back. People can say many things about me, but being fake, phony, or a pretender isn't one of them.

There is a long-held belief that life is like a rollercoaster— it's filled with ups and downs and twists and turns, and oftentimes it's fast and furious. But I think life is far more exhilarating than that. On a rollercoaster you can at least see the path ahead allowing you to grit your teeth and brace for the vertical loops and the steep, gut-wrenching drops. And unless there is some major catastrophic occurrence, you are guaranteed to stay on the tracks and finish off exactly where you started. Life is not that way at all, which makes the journey far more thrilling. It is a wilder ride — more terrifying than any roller coaster. You have to hang on, exercise deep faith, and hope that all of the jolting actually leads you in the direction of your purpose.

You have full control of your life; yet no control at all. I'll say that again-– you have full control of your life; yet no control at all. Let's explore that for a minute. Perhaps the most famous self-help book in the world, *The Secret*, tells us that we can imagine our way to a better state of being—that we can use our mind to create the life that we want. If you release a desire into the universe, with enough faith, it can be realized. Want to become a millionaire? Write yourself a check for a million dollars and post-date it. Want to win a prestigious award? Clear an area on your shelf for it and imagine yourself placing the statue there. It's the fine art of manifesting the life that you want.

But my upbringing teaches me that God is in control of all things. So, which one is it? Do you visualize the life that you want, or do you pray and let God create your life for you? Truthfully, *methinks* it's a mashup of both. If you do your best to obey God and pray for the things that you want out of life, then yes, he will bless you. You must, however, put in the work. And that can look different to different people, depending on your aspirations. A negative, pessimistic, unhappy person may not reach their goals without seeking some counsel first; whereas a person who is optimistically determined to build wealth or get out of debt already knows that toil will help him or her succeed. Either way, it will take effort and it is a joint one between yourself and God — visualizing, manifesting, and working, all the while praying and seeking His guidance. God ultimately will have the final say. Oftentimes he will bless you with far more than you ever could have imagined.

There will no doubt be some unpredictability along the way in life —but if you pay close attention to these moments, they will teach you valuable lessons. All of my heartache has contributed to the better version of myself that I am today. You will not be given more than you can bear.

I have prayed immensely and listened closely for the peace I have now — there is no one who can tell me that a Higher Power hasn't had a hand in guiding me. I have earned every blessing — I have the battle wounds and scars as evidence of this. I am living proof that there is no darkness... too dark for God to wade in with his light.

I have made peace with the arbitrariness of life because I know that the all-knowing all-powerful God is guiding my every move. I am an avid believer that our lives are predestined; I believe that there is a universal torah or ledger that keeps account of our lives and that our ultimate path is already written.

I have realized that there are only two states of being — a suffering state or beautiful state. I make a conscious effort to remain in a beautiful state. Stress, illness, loss, and obstacles will come, but how we deal with these struggles will determine the quality of our lives. Quite often we are so distressed within, that we bring distress into the world. Living in a beautiful state means making the active choice *not* to suffer. Yes, bad times are inevitable, but you cannot allow yourself to stay in that space. Living in a beautiful state means choosing not to engage in negative thinking. It's a commitment to live life through the lens of beautiful emotions, which look different to everyone. For me they include clarity of mind, love in abundance, peace, creativity, and laughter.

When I open my eyes each morning, I thank God for another day and I make it a habit to show gratitude for things big and small, such as being able to spend the night sleeping in a comfortable bed or knowing that I have healthy food awaiting me in the kitchen for myself and my children. I take none of it for granted. I'm learning not to rush and let life be beautiful. I'm more patient and waiting for what is meant for me. Most people that see me out or that feel they know me don't realize the metamorphosis that I've been through. While my personality remains the same my view of things has certainly changed. Suffering loss tends to be a jarring wake up call and it also is very humbling.

I have accepted the fact that trials, setbacks, and ignominies are a part of my journey. I wouldn't change a single thing. The fact that I am still here standing after all I've been through is testament enough that it is possible to smile again even after dealing with some of life's most profound challenges. If you are currently reading this from a suffering state, know that you can and will smile again too.

You will lose love...you will lose friends...you will lose parts of yourself you believed irreplaceable. Then, suddenly, without warning, those components will come back...new and stronger love develops ... new solid and reliable friends will appear...and a new more robust you will be staring out onto a new world of possibility. Keep striving and stay the course. Experience is the best teacher.

I have always aspired for greatness — have always had champagne taste on a beer budget and have always wanted to see and explore places and things that were well beyond my wildest dreams. Over the years, my desire for material possessions has taken a back seat— I don't need the biggest house on the block or the fanciest cars. Instead, I am far more interested in experiences. Seeing the world has opened my eyes to new ideas and concepts, which has expanded my way of thinking. Life is for the living; it is not meant to be taxing or uncomfortable long term... relax, prepare, execute!

As much as I love travelling, I have to admit that the process isn't always pretty or agreeable. Connecting flights pose their share of annoyances. The hustle and bustle of busy, germ-filled airports can be overwhelming. There's screaming babies, body odor, turbulence, and jetlag to contend with. Still, it's always a euphoric adventure for me. There is something about the feeling you get when you finally arrive at your destination safely, and certainly when you awake the next day refreshed and ready to explore a strange, new, and curious place. So much excitement and anticipation.

Whether it is a new country, a new state, a new city, or an unexplored area near your home, I encourage you to venture into some uncharted territory. Go with your heart wide open and energize yourself with the sounds of the people, the food, the culture…and all of the vivid colors. Stimulate and strengthen your mind with new experiences.

I am a chaser of sunsets and peace as I've mentioned — so after my marriage ended, I decided to become the ultimate passport stamper. Most of the global travel that I did before then was predominantly through my work. Despite the countless places I'd visited, I hardly ever took an extra day to learn about the natives, their habits, traditions, culture, or anything about the land. More importantly, I never learned their history. I would always be hopping in and out of cars, searching for things to suit my clients or for souvenirs to bring home to my boys. But I never truly took in the beauty around me. I decided that my first trip would be to Sardinia, Italy in July of 2011. I traveled alone via Rome. I'm an anomaly in that I prefer to travel by myself and have friends join me a day or two— or even three— after I've arrived and settled in. On some trips, especially to places I've never visited before, I like to do as I please for a while on my own. When you travel with people you have to wait for them to get ready, consider what they want to eat, stop for pictures, take bathroom breaks on their schedule, etc. So instead of being selfish, I just beat them there by a few days and get my personal time in. Sardinia is an Italian island with pristine beaches and broad-shouldered mountains. It's an oasis in the Tyrrhenian Sea that remains unscathed by the hip-hop, Gen X-Z crowd. I felt very at home when I traveled there and elsewhere in Italy. I did not feel the same warmth in France, however. The energy there was very cold. I'd dare to say that the French are borderline racist, if not completely racist. On a prior trip to Paris for Fashion Week my friend Diann and I did not get the warm and fuzzy vibe we had hoped for. But I truly enjoyed Italy. I had been to Milan for Fashion Week once and had enjoyed a couple of work-related trips on other occasions, too. I fell in love with Asia in March 2019 while there to commemorate what would have been Kile's 18th birthday. I wanted a calm respite and some reinvigoration too. I took a solo trip to the Indonesian Island of Bali in pursuit of both. I found just that and more. Bali is said to be the center of the universe; it has a magnet at its core and it certainly drew me in. It exudes regal beauty and is a place of complete wonderment. My time there was unlike anything I had ever experienced. The island is carpeted in greenery, surrounded by tall coconut trees, jagged shorelines, and lush landscapes.

The Balinese people are equally enchanting. It's as if they are imbued with the peace of the island. Their spirits are kind and their smiles soft and gentle.

What was planned as a one-week escape turned into three weeks of exploration. All through the towns of Seminyak, Nusa Dua, Canggu and Ubud I went in search of quiet, healing, and sunsets—each place revealing its own distinctive charm, filling my cup with love and light. I literally felt freer; I floated around every day as if I didn't have a care in the world. The natives are warm and polite. The food was so clean and freshly prepared. I was always amicably greeted and addressed with the term "Ibu" which means woman or mother.

Seminyak — a resort town with swank beach clubs, cute cafes, and luxury boutiques— was vibrant and lively. A surfer town — kind of like the California of Bali. I visited the Potato Head Beach Club and stayed at the Alila Hotel where I bore witness to some of the most majestic sunsets I had ever seen—each one more breathtaking than the last. In the quiet and secluded town of Nusa Dua I stayed at the Ritz Carlton in a beautiful suite overlooking the Indian Ocean—the perfect backdrop for my morning prayers and late evening talks with both my angel and God.

Ubud, regarded as the most cultured town on the island, is situated in the leafy uplands of Bali. I spent several days of my "Eat, Pray, Love" journey there at the Ritz Carlton Reserve called the Mandapa in a bungalow on the Ayung River—the same area where the movie was filmed. The peaceful surroundings allowed for the ultimate rejuvenation. I had time to be alone with my thoughts and reflect on my life. I contemplated my upbringing and how it has contributed to my character — good and bad. I thought about karma and how many of the decisions that I have made in the past have come full circle in the form of lessons. And, I thought about my path for the future and how I intend to live purposefully in this next phase of my life. The conversations I had with God were real and unabridged. He spoke to me clearly.

Magic truly permeates the peaceful island of Bali. You cannot help but feel connected to God, because you are surrounded by temples. There are over 20,000 on the island. I visited a few sacred places including the Pura Penataran Sasih in Pejeng Village, the Monkey Forest Sanctuary in Ubud, and the symbolic Handara Gates of Heaven, north of Bali in the Bedugul area.

You are reminded to give thanks, no matter where you are in Bali. Colorful Canang sari adorned the streets as simple, but creative daily offerings to the Hindu Gods. Canang sari are small woven baskets that are made of coconut leaves and filled with flowers and an assortment of gifts. They are topped with a single smoldering stick of incense. It is hard not to notice these selfless and dedicated acts, as they are everywhere — at the hotels, in front of the little shops, and along the streets.

I left Bali feeling cool as a cucumber — at complete peace with myself, and more connected to God than ever before. And can we talk about that Nutella chocolate tan I had?! After years of being broken, Bali held me in the palm of its hand and put me back together again, piece by piece.

Later that year I would take a trip to India that would further restore me.

In the final week of July 2019, my family and I went on a two-week spiritual retreat together. Usher, Usher V, Naviyd, and I had the chance to connect as a family. It also gave us the opportunity to strengthen our co-parenting relationship and to display solidarity for our boys. Before you go check our social media for clues, everything was strictly platonic. No canoodling, creeping or flirting. No funny business! We flew to Chennai in luxury via Emirates Airline. That in itself was an incredible experience, but the awakening I would have in India could not compare. I had no idea how much this trip would refuel me. Before embarking on the experience, though, I was admittedly skeptical. Well, "skeptical" would be an understatement. Usher suggested that we attend the Abundance Festival in India. Now this man knows I am a devout *Jehovah's Baptist* and I'm not always open to new spiritual concepts. So originally, I was vehemently against the idea, because I knew nothing of the trip's agenda and had no interest in getting involved with anything that sounded remotely like a cult. Aside from meditation, dorm rooms, and ayurvedic food, I didn't know what to expect. I was thinking *We are not drinking any of that Jim Jones punch – none, not nary drop!* I thought this was one of the new hippie trends, because in L.A. everyone is suddenly into yoga, afros, moon beams, sound baths, and crystals. The same people just last year were into lying, lace fronts, twerking, and Henny.

I was SO wrong about all of it. This is why it's extremely important to keep an open mind regarding new experiences.

From Chennai we drove to an area called Andhra Pradesh. It was there at the world-renowned philosophy and meditation school, The O&O Academy (also known as Ekam), that I learned the concept of living in a beautiful state. Created by husband and wife duo Preetha-ji and Krishna-ji, the O&O Academy campus is a sacred, serene, and beautiful place, graced by towering mountains and tree-lined courtyards. Secluded in the lap of nature and created mainly for the transformation of human consciousness, it is the ideal place for a spiritual journey. Ekam, the Oneness Temple where people can gather from different parts of the world to meditate in powerful unison, is an architectural wonder. It is a huge, bright, and majestic edifice. The exterior is grand and comparable to the Sheik Zayed Mosque in Abu

Dhabi. The interior of this large, white, castle-like building flows with marble from floor to ceiling.

After meditating at the facility, we were taken a couple miles away to our living quarters. We were welcomed by an amazingly warm and helpful staff. The unpretentious accommodations consisted of spacious one-bedroom apartments with a small kitchenette, dining area, and living room. The décor was retro but comfortable. While there was no central AC, there were air conditioning units mounted on the walls of each room. There was also no shortage of bugs. Rare insects and mosquitoes big enough to stand flat-footed and screw a chicken were plenty. Thankfully, the ceiling fans and mosquito nets helped provide a peaceful night's rest.

One of the first experiences that you participate in at the O&O Academy is a four-day course called the Field of Abundance where you are immersed in what it truly means to be in a beautiful state. You gain insights on how to be a better parent, partner, and leader. You are served with spiritual solutions to overcoming issues in your life. Your consciousness is nurtured with the seeds of calm, connection, and creation. We were taught that when these seeds are cultivated you become a better human being in every sense— you are free from "the suffering state", which are the things that have hurt you in the past, and free from inner wars and conflict. As such, you act in a way that creates greater good in the world and thus a better life for yourself. Water always flows from a higher elevation to a lower elevation. I discovered the importance of looking for answers within myself instead of outside of myself. I also learned the clues to notice when you're not living in the present. (Living in the present seems to be a common challenge.) We often give way to the negative dialogue in our mind. There are only two states of being—the first is in a "beautiful state"; the second is in a "suffering state". In fact, there is no 3rd state. I was taught the power of positive thinking and how important daily meditation is to calm your spirit. There was an example given of two monks who were crossing the river. When they came upon a woman who was crying because she needed to get home to her children they had two different responses. One of the monks was helpful and offered to assist the crying mother, understanding that she needed to cross the river even though the water was too high. The other monk did not offer help. As they continued to walk, the monk who withheld help was annoyed with the one who offered it to the crying woman. The angry monk said, "You carried the woman! Our Master told us we are not to look at a woman or speak to a woman, yet you looked, spoke, *and* carried her!" The helpful monk calmly replied, "I put the woman down a half hour ago; it is YOU that still carries her." The story demonstrates how much we still carry things from our past in our minds. Doing this puts us in a suffering state, whereas moving on and living in the present is the more desired state. Aha! This all made so much sense to me. I finally cracked the code and felt so relieved by the end of my stay. I'm grateful for the suggestion of taking this trip as a family. Things finally felt peaceful between us. Although it seems that whenever he embarks on a new relationship, he can't manage to keep the peace with me. I never even get a chance to vibe with his new love interest. I think it's hard for him to find the balance. Does being awkward with me comfort and quell his new love's insecurities? Do men have to dislike someone in their past in order to love someone new? Why do they always paint their former loves to be the worst villain to their new chick? Revisionist history much? Asking for a friend.

The last decade was a rough stretch, but through the power of manifestation, prayer, and self-realization I am in a much better place now. I am on a distinct spiritual journey, semi-removed from the limelight and away from the glare of cameras and constant backlash.

I live a comfortable and pretty low-key lifestyle. Some days are touch and go, I would be lying if I said that things were always easy. I struggle with my losses daily, just like everyone else I have my bad days, where only pizza and tequila help. Most often, I use my pain as fuel to create. I am a creative at my core, so from time to time various projects require me to tinker within the industry. Even then, I will only do what feels good to my soul. It has been freeing to live this way. The weight and enormous pressure that I once felt has been lifted.

I've been many things over the course of my life: wounded, loved, and misunderstood among them. Looking back over my years, I'd be insincere if I said that I wouldn't do anything differently. I certainly would have considered my boys tender ages more before I left my first husband. They were only four and six years old at the time. In hindsight that was way too young for them to experience such disruption in their home and family life. They've always been good boys, and now Ryan Mekai has grown into a fine young man, but it doesn't mean that the situation didn't rock their core. I also wish that in the days when I had serious money that I had done more good for others with it. Yes, we gave philanthropically to various causes, but what I mean is that I should have done even more kind deeds for the people in my life. One thing I know is that people forget when you help them quicker than a mirror, but will recount a shortcoming with the quickness. Maybe I could have bought a struggling friend something nice for her home— or even something necessary like a washing machine. Or maybe I could have helped a friend with a late car payment. With my access and resources, I had more than enough to help more. A girl really doesn't need all that for herself. No matter how many seeds of good fortune I had scattered, it didn't seem as if I'd sowed enough. What I did spread often landed in shallow soil. I should have dug deeper, laid down better roots, and cultivated more of the kinds of friendships that matter. For as many people as I brought along for the ride in my fast-paced, top-down convertible days, I wish I hadn't left as many in the dust. There are people I didn't see during that time of living at a break-neck speed that I should have kept in touch with and left others where they were. We live and we learn, but the ultimate goal should be to leave people better than we found them.

Most of my early adult years were spent checking boxes. I cruised around in search of love and happiness in all the wrong places. Many times, I appeared fulfilled on the surface, but I was weeping internally because somehow, I had gotten away from the essence of who I was as a person. I was adrift from myself—lost in the hype, fixated on creating the picture-perfect life, and chasing the status quo of celebritydom. These were things that had gotten in the way of my real happiness.

As I write this, we are in the midst of a global pandemic caused by the Coronavirus and much of our country, and the world is under quarantine. We have been forced to drastically change our way of being. Life looks considerably different now than it did a mere few months ago.

I believe the stillness has forced us to look closely at the collective issues around us, at ourselves, and the role that we play in what our society has become and will eventually be. It's helped fuel the fight against another pandemic in America— racism. Following the police killings of George Floyd, Breonna Taylor, Ahmaud Arbery, and Elijah McClain, among others, the Black Lives Matter movement has sparked one of the most honest conversations about race since the Civil Rights Movement in the 1960s.

We've been forced to haul the heavy and painful truths that had been pushed to the periphery of society's attention to the forefront— to exhume and examine them. It's not always easy looking at the truth—especially when it's ugly. But it's better than entertaining delusions. That's a dangerous and costly game. We have seen protests and a global rallying cry for change. I reminisce on the powerful lyrics of love and togetherness in Marvin Gaye's "What's Going on?" often now. What's new is old and old is new. What a time to be alive.

What I can say is that I'm happy with where I am and what I've done. It's important to be true to yourself, but only if the *you* that you know is someone that you can love. If you don't do anything else in this life, you've got to do these two things: *know thy self and love thy self.* When you know who you are and can say that you love that person, your standards change. You have better relationships and you accept less bullcrap from people—even yourself. I love the Tameka that I am today, and my hope is that after reading this you have a better idea of who I am and why.

In loving myself, one of the best things I can do is control the narrative around myself. Obviously, I haven't always been depicted in the best light. I'm not a saint, but who is? It's too easy to point the finger when you're sitting on the sidelines and not on the playing field. We all get a little dirty in life. In all my years I've learned this: you have to be picky about what you're going to give a care about. I'm many things, but pretend ain't one of 'em. This account of my life is my journey and my truth as it stands thus far. I'm excited about the next chapters, what I'm about to do, who I may encounter, and what else I may create and contribute to.

Today's climate has made me think a lot about the last days, mortality, and the importance of living life to the fullest. More than ever, I am encouraged to live boldly, courageously, and freely, and to do so with love.

Like my Aunt Sadie, I too want to sit back when I'm in my 90s and confidently assert: "I have lived a glorious life!"

It's true what they say, *When you leave a beautiful place, you carry it with you wherever you may go.* I will carry pieces of my travels in my heart for the rest of my days.

I can see clearly now. I treasure every moment— the grandiose, the insignificant, and even the minute. Of course, my "heartbeats." I love my children with all that I have in me, just as my parents loved me. My mother gave me a strong foundation with several old-fashioned principles and encouraged me to trust in God. "You just have to pray and be thankful," she would tell me. I do... daily.

My faith has carried me, and my appreciation of all things has allowed me to see the beauty in my life. A lot has gone wrong for me, but a lot has also gone right. Very right.

Stylography

CLIENT LISTING

LAURYN HILL	JAZZE PHA
WYCLEF JEAN	ASHANTI
JAY-Z	NAS
CIARA	GINUWINE
ARETHA FRANKLIN	RAHEEM DEVAUGHN
PATTI LABELLE	DRU HILL
CHAKA KHAN	LETOYA LUCKETT
H-TOWN	NEXT
JANELLE MONÁE	CHRIS BROWN
FUGEES	CHRIS TUCKER
AALIYAH	MAXWELL
USHER	LLOYD
TONI BRAXTON	ANTHONY HAMILTON
MARY J. BLIGE	SAM SALTER
TIMBALAND	SOMETHING FOR THE PEOPLE
TWEET	JESSE POWELL
BRIAN MCKNIGHT	LYFE JENNINGS
BLU CANTRELL	PLIES
JIM CROW	KEVIN GATES
MUSIQ SOULCHILD	

TELEVISION NETWORKS

MTV, BET, CBS, UPN, ABC, NICKELODEON, WGN, NBC, FOX,
VH1, BBC ONE, E ENTERTAINMENT

MAGAZINES

ESQUIRE, HARPERS BAZAAR, THE SOURCE, TOUCH, EBONY, GQ, IN STYLE, VOGUE,
VIBE, IN STYLE, ROLLING STONE, TRACE, SEVENTEEN, PEOPLE, TEEN PEOPLE, DETAILS,
XXL, HONEY, VIBE, PEOPLE, PAPER, GLAMOUR, UPSCALE, ESSENCE

Won't you celebrate with me

won't you celebrate with me
what I have shaped into
a kind of life? I had no model.
born in babylon
both nonwhite and woman
what did i see to be except myself?
i made it up
here on this bridge between
starshine and clay,
my one hand holding tight
my other hand; come celebrate
with me that everyday
something has tried to kill me
and has failed.
by *Lucille Clifton*

Kile—
Keep Chasing Sunsets.